WITH WALT WHITMAN, HIMSELF

Other books by Jean Huets

The Bones You Have Cast Down
The Encyclopedia of Tarot (co-author Stuart R. Kaplan)
The Cosmic Tarot

WITH WALT WHITMAN, HIMSELF

In the Nineteenth Century, in America

JEAN HUETS

CIRCLING RIVERS

RICHMOND, VIRGINIA

Copyright © 2015 by Jean Huets. All rights reserved. No part of this publication may be reproduced or transmitted in any medium, including print and electronic, without permission of the author.

A previous version of *With Walt Whitman, Himself* was published as an interactive book.

ISBN: 978-1-939530-06-6 paperback

ISBN: 978-1-939530-08-0 hardcover (casewrap)

CIRCLING RIVERS

PO Box 8291

Richmond, VA 23226

circlingrivers.com

Visit CirclingRivers.com to subscribe to news of our authors and books, including book giveaways. We never share or sell our list.

Cover and inside design by Jean Huets

Image sources:

Flag – 34 stars. 1861. Curator Branch, Naval History and Heritage Command.

Walt Whitman, 1854: Engraving by Samuel Hollyer of a daguerrotype (now lost) by Gabriel Harrison. Collection Library of Congress.

10 9 8 7 6 5 4 3 2

It avails not, time nor place—distance avails not,
I am with you, you men and women of a generation, or ever so many generations hence.
Just as you feel when you look on the river and sky, so I felt,
Just as any of you is one of a living crowd, I was one of a crowd
…
I consider'd long and seriously of you before you were born.

— *Walt Whitman, from "Crossing Brooklyn Ferry"*

Contents

Dedication | 7
Preface | 11

WALT WHITMAN: HIMSELF | 13

Making a Chart, Making the Man | 16
Seeing Walt Whitman | 18
Hearing Walt Whitman | 20
I see myself | 20

THE CRADLE | 21

Origins | 22

BROOKLYN TO MONTAUK POINT | 29

Rural Long Island | 30
Brooklyn | 34

SHAPING FORCES | 39

American Revolution | 40
Free Thought | 41
Quaker Currents | 43
School | 44
Reading | 47
Printing | 55

THE PARTI-COLORED WORLD | 61

The Streets of New York | 63
Sounds of the City | 67
Entertainment | 69
The Arts | 73

LETTERS | 81

Prose | 82
Literary Scene | 86
Writers of Walt's Time | 88
The Transcendentalists | 105

COMRADES, FRIENDS, SPOUSE | 111

    Comrades | 112
    Friends | 115
    Spouse | 118

VOYAGER | 119

    Transports | 120
    New Orleans | 123
    Voyages | 127

AMERICA | 133

    One Nation | 134
    A changing "us" | 139
    Women's Rights | 142
    Slavery | 143
    Westward | 146
    Roots of Leaves | 150

POETRY | 151

    Coming to Poetry | 152
    Leaves of Grass | 155

THE CIVIL WAR | 157

    Walt as Nurse | 160
    The War at Home | 164
    Writing the War | 165

WASHINGTON, D.C. | 167

    A City of "Things Begun" | 168
    Disciples | 172
    Pete Doyle | 173
    After the War | 176

THE VERSES OWNING | 177

    Calamity & Recovery | 178
    Legacy | 181
    Come, said my Soul | 183

SOURCES | 185

ACKNOWLEDGMENTS | 194

Preface

> "Leaves of Grass" indeed (I cannot too often reiterate) has mainly been the outcropping of my own emotional and other personal nature—an attempt, from first to last, to put a Person, a human being (myself, in the latter half of the Nineteenth Century, in America,) freely, fully and truly on record.
> — *Walt Whitman, from "A Backwards Glance O'er Travel'd Roads"*

Walt Whitman's life spanned a period during which the United States was undergoing profound transformation on nearly every front: geographical, social, political, moral, religious, and cultural. Walt immersed himself in it thoroughly. He wrote for and read voraciously newspapers and magazines; he attended lectures and performances highbrow to lowbrow; he stumped for politicians; he perused exhibitions of photography, art works from contemporary to ancient, demonstrations of technology and trades; he loved baseball, horse-racing, and boating. He traveled extensively in the United States and roved the streets of the cities he loved. He supported libraries and museums, as well as friends in the arts. He immersed himself in the suffering of the American Civil War.

In his life's work, the poetry collection *Leaves of Grass*, he often addresses us, his future readers, for what interested him most of all, above all, was life, human life, whether played out in city streets or rural landscapes, on the bloody pallet of a wounded soldier or in a lover's arms at dawn, in his own life or in ours. His call to us can be direct, confident: "you men and women of a generation, or ever so many generations hence." He can be vulnerable, too; a tentative, haunting phrase recurs throughout *Leaves of Grass:* "whoever you are."

For me, Walt's connection with us, with you and me, echoes the deepest meaning in his poetry: our interconnectedness with each other, regardless of time. We who are now living and we who have lived and died already, including Walt, share our cosmos and all its creatures. From "Song of Myself":

> I pass death with the dying and birth with the new-wash'd babe,
>   and am not contain'd between my hat and boots,
> And peruse manifold objects, no two alike and every one good,
> The earth good and the stars good, and their adjuncts all good.
>
> I am not an earth nor an adjunct of an earth,
> I am the mate and companion of people, all just as immortal and
>   fathomless as myself,
> (They do not know how immortal, but I know.)…

This book is not a biography of Walt Whitman, nor a critique or analysis of his prose or poetry. *With Walt Whitman, Himself* aims to let us join Walt, to answer his call and be with him in the places and events and experiences that inspired and informed him and *Leaves of Grass*.

— Jean Huets / Richmond, Virginia / September 2018

postscript… The arrangement of chapters more or less follows the chronology of Walt's life, but some chapters—for example, "America"—range over Walt's entire life. You won't fall out of step if you skip around some.
Quotations of Walt's poetry are drawn from the 1891–92 edition of *Leaves of Grass*, unless otherwise indicated.

CHAPTER 1

Walt Whitman: Himself

I CELEBRATE myself, and sing myself,
And what I assume you shall assume,
For every atom belonging to me as good belongs to you.

I loafe and invite my soul,
I lean and loafe at my ease observing a spear of summer grass.

My tongue, every atom of my blood, form'd from this soil, this
    air,
Born here of parents born here from parents the same, and their
    parents the same,
I, now thirty-seven years old in perfect health begin,
Hoping to cease not till death.
…

— *opening of "Song of Myself"*

THE AMERICAN POET Walt Whitman, born 1819, died 1892, enjoyed during his life affection and acclaim. He also faced ridicule, contempt, failure, and censure.

His prose works were less controversial than his poetry. The memoirs *Specimen Days* and *Memoranda during the War* offer vivid impressions of his life and of the American Civil War. He also wrote many, many articles, including reviews of books, art, music, and theatre, dispatches from Washington, D.C., during the Civil War, and a loving history of Brooklyn, New York. But the work he lavished the most care on, the work that he held closest to his heart, is his volume of poetry, *Leaves of Grass*.

With an optimism any new writer can surely understand, Walt self-published in 1855 the first edition of *Leaves of Grass* as a large-format book, with a beautiful embossed and gilded cover. Sales were poor. But Walt continued to alter, embellish, rework, and rearrange *Leaves* throughout his adult life, taking in and expressing the events, personal and global, of his life. He self-published some editions, managed to find publishers for other editions. He never did sell many copies, but he gathered around himself a group of "disciples" who groomed his legacy and ensured his work would live after his body's death. At the end of his life he wrote:

That I have not gain'd the acceptance of my own time, but have fallen back on fond dreams of the future—anticipations…That from a worldly and business point of view "Leaves of Grass" has been worse than a failure—that public criticism on the book and myself as author of it yet shows mark'd anger and contempt more than anything else—("I find a solid line of enemies to you everywhere,"—letter from W. S. K., Boston, May 28, 1884)—And that solely for publishing it I have been the object of two or three pretty serious special official buffetings—is all probably no more than I ought to have expected. I had my choice when I commenc'd. I bid neither for soft eulogies, big money returns, nor the approbation of existing schools and conventions.

— *from "A Backwards Glance o'er Travelled Roads"*

Of the frontispiece illustration to the first edition of Leaves of Grass, Walt said later, "That standing portrait of me was much hatcheted by the fellows at the time—war was waged on it…." Besides the defiant stance, the picture shows Walt without vest, jacket, tie, without even suspenders to hold up his trousers—scandalous! At least in mid-nineteenth-century America.

A circa 1870 portrait of Edward James Roye illustrates conventional attire for a mid-nineteenth-century gentleman: a white "boiled" shirt, its hard-starched collar attached by buttons and bound by a cravat (which conceals attachment), a vest or waistcoat (which conceals trouser suspenders), and a coat. Roye was an American who emigrated to Liberia and became its fifth president.

Walt particularly aimed to overthrow European-based conventions that weighed on American poetry; he wanted to make something new, and he wanted his poetry to affirm and inspire his country.

The men and women who loved Walt's work were dedicated. Walt called them, "a small band of the dearest friends and upholders ever vouchsafed to man or cause—doubtless all the more faithful and uncompromising—this little phalanx!" They had to be "faithful and uncompromising," just as Walt was. Though the American Civil War era was not nearly as "Victorian" as it may seem on first glance, anyone defending Walt's poetry—which mentioned a prostitute's "pimpled neck," and "limitless limpid jets of love hot and enormous, quivering jelly of / love, white-blow and delirious juice"—risked public disgust and hostility.

The very qualities that frustrated and even enraged people of his time continue to frustrate and even enrage people of our time. Coarse or lyrical; conservative or liberal; racist and sexist or lovingly inclusive; compassionate, wrathful, forgiving, Walt's poetry cannot be forced to an agenda or ideology.

Maybe it is too vast to fit a cause. *Leaves of Grass* embraces the earth and every leaf of grass upon it, and every man and every woman near and far, including himself. Especially himself. It is a cosmos of a man's body and soul, intense, passionate, violent, and tender. It embraces, as Walt said, "the latter half of the Nineteenth Century, in America," a place and time that saw every extreme of human folly, endeavor, optimism, hatred, fury, romance, exploration, ecological disaster, rural idyll, exploitation and opportunity. Vivid as are Walt's evocations of his own milieu, they transcend it to offer relevance to our own place and time, "whoever you are," as Walt often says in his poetry.

Walt Whitman, circa 1871

Two hundred years after his birth, Walt Whitman is called America's bard. His work lives all over the world. The poems "Song of Myself," "When Lilacs Last in the Dooryard Bloom'd," "Out of the Cradle Endlessly Rocking," "I Hear America Singing," "I Sing the Body Electric," "Beat! Beat! Drums!" are among his most well-known works.

Walt's *Leaves of Grass* never came close to best-seller status, but by the time he died, Walt seemed to know his words would live.

The poem "Song of Myself" is considered Walt Whitman's masterpiece. As Whitman scholar James E. Miller says, it dominates *Leaves of Grass* "not only by its sheer bulk, but also by its brilliant display of Whitman's innovative techniques and original themes."

The "most notorious stylistic feature" of his poetry, as scholar John. B. Mason puts it, are the "catalogues": lists that at times seem disconnected, even random, but whose cadence and vivid language and sheer cumulative energy bring the reader right into Whitman's intention to include us in his experience.

> The blab of the pave, tires of carts, sluff of boot-soles, talk of the promenaders,
> The heavy omnibus, the driver with his interrogating thumb, the clank of the shod horses on the granite floor,
> The snow-sleighs, clinking, shouted jokes, pelts of snow-balls,
> The hurrahs for popular favorites, the fury of rous'd mobs,
> …

James E. Miller concludes his insightful exposition of the various themes and sections of the poem: "In the final analysis, readers must find their own way through 'Song of Myself.' They will know they are on the right path when they begin to feel something of the 'great power' that Ralph Waldo Emerson felt in 1855."

Making a Chart, Making the Man

> This man has a grand physical constitution, and power to live to a good old age. He is undoubtedly descended from the soundest and hardiest stock....Leading traits of character appear to be Friendship, Sympathy, Sublimity and Self-Esteem, and markedly among his combinations the dangerous faults of Indolence, a tendency to the pleasure of Voluptuousness and Alimentiveness, and a certain reckless swing of animal will, too unmindful, probably, of the conviction of others.
>
> —from Lorenzo Fowler, "Phrenological Notes on W. Whitman"

In July 1849, Walt Whitman visited the consultation room of Lorenzo Fowler to get his head examined. Using special instruments, Fowler painstakingly measured and mapped Walt's skull. The skull's contours, according to Fowler's phrenology practice, reflect the psyche's contours, with different mental faculties assigned to different areas of the head. For example, if the bony protrusion behind the bottom of the ears was large, the subject was highly "amative," interested in love and sex.

"Know thyself" was not an end in itself to Lorenzo Fowler or to Walt Whitman. The phrenological chart was a diagnostic tool, indicating weaker faculties of personality and character to be "cultivated" and overbearing faculties to be "diminished," though without unhealthy repression.

Phrenology (from Greek: *phren*, "mind," and *logos*, "knowledge") was considered a science by its followers and enjoyed wide popularity in the early and mid-nineteenth century. Brothers Orson Scott Fowler and Lorenzo Fowler were celebrated American phrenologists, authoring several books and running a successful practice in Manhattan. They were also publishers who issued the 1856 edition of *Leaves of Grass*.

Phrenology united for Walt three strong-driving personal interests: the latest scientific studies, self-knowledge, and self-creation. Today, he would likely be an avid reader of self-help books. Phrenology was self-help nineteenth-century style: a bracing combination of moral, physical, and mental improvement.

By the end of the nineteenth century few believed in phrenology, but Walt continued to cite Lorenzo's chart. He said, "I guess most of my friends distrust it—but then you see I am very old fashioned—I probably have not got by the phrenology stage yet."

Like many writers, especially poets, Walt closely observed himself in relation to the world both natural and molded by humans. Through raw self-understanding, his mind, body, and spirit found correspondences in nature, people, art, and science.

Samuel R. Wells, Charlotte Fowler Wells, and Lorenzo N. Fowler with two other men, standing in the doorway of S.R. Wells & Co., late Fowler & Wells, Phrenologists and Publishers. Circa 1880

WALT'S CHART

On a scale of 1 to 7, the larger the number, the more dominant the faculty.

Adhesiveness 6: "One having adhes. large exercises strong and ardent attachment; is eminently social and affectionate: seeks every opportunity to enjoy the company of friends, and feels very unhappy when deprived of it; does and sacrifices much for their sake; sets much by them, and goes far to see and help them; and makes a real, true, warm-hearted, and devoted friend." Comradeship, an expression of adhesiveness, runs deep in Walt's poetry and in his life.

Alimentiveness 7: "Very fond of the good things of this life, and frequently eats more than health and comfort require…." Walt prided himself on his weight—at six feet tall, in his prime he weighed 200 pounds. Later, his friend John Burroughs fretted that "you eat too heartily and make too much blood and fat."

Amativeness 6: "One who has amativeness large, will be alive to the personal charms and accomplishments of the other sex; a great admirer of their beauty of form, elegance of manners, &c.…can easily ingratiate himself into their good will, become acquainted, exert an influence with them, and kindle in them the passion of love, or, at best, create favourable impression…. With adhesiveness also large, he will mingle pure friendship with devoted love…." Walt's sexual longings may not have embraced women, but women were drawn, often with "devoted love," by his poetry's frank appreciation of sexuality, femininity, and the human physique.

Benevolence 6–7: "Kindness; humanity; desire to make others happy; an accommodating, neighborly spirit; sympathy for distress; a self-sacrificing disposition; philanthropy; generosity…. cannot witness pain or distress; and does all it can to relieve them…." Nowhere is Walt's benevolence more apparent than in his nursing of injured working men and sick and wounded soldiers.

Cautiousness 6: "Watchfulness; prudence; carefulness; precaution; solicitude; provision against want, danger, and a rainy day; fleeing from prospective evils; apprehension; fear; irresolution; procrastination; suspense." To his friend Horace Traubel, Walt expressed a different interpretation of caution: "I know your habits are all cautious, judicial: that you are careful not to go astray—are not tinged by outside influences."

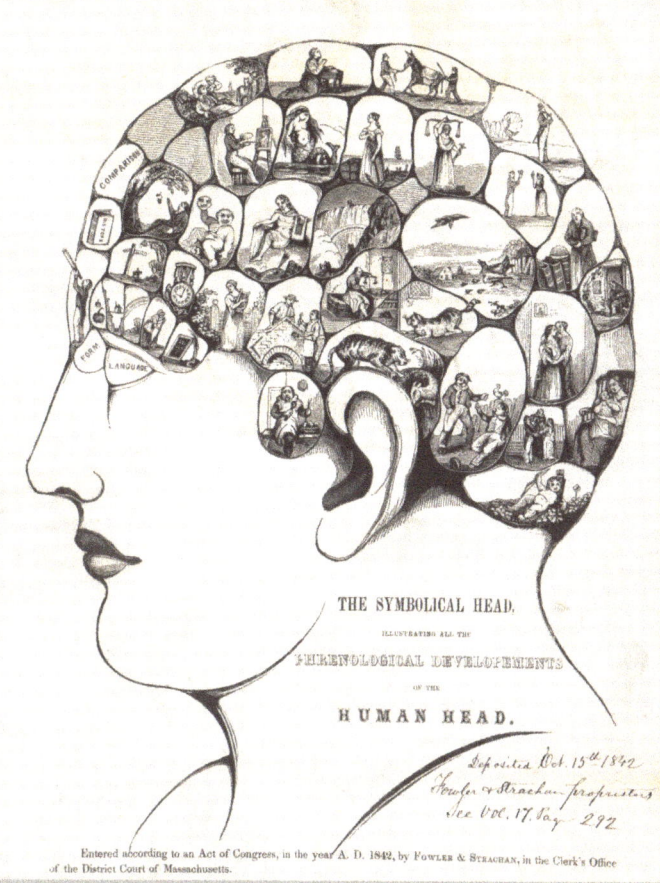

Concentrativeness 6: "… Is able and inclined to apply his mind to one, and but one, subject for the time being, till it is finished; changes his mental operations with difficulty; is often prolix…."

Self-esteem 6–7: "One having self-e[steem] large, will be independent, and place a high value upon himself; feel that whatever he thinks or does, is well thought and done; throw himself back upon his own unaided resources, and rely upon his own judgment and strength; will never knowingly degrade or demean himself; aspire at something commanding; never be content to be dependent or to serve, but rather aspire to be himself a leader and commander of others; will despise and detest meanness, and shrink from it; and assume an appearance of dignity and manliness, calculated to command respect."

Indolence wasn't numbered, but Fowler noted it as among the "dangerous faults" in Walt's "combinations." Fowler wasn't the only one. The editor of the *Aurora*, where Walt worked for a short time, declared him "the laziest fellow who ever undertook to edit a city paper." Said Walt's brother George, "He would lie abed late, and after getting up would write a few hours if he took the notion—perhaps would go off the rest of the day. We were all at work—all except Walt."

Seeing Walt Whitman

THE AMERICAN PHILOSOPHER Amos Bronson Alcott described Walt in 1856, after the first edition of *Leaves of Grass* had been published: "He is too brawny and broad to be either high or deep, and must rank with the sensuous school of thought and style. Yet, a majestic presence, and worthy of his fame."

Few people possess majesty at age thirty-seven—or any age—especially, as Alcott observed, in a messy bedroom with a dirty chamber pot in sight. Alcott was one of many people impressed by Walt's charisma and presence. Grace Gilchrist, whose mother was close friends with Walt, described his personality as "a very grand one, magnetic, and charged with the great elemental forces, which drew in great and small natures to minister to his omnivorous humanity."

Walt's ideal of personal appearance rested not on fashion but on an aura of well-being, which he believed had healing powers.

During the war I possess'd the perfection of physical health. My habit, when practicable, was to prepare for [nursing sick and wounded soldiers] by fortifying myself with previous rest, the bath, clean clothes, a good meal, and as cheerful an appearance as possible.

He wore a beard most of his adult life, unwilling to be a "latherer." Tall and ruddy-faced, he was slender in his youth, robust in his prime, heavyset in his age. In contrast to his untidy living quarters, he kept his body and clothes clean.

After passing through a youthful dandy phase, Walt favored an open-necked shirt, sometimes with a loose necktie, a waistcoat, a sack coat (a straight-sided suit jacket, like those worn today, versus the frock coat, which nipped in at the waist), baggy trousers tucked into boots, and a shapeless wide-brimmed hat. An editorial in Appleton's Journal, a literary magazine, mocked Walt's appearance as a phony play at being "a hero among roughs." Yet the "red flannel shirt, conspicuously open," cited in the article, was more true to his roots, his father a farmer and carpenter, than a dress shirt.

Above all, Walt strove to radiate kindness, cheer, and vigor.

No man has any excuse for looking morose or cruel: he should do better…. That is so important to me: to not look downcast—cloud up things.

Walt's attention to his physical persona reflected his joy in self-expression, and his life-long determination to mold his outer and inner selves into what he valued and loved.

PHOTOGRAPHS

WALT WHITMAN SCHOLAR Ed Folsom points out a startling yet obvious fact: "Whitman's generation was the first to be able to watch itself age, to actually look back on its youth in a distant mirror." Before photography became popular, only people with the time and money to sit for and pay a painter could gaze upon a past self: the child, the youth, the mature man or woman.

Photographers took portraits in studios or in homes and workplaces, including

One of Walt's friends called this circa 1854 photo "the Christ likeness," believing that it captured the "moment this carpenter too became seer…."

LEFT: Louis Jacques Mandé Daguerre (1787-1851) kept his photoprocessing technique open source. As a result, and because of their clarity, daguerrotypes became the dominant photograph type in the mid-nineteenth century. Photo of Daguerre is dated 1844.

RIGHT: Portraits made by Mathew Brady included eminent men and women, such as Abraham Lincoln and the Civil War commanders Ulysses S. Grant and Robert E. Lee. Walt visited Brady's galleries in Manhattan and Washington, D.C., both to view the pictures and to be photographed. Photo of Mathew Brady circa 1875

military camps. Prints mounted on cardboard, called cartes de visites, made gifts to friends and family, as did photographs framed in cases small enough to slip into a pocket. Photographs did not dominate media until the twentieth century, but etchings reproduced photographs for newspapers and magazines. Galleries displayed original prints.

We love to dwell long upon [photographs]—to infer many things, from the text they preach—to pursue the current of thoughts running riot about them.

Of photographer John Plumbe's gallery, Walt wrote in 1846:

You will see more life there, more variety, more human nature, more artistic beauty (for what can surpass that masterpiece of human perfection, the human face?) than in any spot we know of.

During the Civil War, photographers set up shop anywhere they could. Families could keep the face of their soldiers before them; and many pictures survive of men in uniforms, often posed holding pistols, sometimes mocking conventional morality with booze and playing cards. Photographs let the public see, for the first time, war ungarnished and undisguised by beautiful paint: bloated corpses on battlefields, soldiers at gritty campfires and primitive huts, wounded and maimed men bedded on the grounds of overflowing field hospitals.

Walt shared with his beloved President Lincoln the urge to be photographed "until the cameras themselves are tired of me." He pored over "this heart's geography's map," and gave photographs of himself to friends and admirers.

Walt preferred a close physical likeness in portraits. Of this 1889 portrait by Frederick Gutekunst, Walt said: "Nowadays photographers have a trick of what they call 'touching up' their work—but, at my special request, that has not been interfered with in any way, and, on the whole, I consider it a good picture.... To a person who gets only one picture, this picture is in more ways than any other spiritually satisfactory and physically representative." Walt's inscription on the photo reads: "My 71st year arrives; the fifteen past months nearly all illness or half illness — until a tolerable day (Aug 6, 1889) & conveyed by Mr. B. & Ed. W. I have been carriaged across to Philadelphia (how sunny & fresh & good looking the river, the people, the vehicles & Market & Arch streets!) & have sat for this photo: wh- satisfies me. Walt Whitman"

Hearing Walt Whitman

Thomas Edison circa 1878. A recording on a wax cylinder had to be made complete, without mistakes all the way through each track: no backtracking, no overdubbing, no editing.

THE VOICE on a circa 1890 recording of Walt's poem "America" may be that of Walt himself. The physical evidence is controversial. The earliest extant artifact is a cassette tape recording made in the 1970s from a now-lost wax cylinder. Library of Congress experts found the recording to be too high-fidelity for the late nineteenth century. However, sound engineer Dave Beauvais asserts the recording is authentic, comparing it to other Edison recordings of the period. Beauvais also finds the accent true to the period: "It exhibits a quaint and subtle regional inflection…which has quite literally disappeared in our age. No one speaks this way any more."

Assuming that the recording itself dates from the late nineteenth century, the question is whether the voice is Walt's. In a letter dated February 14, 1889, Thomas Edison's secretary assured Walt's friend Sylvester Baxter that Edison would "endeavor to carry…out" Baxter's suggestion of "obtaining a phonographic record of the poet Whitman." Walt himself surely would not have resisted co-creating an audible equivalent of his many visual portraits.

Friends agreed that Walt spoke with "no local peculiarity of accent or pronunciation." Yet today, any American, at least outside of New England, would hear an accent in the recording. A nineteenth-century New Englander might not.

People who knew Walt variously described his voice as "musical and resonant"; "high-pitched, but agreeable and without twang; a sort of speaking tenor"; "a full-toned, rather high, baritone voice, a little harsh…." Overall, Walt's voice was described as resonant, manly, deliberate, musical. All these qualities tally with the voice on the recording.

You can listen to the recording on-line at jeanhuets.com/walt-whitman

America
Centre of equal daughters, equal sons,
All, all alike endear'd, grown, ungrown, young or old,
Strong, ample, fair, enduring, capable, rich,
Perennial with the Earth, with Freedom, Law and Love.

I see myself

WALT'S ULTIMATE source of insight and expression was his poetry. There, he fluidly identifies himself as himself, and as others: slave and master, a fireman crushed by a beam, a woman awaiting her lover, birds flying, prostitutes, sailors and ships' captains, old women and young brides, addicts—all.

> In all people I see myself, none more and not one a barley-corn less,
> And the good or bad I say of myself I say of them….
> — *from "Song of Myself"*

Leaves of Grass is modeled on Walt Whitman, but Walt Whitman is also modeled on *Leaves of Grass*.

CHAPTER 2

The Cradle

I estimate three leading sources and formative stamps to my own character, now solidified for good or bad, and its subsequent literary and other outgrowth—the maternal nativity-stock brought hither from far-away Netherlands, for one, (doubtless the best)—the subterranean tenacity and central bony structure (obstinacy, willfulness) which I get from my paternal English elements, for another—and the combination of my Long Island birth-spot, sea-shores, childhood's scenes, absorptions, with teeming Brooklyn and New York—with, I suppose, my experiences afterward in the secession outbreak, for the third.

— *from Specimen Days*

Long Island Homestead. 1859.
Painting by Andrew W. Warren.

Origins

Walt was born on May 31, 1819, into a family of farmers and artisans who took pride in descent from New York's earliest settlers. For more than a century, his ancestors farmed land on Long Island with a labor force that included slaves up to Walt's grandparents' generation.

Walt's father's generation saw the family wealth nibbled away by national economic downturns, hereditary divisions, bad business decisions, perhaps emancipation, and perhaps bad luck. By turns a carpenter, a farmer, and a real estate speculator, Walter Whitman, Sr., shifted his family back and forth between Long Island and Brooklyn in vain attempts to win financial security.

Like many people of his time, Whitman believed in the theory of hereditarianism, which held that the parents' inherent makeup—including ethnicity and national

Slavery in New York lasted from 1626, when the Dutch West India Company brought enslaved Africans to present-day Manhattan, until July 4, 1827. According to the New York Historical Society, "In 1799, New York passed a Gradual Emancipation act that freed slave children born after July 4, 1799, but indentured them until they were young adults. In 1817 a new law passed that would free slaves born before 1799 but not until 1827. By the 1830 census there were only 75 slaves in New York and the 1840 census listed no slaves in New York City."

WALT'S FAMILY
Walter Whitman (1789-1855) + Louisa Van Velsor Whitman (1795-1873)
Jesse Whitman (1818-1870)
Walter (Walt) Whitman (1819-1892)
Mary Elizabeth Whitman Van Nostrand (1821-1899)
Hannah Whitman Heyde (1823-1908)
Andrew Jackson Whitman (1827-1863)
George Washington Whitman (1829-1901)
Thomas Jefferson (Jeff, Jeffy) Whitman (1833-1890)
Edward Tobias (Eddy, Eddie, Toby) Whitman (1835-1892)

The house in West Hills, Long Island, where Walt was born. His father Walter was a carpenter who built the house himself around 1810. The building is typical of the region and period. This circa 1933 photograph is the earliest known of the Whitman home.

origin—and the parents' behavior even before conception imprinted their children physically, emotionally, intellectually, and spiritually. This current of thought imbued many people with a sense of responsibility and wholesome conduct, but also bolstered racism and ethnic stereotyping.

Memoirs and biographies of the period often begin with a family lineage. Wealthy southerners preferred to descend from the "Cavaliers" (English by way of the Norman conquest). Status for New Englanders lay in English Puritan roots. New Yorkers prized ancestors from Holland, since the Dutch were the first Europeans to settle Manhattan. ("Dutch" in nineteenth-century America usually meant German, from the German word *deutsch;* many Americans looked down on German immigrants.)

In middle age, Walt drifted away from hereditarianism, maybe because the disasters that befell his immediate family did not reflect well, in hereditarian terms, on his mother and father. The members of Walt's immediate family ranged from normal to eccentric to utterly dysfunctional. His father's early illness and demise and his elder brother's fits of violence meant that Walt partnered with his mother to pilot the family through its crises and its everyday needs. He called his siblings "my boys and girls"; younger brother George found that "now and then his guardianship seemed excessive." When physically distant from his family, Walt wrote often, sent what money he could, and intervened through the domestic catastrophes that unfolded over the years.

Walt did not count on his family for artistic affirmation. "No one of my people—the people near to me—ever had any time for *Leaves of Grass*—thought it more than an ordinary piece of work, if that," he claimed. His mother and father and brothers and sisters formed the poet's cradle, as did the places they lived, worked, and played.

LOUISA VAN VELSOR WHITMAN (1795–1873)

Louisa Van Velsor Whitman, circa 1855. The picture shows half of a case frame, which can close, booklike, with hinges (LEFT) and a latch (RIGHT). It was a very common type frame in the Civil War era.

Leaves of Grass is the flower of her temperament active in me. My mother was illiterate in the formal sense but strangely knowing: she excelled in narrative—had great mimetic power: she could tell stories, impersonate: she was very eloquent in the utterance of noble moral axioms—was very original in her manner, her style.

Maternal, vigorous—"a daily and daring rider" in her youth—intelligent and well-informed, though with little if any formal education, Louisa Van Velsor Whitman was to Walt "the ideal woman, practical, spiritual, of all of earth, life, love, to me the best." Walt embraced his mother's sunny outlook. The word "cheer" resounds throughout his writings, and he cultivated cheer in himself, to share with friends, to infuse his poetry, and to bolster the spirits of the thousands of hospitalized workers and soldiers he visited.

By "illiterate" Walt meant, not formally educated. Louisa Whitman could and did read, and Walt supplied her with periodicals of all kinds. He claimed that she was "mystified, defeated" by *Leaves of Grass*. Yet she did read and cherish at least some of his poetry.

so your writing again leaves of grass well if it dont hurt you i am glad...

i used to read some in [Drum Taps] almost every night before i went to bed

...i have the whisper of heavenly death it lays here on the table by my side i have read it over many times i liked it it was so solemn ...
— *Louisa Whitman, letter to Walt*

> "Whispers of Heavenly Death" was the first of a cluster of five poems Walt wrote for the October 1868 issue of *The Broadway: A London Magazine*.
>
> WHISPERS of heavenly death, murmur'd I hear;
> Labial gossip of night—sibilant chorals;
> Footsteps gently ascending—mystical breezes, wafted soft and low;
> Ripples of unseen rivers—tides of current, flowing, forever flowing;
> (Or is it the plashing of tears? the measureless waters of human tears?)
>
> I see, just see, skyward, great cloud-masses;
> Mournfully, slowly they roll, silently swelling and mixing;
> With, at times, a half-dimm'd, sadden'd, far-off star,
> Appearing and disappearing.
>
> Some parturition, rather—some solemn, immortal birth:
> On the frontiers, to eyes impenetrable,
> Some Soul is passing over.

Walter Whitman, Sr., circa 1850. Walter Whitman's drooping eye may indicate he suffered a stroke, a tendency inherited by Walt and possibly his brother Jesse.

WALTER WHITMAN (1789–1855)

A few old-timers remembered Walt's father, Walter Whitman, as "a large-limbed, heavy man, even taller and broader than Walt; strong of arm and slow of speech,...a taciturn Colossus, who attended no church and did not seek the society of his fellow townsmen." Some biographers speculate that Walter was a binge-drinker with a quick temper.

The "taciturn Colossus" had a genial side, and he loved to give wagon rides to children when he farmed on Long Island. Years after Walter's death, his wife recalled in a letter to Walt, "Good luck to you walter dear dont you remember your poor old father always wished that wish to every one." Walt compared his father to a soldier he later met: "a large, slow, good natured man...shrewd, very little to say...."

Walt didn't write often of his father, but always did so with affection and respect. His brother George affirmed that Walt's relations with his father were "always friendly, always good." Still, Walt rejected, without entirely suppressing in himself, his father's stolidly gloomy outlook: "Keep good heart," Walter liked to say, "the worst is to come."

Walter Whitman passed to his son Walt an individualistic turn of mind, pro-labor political views, and unyielding skepticism—sometimes outright hostility—toward organized religion. His string of financial failures may have instilled in Walt a stoic indifference to personal wealth.

Walter probably read his son's newspaper articles, but his opinion of Walt's writing is unknown. He died only a week after the first publication of *Leaves of Grass*.

JESSE WHITMAN (1818–1870)

Only one year in age lay between Walt and Jesse, yet Walt rarely mentioned his older brother in his writing.

Jesse went to sea as a sailor, perhaps in his teens when the family moved from Brooklyn back to Long Island. On his return, he worked in the Brooklyn Navy Yard, probably beginning in the late 1830s.

His mental decline in the late 1850s has been attributed to a head injury received as an adult. When the Navy Yard discharged him in 1861, Walt wrote a letter asking that the Yard "continue him on in employment," describing Jesse as "a laboring man…has for some time been working in the provision store." The Yard did not relent.

Jesse might have served as crew aboard a schooner like this one.

Jesse's behavior grew erratic, and he threatened and verbally abused his mother and others. His violent fits reached a crescendo on his brother Andrew's death in 1863. In 1864 Walt committed Jesse to Kings County Lunatic Asylum, where he died.

o walt aint it sad to think the poor soul hadent a friend near him in his last moments and to think he had a pauper's grave… hes done poor fellow i was thinking of him more lately than common… i feel very sad of course walt if he has done ever so wrong he was my first born…

— *Louisa Whitman, letter to Walt*

MARY ELIZABETH WHITMAN VAN NOSTRAND (1821–1899)

At age nineteen, Mary married shipbuilder Ansel Van Nostrand and settled at the whaling village of Greenport, Long Island. Her husband was a hard worker and a hard drinker. Walt may have found their home a comfortable haven to visit, when he still lived in New York. According to a family website, however, "Ansel Van Nostrand was … an alcoholic whose regular binges gave Walt Whitman another reason to visit the elder of his two sisters in Greenport."

Reliable, sturdy, dutiful, tender, and maternal, Mary seems cast from her mother's mold. Of her conduct at Andrew's deathbed, Jeff wrote, "Mary has acted like the best of women." Like her parents, she and her husband endured economic downturns, with Ansel out of work for long periods.

Unless Walt's claim to have fathered children is true (he named none), Louisa and Walter Whitman's living descendants all come from Ansel's and Mary's children.

Mount Mansfield, by Charles L. Heyde. When Heyde did this painting, circa 1857, he was five years into his marriage to Hannah and still on good terms with Walt.

HANNAH WHITMAN HEYDE (1823–1908)

Hannah received more formal education than anyone else in the family and, like Walt, taught school for a while. She moved to Vermont on marrying landscape painter Charles L. Heyde. The relationship eventually deteriorated into mutual misery, with Charles abusive and controlling, and Hannah's self-esteem and volition crumbling. Walt, who introduced the two, ended up heartily detesting his brother-in-law, whose letters to Walt soured into scathing, petty diatribes. Walt's brothers George and Jeff seethed over Heyde's treatment of their sister, with Jeff calling Charles "a miserable skunk." Although Hannah wrote in letters of being mortally ill, she outlived all of her siblings and corresponded with Walt until his death.

Your Book came last night, I was just delighted I prize it greatly.... It will be successful, many speak of it, here. We looked it over all the evening, Charlie taking it, then I. he read aloud (appreciatively) the Song of Myself. I wanted to read the Ox Tamer and others I liked.

— *Hannah Whitman Heyde, letter to Walt, 1881*

The Brooklyn Navy Yard dominated the financial life of Walt's family. The image shows the inside of a boat shed at the Brooklyn Navy Yard in 1861, the year Jesse was discharged. Andrew was fired from the Yard in February 1863, "on account of his not being there much of the time," as Jeff wrote.

ANDREW JACKSON WHITMAN (1827–1863)

Like his brother Jesse, Andrew worked at the Brooklyn Navy Yard; like Jesse, he got fired; and like Jesse, his demise was a family tragedy. Always sickly, after a short stint in the Union army his health failed completely. He died at age thirty-six with a diagnosis of "laryngitis," possibly a result of tuberculosis. Walt's mother lamented the squalor of Andrew's home and his wife Nancy's slovenliness. A more orderly life might have delayed but probably not prevented his early death. Andrew had three sons, one of whom lived long enough to be named in Walt's will. The youngest was killed by a brewery wagon.

GEORGE WASHINGTON WHITMAN (1829–1901)

George served the Union through the entire Civil War, staying in despite a wound, imprisonment, and his family's pleas. After the War, and a few false starts in the building business, he prospered as a municipal pipe inspector in Camden, New Jersey.

George and Walt had little in common—"George believes in pipes, not in poems"—and George hung on to a notion that Walt used poetry writing as an excuse not to work. Walt could have made something of himself, George believed, if only he didn't waste time scribbling poems. Still, the brothers got along with each other.

George and his wife Louisa, of whom Walt was very fond, cared for Walt when a stroke felled him in 1873. They also took in Mrs. Whitman and the youngest brother Eddy. Mrs. Whitman chafed at Louisa's fastidious housekeeping and penny-pinching, and resented being dependent on her son.

George and Louisa had one child who died in infancy and another stillborn. In 1884, they retired from Camden to a farm in rural New Jersey. They invited Walt, but he opted for independence in Camden.

Wednesday night Feb 25th/63
Walt we have a splendid camp here. I have a bran new tent and when I get it fixed up to suit me, it will just be gay I tell you. If I find out for certain, that I cant get home very soon you must come down here and see a feller, and if I do go home you must come as soon as I get back, I shall have my tent fixed up Bully in a day or two, we have had a grand revieu to day by Gen Dix the whole Army Corps was out, and as there is splendid grounds here for that kind of work we made a first rate appearance and everything went off with great applause &c

— *George Whitman, 1863 letter to Walt*

Although George Washington Whitman posed in uniform, the photograph was taken years after the War, circa 1870-80.

THOMAS JEFFERSON (JEFF, JEFFY) WHITMAN (1833–1890)

… When Jeff was born I was in my 15th year, and had much care of him for many years afterward, and he did not separate from me.… As he grew a big boy he liked outdoor and water sports, especially boating.… I loved long rambles, and he carried his fowling-piece. O, what happy times, weeks!

— *Specimen Days*

Jeff Whitman, circa 1863

Walt's favorite brother was also his surrogate son. Their strong bond instilled in the younger man a love of music, especially opera, and shared political views. The two traveled to New Orleans when Jeff was still a teenager.

Jeff married in 1859. During the War, the couple and their baby daughter lived in the Whitman household. As the increasingly dysfunctional family spun out of control, he begged his big brother Walt, living in D.C., to come home and fix things, which Walt did; on one visit he committed eldest brother Jesse to an asylum.

Despite Jeff's pleas that Walt (and George) return home, he heartily endorsed their War duties. He faithfully wrote both brothers, and he collected money for Walt to distribute as cash and gifts to the soldiers he nursed. "I am thankfull that you are there," he wrote Walt in 1863. "Somehow I feel that as if George, God bless him, was a little safer while you are so near him and while you are doing so much good."

In 1867 Jeff moved to St. Louis as superintendent of the city's Water Works. He likely did not miss the domestic chaos of his birth family. Among Walt's siblings, Jeff achieved the highest material success, earning national distinction as a civil engineer.

Walt counted Jeff's wife Mattie, with Louisa Whitman, as "the two best and sweetest women." Mattie died in 1873, only three months before Walt's mother. Jeff's two young daughters spent several summers in Camden with their uncles George and Walt. Manahatta died in 1886. Jessie, who never married, lived until 1957.

Jeff supported Walt enthusiastically throughout his career, despite Walt's claim that no one in his family considered *Leaves of Grass* "more than an ordinary piece of work."

> I am truly glad Walt, that you are comfortably situated and the more so that you are having things done to suit you in the way of publishing your book. I quite long for it to make its appearance. What jolly times we will have reading the notices of it wont we. you must expect the "Yam Yam Yam" writer[s] to give you a dig as often as possible but I dont suppose you will mind it any more than you did in the days of your editorship of the B.[rooklyn] Eagle when the Advertiser Lees used to go at you so roughly Do you remember those days Walt.
>
> — *Jeff Whitman to Walt, 1860*

EDWARD TOBIAS (EDDY, EDDIE, TOBY) WHITMAN (1835–1892)

Although Eddy was born on Long Island while Walt was living in Brooklyn, Walt seems to have known the traumatic event that left Eddy mentally retarded, probably epileptic, and with a leg and an arm partially paralyzed. A close friend claimed that Walt attributed Eddy's disabilities to the father's alcoholism, but Jeff's daughter Jessie dismissed that idea. She said that Eddy's "childishness, and the dragging of one foot" followed a scarlet fever attack when Eddy was three.

Jeff encouraged Eddy to "go to school and learn to read and write," but Eddy did not, probably could not. He was able to roam about on his own, do errands for his family, and attend church regularly.

In a time when medicine and education offered little to special-needs children, Walt saw no potential in Eddy.

This house at the Camden County Insane Asylum dates from the early nineteenth century and would have housed up to thirty inmates. After 1878, inmates occupied a new brick building.

> Eddy is helpless…was a poor, stunted boy almost from the first. He had the convulsions—it was all up with him—the infernal, damnable, fits, that left him not half himself from that time on forever…. Eddy, who practically has never had any mental life at all: who has lived in darkness, eclipsed almost from the start…. And so I turn every thing I can into provisioning for him. The little property—Lord knows it's little enough: all, all, for Eddy—for such boon as it may bring to him after I am gone.

After Mrs. Whitman died in 1873, Walt paid for Eddy to be boarded at a private home, then institutionalized.

Descriptions of mental asylums of the time read like horror stories, yet Walt wrote to a friend that his brother was "well, and seems to be off & satisfied." In the only extant letter from Walt to Eddy, Walt says, "I often think of you & hope you have comfortable times—I have heard you have a good kind attendant who has been there some time in the asylum…."

At least Eddy's confinement followed reforms in treatment of mental illness, including a new facility at Camden County that replaced the "barnlike cells" of the previous institution.

Eddy died at Camden County Insane Asylum at Blackwood, New Jersey, only eight months after Walt died.

CHAPTER 3

Brooklyn to Montauk Point

I was down Long Island more or less every summer, now east, now west, sometimes months at a stretch.... The successive growth-stages of my infancy, childhood, youth and manhood were all pass'd on Long Island, which I sometimes feel as if I had incorporated. I roam'd, as boy and man, and have lived in nearly all parts, from Brooklyn to Montauk point.

— *Specimen Days*

On Long Island Sound near Shelter Island
Painting by John Carleton Wiggins, circa 1860

Rural Long Island

As I write, the whole experience comes back to me after the lapse of forty and more years—the soothing rustle of the waves, and the saline smell—boyhood's times, the clam-digging, bare-foot, and with trowsers roll'd up—hauling down the creek—the perfume of the sedge-meadows—the hay-boat, and the chowder and fishing excursions…

Shortly after Walt died, a visitor to his birthplace described the Long Island landscapes that nurtured the poet as child: "Numerous copses and hedgerows conceal the cultivated fields and the steadings, so that the prospect is that of a wild, scarce-cultured scene, imparting a sense of rude nature and free growth to the mind."

Except for Brooklyn, Long Island in Walt's childhood was sparsely populated, mostly by farmers and fishermen. Stagecoach lines kept the main roads serviceable. Secondary roads were little more than parallel ruts made by carts. People traveled on foot or horseback, by cart or stagecoach, or by boat.

The Whitman family's 1823 move to Brooklyn added cityscapes to Walt's world, but he returned most summers to the old family haunts of rural Long Island. His recollections of childhood, given in *Specimen Days* (quoted in this section), revolve around woods, fields, pastures, and farmhouses, all girded and ribboned by water.

A Sunny Afternoon, Shinnecock Hills. Painting by William Merritt Chase. 1898

Although the paintings reproduced in this chapter were made after Walt grew up, they capture the terrain of his childhood: rugged, rural, a giant playground for an active, adventurous child.

Long Island map made in 1815, four years before Walt was born

Today's Long Island comprises the New York City boroughs of Brooklyn and Queens (contiguous with Kings and Queens counties), and Nassau and Suffolk counties. Brooklyn lies at the western tip across the East River from Manhattan. From end to end, Long Island measures about 118 miles.

1. MANHATTAN: Although Walt lived in Manhattan only briefly, he commuted there from Brooklyn almost every day, to work, to take in cultural attractions, and to loaf.

2. EAST RIVER: One of Walt's most wondrous poems, "Crossing Brooklyn Ferry," was inspired by his daily commute over the East River to and from Brooklyn and Manhattan.

3. BROOKLYN: Walt and his family moved to Brooklyn in 1823. Walter, Sr., Jesse, and Andrew died there. The rest eventually scattered away.

4. CONEY ISLAND: "I went regularly every week in the mild seasons down to Coney island, at that time a long, bare unfrequented shore, which I had all to myself, and where I loved, after bathing, to race up and down the hard sand, and declaim Homer or Shakspere to the surf and sea gulls by the hour." — *Specimen Days*.

5. HUNTINGTON: The Whitman house, Walt's birthplace, stands today as a historic site.

6. FIRE ISLAND: A barrier island constantly reshaped by storm.

7. GREENPORT: Walt's sister Mary settled in this fishing and whaling village.

8. SHELTER ISLAND: Lying at the east end of Long Island, between the North and South forks, Shelter Island was a remote fishing settlement in Walt's day.

9. MONTAUK: Situated on the easternmost point of Long Island, wild and sea-beaten Montauk was the last outpost of Long Island's Native Americans, who were nearly extinct by the time Walt was born.

Long Island Sound at Dawn. Circa 1865 painting by John Frederick Kensett

SPECIMEN DAYS

…I spent intervals many years, all seasons, sometimes riding, sometimes boating, but generally afoot, (I was always then a good walker,) absorbing fields, shores, marine incidents, characters, the bay-men, farmers, pilots—always had a plentiful acquaintance with the latter, and with fishermen.

Sail'd more than once around Shelter island, and down to Montauk—spent many an hour on Turtle hill by the old light-house, on the extreme point, looking out over the ceaseless roll of the Atlantic. I used to like to go down there and fraternize with the blue-fishers, or the annual squads of sea-bass takers. Sometimes, along Montauk peninsula, (it is some 15 miles long, and good grazing,) met the strange, unkempt, half-barbarous herdsmen, at that time living there entirely aloof from society or civilization, in charge, on those rich pasturages, of vast droves of horses, kine or sheep, own'd by farmers of the eastern towns. Sometimes, too, the few remaining Indians, or half-breeds, at that period left on Montauk peninsula, but now I believe altogether extinct.

Montauk Lighthouse. 1877 painting by Sanford Robinson Gifford. The structure, built in 1796, was extended 14 feet in 1860 and a new lantern room was installed. Gifford's painting is among the earliest known images of the lighthouse.

On the ocean side the great south bay dotted with countless hummocks, mostly small, some quite large, occasionally long bars of sand out two hundred rods to a mile-and-a-half from the shore. While now and then, as at Rockaway and far east along the Hamptons, the beach makes right on the island, the sea dashing up without intervention.

TOP: Fire Island Beach. 1878 painting by Sanford Robinson Gifford

Pool in the Forest. 1883 painting by Thomas Moran

I...can yet recall in fancy the interminable cow-processions, and hear the music of the tin or copper bells clanking far or near, and breathe the cool of the sweet and slightly aromatic evening air, and note the sunset.

33

A circa 1837 view from Brooklyn Heights, over the East River toward Manhattan, shows a slice of life as it was when Walt was a young man. The woman on the roofwalk wears a more relaxed dress than the later form-fitting dress undergirded by corset and skirt hoops. Watercraft of all kind, steam and sail, ply the river. Church steeples, still the tallest structures, poke up over Manhattan's crowd of commercial and residential buildings. The Brooklyn buildings are mostly timber framed, the kind Walt's father would have built. Art by John William Hill.

Brooklyn

Its situation for grandeur, beauty and salubrity is unsurpassed probably on the whole surface of the globe; and its destiny is to be among the most famed and choice of the half dozen of the leading cities of the world. And all this, doubtless, before the close of the present century.

— *from Brooklyniana*

In 1823, Walt's family—then comprising parents Walter and Louisa, older brother Jesse, four-year-old Walt, and his two younger sisters Hannah and Mary—moved from rural Long Island to Brooklyn.

A history published in 1869 describes the "little village" as it was when the Whitmans arrived:

Its streets were poorly regulated, unpaved, without sidewalks. It had no market, no watch, a police without organization, and consequently inefficient; an apology for a fire department.... Those whose business called them abroad in the night, were obliged to carry their own lanterns, and cautiously to pick their winding way through streets well nigh impassible from mud and mire.

The retrospect reflects the transition of rural to urban, the passing of a cozy world of wooden buildings, barnyards, pastures, dirt roads, and gentle small-town disorder.

Winter Scene in Brooklyn. Ca 1820. Painting by Guy Francis

Devastating fires and urban development swept away the 1830s Brooklyn Walt remembered decades later, in *Specimen Days*:

Hardly anything remains, except the lines of the old streets. The population was then between ten and twelve thousand. For a mile Fulton street was lined with magnificent elm trees. The character of the place was thoroughly rural.... At that time broad fields and country roads everywhere around.

At the opening of the nineteenth century, the Wallabout, the neighborhood that the Whitmans usually lived in when in Brooklyn, was a sleepy farm village encircling a small bay. The Brooklyn Navy Yard changed that. Founded in 1809, the Yard eventually consumed much of the original Wallabout. Employment at the Yard spurred development of a diverse neighborhood of artisans and laborers, including the Whitmans as well as German and Irish immigrants.

The foreground of an 1847 engraving shows the Navy Yard at the left, and the Wallabout at the right. The East River and Manhattan lie in the distance.

Walter Whitman would have noticed Dr. James Tillary's house at number 15 and possibly modeled his building after it. The Library of Congress description of Tillary's house says, "The style...exhibits many forms and details common to this period and found in Brooklyn, Washington Square (New York City), and parts of Long Island—especially in and around Hempstead," Walt's birthplace.

Opportunities in Brooklyn seemed abundant—but not for Walt's father. Walter Whitman bought several lots and built houses on them. "We occupied them," Walt said, "one after the other, but they were mortgaged, and we lost them." In the 1850s, Walt bought his mother a house on Ryerson Street, "without concurrence of her husband at any time," the deed said, possibly to shield the property from Walter Whitman's creditors. (There Walt prepared the first edition of *Leaves of Grass*, and there his father died in 1855.)

BASEBALL

It's our game, that's the chief fact in connection with it: America's game: has the snap, go, fling, of the American atmosphere—belongs as much to our institutions, fits into them as significantly, as our constitutions, laws: is just as important in the sum total of our historic life.

During the Civil War the communal restlessness of thousands of men encamped together launched baseball as a national sport. But in Walt's hometown of Brooklyn, baseball (back then, spelled base ball) was snapping, going, and flinging for decades before the War. A Brooklyn mayor recalled, "I went to school in 1820–1.... Foot racing and base ball used to be favorite games in those days."

As a boy, Walt surely played some form of the evolving game. As a man he embraced baseball with fervor. Confined by illness, he told his friend Horace Traubel, "I can't forget the games we used to go to together: they are precious memories."

Baseball game, circa 1887

1. Tillary Street • Walter Whitman lost the house he built on Tillary Street to foreclosure.
2. District School No. 1 • Walt attended school at Adams and Concord Streets for six years.
3. Morrison Hotel • Walt's parents brought him to hear the controversial Quaker preacher Elias Hicks speak at the ballroom overlooking New York harbor.
4. Apprentice's Library • After he left school, Walt's education continued with borrowed books.
5. Fulton Ferry • Also known as the Brooklyn Ferry, Walt traveled on it nearly daily, to work, to carouse, to immerse himself in the streets of Manhattan.
6. Rome's printshop • Andrew Rome printed the first edition of Leaves of Grass, in 1855.
7. Clarke's Law Office • Walt's first professional job was here, as an office boy.
8. Brooklyn Navy Yard • The hub of the Wallabout.
9. Ryerson Street • Walt lived here with his mother and little brother Eddy in 1855, when he published the first edition of Leaves of Grass. The house is still extant.
10. Classon Avenue • Amos Bronson Alcott and Henry David Thoreau visited Walt here, where he lived with his mother and youngest brother Eddy.

The white squares indicate the locations of some of the other Whitman homes. New York City map, 1866

COMING OF AGE IN BROOKLYN

As an adult, even with loyalties divided between Manhattan and Brooklyn, Walt became a strong booster of his hometown, supporting libraries and the founding of the Brooklyn Museum. In the early 1860s, he wrote "Brooklyniana," a (somewhat stodgy) history of Brooklyn serialized in the *Brooklyn Standard*. His father's failures in the housing industry didn't stop him from extolling local residential architecture.

> We have not, in a modern city like Brooklyn, such marked specimens of magnificent architecture as the ancient or mediaeval cities presented, and many of whose ruins yet remain. For our architectural greatness consists in the hundreds and thousands of superb private dwellings, for the comfort and luxury of the great body of middle class people—a kind of architecture unknown until comparative late times, and no where known to such an extent as in Brooklyn, and the other first class cities of the New World.

In 1830, with family finances shaky, Walt left school at eleven years old to become an office boy for a lawyer. Leaving school to enter a trade at such an early age was not unusual in those days, especially in working-class families. Four years later, Walt apprenticed to a printer. It was his entry into a world he never left: the world of letters.

Walter Whitman and most of his burgeoning family returned to Long Island in 1833 to give farming another try. As much as Walt extolled country life, he heartily disliked farm work. He stayed in Brooklyn.

At age fifteen Walt was self-supporting, independent, ready to launch what looked to be a secure career in publishing.

CHAPTER 4

Shaping Forces

THERE was a child went forth every day,
And the first object he look'd upon, that object he became,
And that object became part of him for the day or a certain part
   of the day,
Or for many years or stretching cycles of years.
                    —from *"There Was a Child Went Forth"*

PREVIOUS PAGE:
Young America. Painting by Thomas Le Clear, circa 1860

American Revolution

Walt Whitman considered himself a man of nineteenth-century America, but his deepest roots lay in the American Revolution, with its battle cry of liberty. The founding of his beloved country was still in living memory; Walt could ask his own grandparents about it. He returned to it again and again in poetry and prose. George Washington in particular attracted his devotion. Standing on an old battleground in Brooklyn:

> And is this the ground Washington trod?
> And these waters I listlessly daily cross, are these the waters he
>   cross'd,
> As resolute in defeat as other generals in their proudest triumphs?
>
> I must copy the story, and send it eastward and westward,
> I must preserve that look as it beam'd on you rivers of Brooklyn....
>
> — from "The Centenarian's Story"

Washington's brother-in-arms, the French general the Marquis de Lafayette, was considered one of the heroes of the American Revolution. Lafayette combined with George Washington for significant victories in Virginia and helped negotiate trade agreements between America and France after the War. His visit to the United States brought thousands of people to cheer him. Walt cherished life-long a memory of Lafayette's stop in Brooklyn.

> It was on that occasion that the corner-stone of the Apprentices' Library, at the corner of Cranberry and Henry streets—since pull'd down—was laid by Lafayette's own hands. Numerous children arrived on the grounds, of whom I was one, and were assisted by several gentlemen to safe spots to view the ceremony. Among others, Lafayette, also helping the children, took me up—I was five years old, press'd me a moment to his breast—gave me a kiss and set me down in a safe spot.
>
> — *Specimen Days*

Walt's connection with Lafayette was strengthened by his reverence for Lafayette's woman friend, the social philosopher Frances Wright.

America's struggle for independence lived vividly in Walt's childhood. His grandparents' lives bridged Colonial times and the Revolution, and they and his parents personally knew some of the most important essayists and speakers of that time, including the Free Thinkers Thomas Paine and Frances Wright.

General George Washington and the General Marquis de Lafayette at winter quarters in Valley Forge, Pennsylvania. Reproduction of 1907 painting by John Ward Dunsmore

Free Thought

I swore when I was a young man that I would sometime—I could not say when but as the opportunity appeared—do public justice to three people—three of the superber characters of my day or America's early days who were either much maligned or much misunderstood. One of them was Thomas Paine: Paine the chiefest of these: the other two were Elias Hicks and Fanny Wright.

The Free Thought movement arose in the United States during the early nineteenth century. Free Thought centers on the conviction that truth must be sought through individual investigation founded on reason and experience, rather than through conventions, dogma, and authority.

Because of their rejection of the religious establishment, Free Thinkers were usually equated with atheists. However, atheism is not a tenet of Free Thought. The American writer Thomas Paine is considered a father of Free Thought, for example, yet he professed a personal belief in a supreme being. Walt's father was a Free Thinker, yet he attended public teachings by the Quaker Elias Hicks.

THOMAS PAINE (1737–1809)

Thomas Paine ranks with the Founding Fathers for his patriotic writings, especially *Common Sense*, which inspired American patriots to join their hearts, minds, and bodies to the struggle for independence and a form of government "of the people, by the people, for the people," as Abraham Lincoln would say a century later.

Paine's religious opinions, however, cast him out of the mainstream. About him, Walt "heard many, many, many a fight,…warmest espousals, hottest denunciations." Just one line from Paine's *The Age of Reason* shows why its author was denounced "by preachers whose words got hot in the mouth."

"I have shown [in The Age of Reason], that the Bible and Testament are impositions and forgeries….

Paine placed reason and personal insight above dogma and "revealed" teachings. In *The Age of Reason*, he makes a "voluntary and individual profession of faith":

I believe in one God, and no more; and I hope for happiness beyond this life.

I believe in the equality of man; and I believe that religious duties consist in doing justice, loving mercy, and endeavoring to make our fellow-creatures happy.

My own mind is my own church. All national institutions of churches, whether Jewish, Christian or Turkish, appear to me no other than human inventions, set up to terrify and enslave mankind, and monopolize power and profit….

It is a contradiction in terms and ideas, to call anything a revelation that comes to us at second-hand, either verbally or in writing….

Circa 1792 portrait of Thomas Paine, by Laurent Dabos

THE WORD OF GOD IS THE CREATION WE BEHOLD and it is in this word, which no human invention can counterfeit or alter, that God speaketh universally to man....

It has been by wandering from the immutable laws of science, and the right use of reason, and setting up an invented thing called revealed religion, that so many wild and blasphemous conceits have been formed of the Almighty.

1824 portrait of Frances Wright by Henry Inman

FRANCES WRIGHT (1795–1852)

Walt described Frances Wright as "one of the few characters to excite in me a wholesale respect and love: she was beautiful in bodily shape and gifts of soul."

Born in Scotland, Frances Wright visited and lived in America on and off from the age of twenty-three. The Whitmans knew her especially from her career as a public speaker and essayist. She published in New York a newspaper called the *Free Inquirer*, "which my daddy took," Walt said, "and I often read."

Wright possessed the charisma that Walt so highly prized: "She has always been to me one of the sweetest of sweet memories: we all loved her: fell down before her.... Her very appearance seemed to enthrall us."

Her high opinion of the United States won Walt over, but her treatment of three issues in particular wove into Walt's outlook and writing: pro-labor, anti-slavery, and feminist. She made the case for equality in her lectures:

However novel it may appear, I shall venture the assertion, that, until women assume the place in society which good sense and good feeling alike, assign to them, human improvement must advance but feebly.

All men are born free and equal! That is: our moral feelings acknowledge it to be just and proper, that we respect those liberties in others, which we lay claim to for ourselves; and that we permit the free agency of every individual, to any extent which violates not the free agency of his fellow creatures.

— *from Course of Popular Lectures*

> I see something of God each hour of the twenty-four, and each
>   moment then,
> In the faces of men and women I see God, and in my own face in
>   the glass,
> I find letters from God dropt in the street, and every one is sign'd
>   by God's name,
> And I leave them where they are, for I know that wheresoe'er I go,
> Others will punctually come for ever and ever.
>
> — *from "Song of Myself"*

Quaker Currents

Sometimes Walt made much of Quaker roots on his mother's side; sometimes he admitted he made too much of them. He clearly rejected Quaker pacifism in his stance on the Mexican and Civil wars. Yet he opposed slavery, lived simply, advocated temperance (and drank moderately), and adhered to the equality of men and women: all Quaker values.

> Did you know (but I guess you did not) that when I was a young fellow up on the Long Island shore I seriously debated whether I was not by spiritual bent a Quaker?—whether if not one I should not become one? But the question went its way again: I put it aside as impossible: I was never made to live inside a fence…. We must go outside the lines before we can know the best things that are within.

ELIAS HICKS (1748–1830)

Walt's parents passed to him veneration for the teachings of a most radical Quaker, Elias Hicks.

> Though it is sixty years ago since—and I a little boy at the time in Brooklyn, New York—I can remember my father coming home toward sunset from his day's work as carpenter, and saying briefly, as he throws down his armful of kindling-blocks with a bounce on the kitchen floor, 'Come, mother, Elias preaches to-night.' Then my mother, hastening the supper and the table-cleaning afterward, gets a neighboring young woman, a friend of the family, to step in and keep house for an hour or so—puts the two little ones to bed—and as I had been behaving well that day, as a special reward I was allow'd to go also.
>
> — *Specimen Days*

Elias Hicks, circa 1827. Walt possessed a print of this portrait by Henry Inman, engraved by Peter Maverick

The little boy Walt was deeply affected by Hicks' "magnetic stream of natural eloquence, before which all minds and natures, all emotions, high or low, gentle or simple, yielded entirely without exception…."

A passage in a letter by Hicks, which Walt quoted in an essay on the preacher, reveals what Walt found supreme among all values Hicks taught. Hicks places realization not with the man in the pulpit but with the people in the pews—and the people outside the pews, people like Walt. It's hard not to see in Hicks' teachings parallels with the writings of Thomas Paine.

> Some may query, What is the cross of Christ? To these I answer, It is the perfect law of God, written on the tablet of the heart and in the heart of every rational creature, in such indelible characters that all the power of mortals cannot erase nor obliterate it. Neither is there any power or means given or dispens'd to the children of men, but this inward law and light, by which the true and saving knowledge of God can be obtain'd.

School

The schoolroom of District School No. 1, which Walt attended for five years, was simple, crowded, and segregated. All ages shared the room, with student monitors to tutor and keep discipline. The windows stayed shut against heat or cold, street noise, insects and, unfortunately, fresh air. One stove provided heat. Black children attended school in a room upstairs.

One of Walt's teachers remembered him as big, sloppy, and good-natured, but without much potential. Of Walt's later renown, he remarked, "We need never be discouraged over anyone."

Learning meant memorizing and reciting lessons. Morality got folded in with questions such as, "How does History incite to virtue, and warn against vice?"

Walt advocated tax-supported free schools, but bitterly criticized the tyranny of the system: obedience enforced by beatings, and hours of physical confinement. Raised by radically minded parents and used to roaming outdoors, Walt described school as "child torture." During his several years as a schoolmaster, he relied on educational games, storytelling, and discussion. He did not beat the children.

Walt's brief formal education was not unusual for his time, and it didn't disqualify him as a grammar school teacher. His lack of university credentials did bar him from the literary eminence of writers such as Ralph Waldo Emerson and Henry Wadsworth Longfellow.

Walt's schoolroom may have looked like this one in Rhode Island.

QUESTIONS.

The more important Questions are in Roman Letters.

QUESTIONS ON INTRODUCTION.

How does History incite to virtue, and warn against vice? How does it instruct us in politicks? In what way does it display the dealings of God with mankind? What other advantages are to be derived from the study of history?

GENERAL DIVISION

Into how many periods may the history of the United States be divided? What will be the extent of the first, (*second, third, &c.*) period, and for what is it distinguished? *Repeat this last question on every period.*

Period I.

What is the extent of this Period, and for what is it distinguished?
Section I. Who made the early discoveries on the continent of America? Who took the lead? Who was Christopher Columbus? Under whose patronage did he sail? In what year? What place did he first discover? *Relate the most remarkable circumstances of his voyage. Give an account of Americus Vespucius.*
II. What were the first discoveries made under English patronage? When? By whom?
III. *What is said of the early discoveries of the French in America?*
IV. *What is said of Sir Walter Raleigh's expedition to America in 1584? Whence had Virginia its name?*
V. When and by whom was Cape Cod discovered?

NOTES.

VI. What was the state of the country on the arrival of the first settlers?
VII. By whom was the country inhabited? What was their number? physical character? general character? *What can you say of their literature? arts and manufactures? agriculture? skill in medicine? employments? amusements? dress? habitations? domestick utensils? food? money? society? war? government? religious notions? marriage? treatment of females? rites of burial? origin?*

156

Varieties of the Human Race. (Continued.)

THE *sixth* and last grand division of the human race, and the most elevated in the scale of being, comprehends the Europeans, and those of European origin; among whom may be classed the Georgians, Circassians and Mingrelians, the natives of Asia Minor, and those of the northern parts of Africa, together with a part of those countries that lie north west of the Caspian Sea.

The inhabitants of countries so extensive, and so widely separated, must be expected to vary a good deal from each other; but in general, there is a striking uniformity in the fairness of their complexions, the beauty and proportion of their limbs, and the extent of their capacity. Arts which are but partially practised, or little known, in other countries, are here brought to great perfection: and among the natives of the countries now under consideration, the highest endowments of the understanding, the best virtues of the heart, whatever can improve or adorn human nature, are to be found in an eminent degree.

To some one of the classes already enumerated, the people of every country may be referred; and in proportion as nations have been less visited by strangers, or have maintained less intercourse with the rest of mankind, we find their persons and manners more strongly impressed with some of the characteristics above mentioned. On the contrary, in those places where trade has long flourished, or which have been exposed to frequent hostile invasions, the races usually appear blended; and probably fall under no one particular variety, but partake in some respect of all.

It is undeniable, that of all colors by which mankind is diversified, white is not only the most beautiful, but also the most expressive. The fair complexion becomes like a transparent veil to the soul; through which every shade of passion, every change of health, may be seen without the necessity of oral utterance: whereas in the African black, and the Asiatic olive complexion, the countenance is found

---

A History of the United States of America, on a Plan Adapted to the Capacity of Youth, and Designed to Aid the Memory by Systematick Arrangement and Interesting Associations, by Rev. Charles A. Goodrich, 1825

Although many Americans opposed exploitation of Native Americans and enslavement of African-Americans, belief in equality of all men and women was rare in Walt's time. Racism formed part of education. Thomas Kimber's 1812 *The American Class Book* extols Europeans "and those of European origin" as "most elevated in the state of being."

The Student's Manual subtitle says what it's about: *designed by specific directions, to aid in forming and strengthening the intellectual and moral character and habits of the student.* Rev. John Todd's 1835 "self-help" book offered advice particularly relevant to a rising and ambitious generation of American men whose social status was more mutable than that of their Old World cousins, and who needed advice that less refined elders couldn't offer. Walt may not have read this particular book, but his own manners resonate with it. The book also reflects the growing preoccupation with contrasting North and South.

Walt might have approved of Rev. Isaac Taylor's 1848 children's book, *Scenes in America*, which reflects the beliefs of his generation, and educates in a playful manner.

HIGHER EDUCATION

Walt's education didn't stop when he left the schoolroom. He read omnivorously and attended lectures and exhibitions on everything from art to technology to natural history. He absorbed music and drama by attending and reviewing for various publications live performances of the best (and worst) artists of his day.

Oratory was a cornerstone of popular education in the nineteenth century. Lectures and inspiring sermons were well-attended, and Walt's parents took him, and probably the other children, to both. In the 1870s, Walt himself took to the podium with "The Death of Lincoln," a lecture that ended with his poem "O Captain!"

Reading

In the nineteenth century, as now, the world of literature had two poles: works praised by academia—Shakespeare, Pope, Milton—and mass media—sensational journalism, penny novels, sentimental poetry, melodramas. To be complete, there were (and are) works that shuttle between the two—for example, novels by Charles Dickens and Walter Scott.

As a reader and theater-goer, a newspaper editor and a typesetter, Walt absorbed the highs and the lows of American letters. He read newspapers, magazines, the Bible, Shakespeare, Dante and Homer, penny novels, popular novels now considered classics, scientific journals, history, poetry, and philosophical essays. Even one of Walt's own poetic catalogues can't touch the scope of his reading.

A visitor to Walt's home was surprised to see how few books he possessed. Yet Walt read books by the stack, mostly borrowed from public libraries. In January 1835, the minutes of the Brooklyn Apprentices' Library record "Walter Whitman" as acting librarian; this may have referred to Walt himself, who at fifteen years old had been employed by two printers active in the Library.

The Library provided "a repository of books, maps, drawing apparatus, models of machinery, tools and implements generally, for enlarging the knowledge, and thereby improving the condition of mechanics, manufacturers, artisans and others." Today the Library (rehoused in a late 19th-century building) is the Brooklyn Museum.

KOSMOS

Alexander von Humboldt (1769–1859), wrote in a letter:

I have the crazy notion to depict in a single work the entire material universe, all that we know of the phenomena of heaven and earth, from the nebulae of the stars to the geography of mosses and granite rocks—and in a vivid style that will stimulate and elicit feeling.

Humboldt devoted himself to his "crazy notion" as passionately as Walt devoted himself to his volume of poetry. *Kosmos*, the most widely read scientific treatise of the nineteenth century, sent him on epic expeditions and won him friendships with the most prominent men of his day, including Thomas Jefferson and James Madison, Charles Darwin, Johann Wolfgang von Goethe, and Friedrich von Schiller.

Alexander von Humboldt in his library. Chromolithograph copy of watercolor drawing by Eduard Hildebrant, 1856

Nature considered "rationally," that is to say, submitted to the process of thought, is a unity in diversity of phenomena; a harmony blending together all created things, however dissimilar in form and attributes; one great whole...animated by the breath of life....

In the sphere of natural investigation, as in poetry and painting, the delineation of that which appeals most strongly to the imagination, derives its collective interest from the vivid truthfulness with which the individual features are portrayed.

— *from Kosmos*

The first volume of *Kosmos* observed nature "stripped of all additions derived from the imagination." The second volume of *Kosmos* considers "the impression which the image received by the external senses produced on the feelings, and on the poetic and imaginative faculties of mankind." Humboldt makes clear, he's not aiming at psychology. Rather he wants to investigate why we enjoy nature, and why (in his time) there was a surge of interest in the natural world.

Ranging from the Middle East to Europe, the first section outlines "Incitements to the Study of Nature" in parts: "Poetical Descriptions of Nature," "Landscape Painting," and "Culture of Characteristic Exotic Plants" (landscape gardening). The second section of the book is "History of the Physical Contemplation of the Universe," meaning natural science as practiced from the ancients to Newton.

David S. Reynolds traced the influence of Humboldt's *Kosmos* on Walt, who in "Song of Myself" named himself "Walt Whitman, a kosmos, of Manhattan the son." He also noted Walt's marginal note (of a note by Humboldt, on Schiller, on the Greeks):

> Humboldt, in his Kosmos, citing Schiller, has observed of the Greeks: "With them the landscape is always mere background, of a picture, in the foreground of which human figures are moving."

Walt shared with Humboldt the urge to encompass all, from great to tiny. Although his emotional compass pointed always to men and women and children, far from consigning "the landscape," or the cityscape, to "mere background," in his poetry, Walt audaciously mixed himself, and us, with the natural word and all the seemingly random stuff of it.

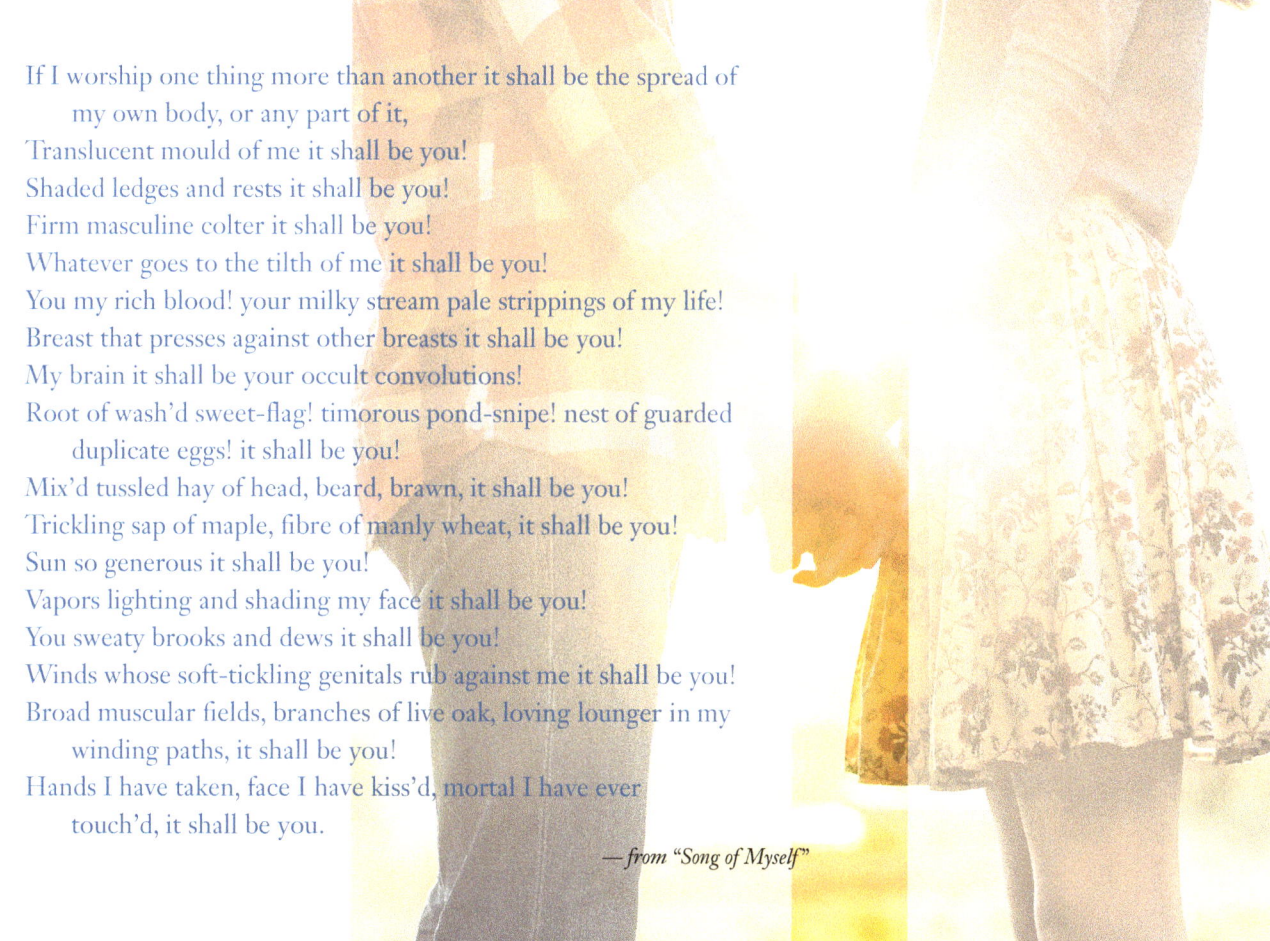

> If I worship one thing more than another it shall be the spread of
>   my own body, or any part of it,
> Translucent mould of me it shall be you!
> Shaded ledges and rests it shall be you!
> Firm masculine colter it shall be you!
> Whatever goes to the tilth of me it shall be you!
> You my rich blood! your milky stream pale strippings of my life!
> Breast that presses against other breasts it shall be you!
> My brain it shall be your occult convolutions!
> Root of wash'd sweet-flag! timorous pond-snipe! nest of guarded
>   duplicate eggs! it shall be you!
> Mix'd tussled hay of head, beard, brawn, it shall be you!
> Trickling sap of maple, fibre of manly wheat, it shall be you!
> Sun so generous it shall be you!
> Vapors lighting and shading my face it shall be you!
> You sweaty brooks and dews it shall be you!
> Winds whose soft-tickling genitals rub against me it shall be you!
> Broad muscular fields, branches of live oak, loving lounger in my
>   winding paths, it shall be you!
> Hands I have taken, face I have kiss'd, mortal I have ever
>   touch'd, it shall be you.
>
> —*from "Song of Myself"*

ARABIAN NIGHTS

… Employ'd as a boy in an office, lawyers', father and two sons, Clarke's, Fulton street, near Orange. I had a nice desk and window-nook to myself; Edward C. kindly help'd me at my handwriting and composition, and, (the signal event of my life up to that time,) subscribed for me to a big circulating library. For a time I now revel'd in romance-reading of all kinds; first, the "Arabian Nights," all the volumes, an amazing treat. Then, with sorties in very many other directions, took in Walter Scott's novels, one after another, and his poetry, (and continue to enjoy novels and poetry to this day.)
— *Specimen Days*

The folk story cycle *One Thousand and One Nights* came to English-language readers in the early eighteenth century under the title *The Arabian Nights' Entertainment*. The stories and their fabulous characters and settings continue today to sow nightmare and fantasy among children and adults, and to inspire adaptations in media from ballets to comic books to films.

On the third day, regarding his death as certain, [Aladdin] lifted up his hands, and joining them, as in the act of prayer, he wholly resigned himself to the will of God, and uttered, in a loud tone of voice, "There is no strength or power but in the high and great God." In this action of joining his hands he happened, without at all thinking of it, to rub the ring which the African magician had put upon his finger, and of the virtue of which he was as yet ignorant. Upon its being thus rubbed, a Genius of a most enormous figure, and a most horrid countenance, instantly rose as it were out of the earth before him; he was so tall that his head touched the vaulted roof, and he addressed these words to Aladdin. "What do you wish? I am ready to obey you as your slave; as the slave of him who has the ring on his finger, both I and the other slaves of the ring."

— *from The Arabian Nights, translated by Edward Forster*

The Arabian Nights. Chiswick, U.K.: C. Whittingham, College House, 1828.

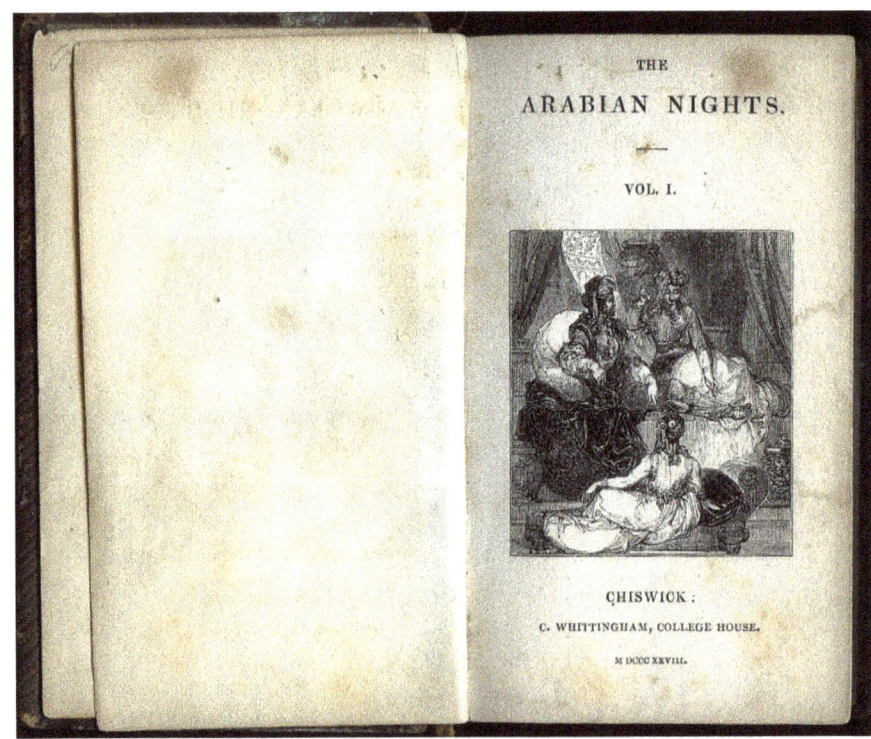

SIR WALTER SCOTT (1771–1832)

How much I am indebted to Scott no one can tell. If you could reduce the Leaves to their elements you would see Scott unmistakably active at the roots.

Walter Scott was *the* novelist of the nineteenth century. Anyone who read novels at all read Scott's, especially the historical adventures set in medieval Britain. Walt enjoyed Scott's poetry and fiction, reading them in his Brooklyn childhood haunts, in a Missouri lodging-house, in his urban cottage in Camden. "Scott does not stale for me." Walt found Scott's "richest vein" in *The Minstrelsy of the Scottish Border*, a collection of Scottish folk ballads. Scott warned: "The reader must not expect to find, in the border ballads, refined sentiment, and, far less, elegant expression." This rawness held for Walt "something even wild, even barbaric…elements of virile emotionalism."

> The American wilderness of Indian Glen, on the Hudson River, provides a setting for Walter Scott's poem, "The Lord of the Isle." The reverse of this 1859 stereo card quotes Scott:
>
> Huge terraces of granite black,
> Afforded rude and cumbered track;
> Far from the mountain hoar,
> Hurled headlong in some night of fear,
> When yelled the wolf, and fled the deer,
> Loose crags had toppled o'er.

> Now Liddesdale has ridden a raid,
> But I wat they had better hae staid at hame;
> For Michael o' Winfield he is dead,
> And Jock o' the Side is prisoner ta'en.
> For Mangerton house Lady Downie has gane,
> Her coats she has kilted up to her knee;
> And down the water wi' speed she rins,
> While tears in spaits fa' fast frae her e'e.
> Then up and spoke our gude auld lord—
>
> "What news, what news, sister Downie, to me?"
> "Bad news, bad news, my Lord Mangerton;
> "Michael is killed, and they hae ta'en my son Johnie."
> "Ne'er fear, sister Downie," quo' Mangerton;
> "I have yokes of ousen, eighty and three;
> "My barns, my byres, and my faulds a' weil fill'd,
> And I'll part wi' them a' ere Johnie shall die.
>
> *— from "Jock o' the Side" in Ministrelsy of the Scottish Border*

JAMES FENIMOORE COOPER (1789–1851)

Like Walter Scott, James Fenimore Cooper wrote historical novels, but his were set in early America. His most famous was *The Last of the Mohicans: A Narrative of 1757*, published in 1826. In the book, a frontiersman and two Mohican Indians set out to free two sisters, one mixed-race and one white, abducted by Huron Indians.

Walt didn't name Cooper as an influence on his own work, but Cooper's transformation of the American frontier into the setting of a romantic epic confirmed Walt and other nineteenth-century writers and artists in viewing America as a new font of inspiration.

The eyes of the old man opened heavily, and he once more looked upward at the multitude. As the piercing tones of the suppliant swelled on his ears, they moved slowly in the direction of her person, and finally settled there in a steady gaze. Cora had cast herself to her knees; and, with hands clenched in each other and pressed upon her bosom, she remained like a beauteous and breathing model of her sex, looking up in his faded but majestic countenance, with a species of holy reverence. Gradually the expression of Tamenund's features changed, and losing their vacancy in admiration, they lighted with a portion of that intelligence which a century before had been wont to communicate his youthful fire to the extensive bands of the Delawares. Rising without assistance, and seemingly without an effort, he demanded, in a voice that startled its auditors by its firmness:

"What art thou?"

"A woman. One of a hated race, if thou wilt—a Yengee. But one who has never harmed thee, and who cannot harm thy people, if she would; who asks for succor."

— *from The Last of the Mohicans*

Scene from The Last of the Mohicans: Cora Kneeling at the Feet of Tamenund. 1827 painting by Thomas Cole. Cole is one of the best-known of the Hudson River School painters. The landscape dwarfs humans in scale and magnificence, an effect intended to express the sublime in nature.

HOMER (CIRCA 850 BCE)

Walt enjoyed declaiming Homer while running naked up and down a beach on Coney Island. (How rural Long Island was in Walt's time—that a man could skinny-dip off Coney Island with only seagulls to squawk about it!) Walt most likely read Homer translated by the English poet Alexander Pope.

Page from The Odyssey, by Homer. Translated by Alexander Pope. 1853

GEORGE SAND (1804–1876)

George Sand was the pen name of French writer Amantine-Lucile-Aurore Dupin. Her books reached wide circulation in England as "shilling novels," ancestors of the mid-nineteenth-century American "dime novels." Of George Sand, Walt said:

I regard her as the brightest woman ever born…. Why, read Consuelo: see if you don't think so yourself: it will open your eyes: it displays the most marvellous verity and temperance: no false color—not a bit: no superfluous flesh—not an ounce: suggests an athlete, a soldier, stripped of all ornament, prepared for the fight—absolutely no flummery about her. She was Dantesque in her rigid fidelity to nature—her imagery: she led a peculiar life—obeyed the law of her personal temperament: she redeems woman. [Answering the question, "Do you think woman needs redeeming?"] No indeed: no, no, no: I do not use the word in that sense: I had in mind the question, what is woman's place, function, in the complexity of our social life? Can women create, as man creates, in the arts? rank with the master craftsmen? I mean it in that way. It has been a historic question. Well—George Eliot, George Sand, have answered it: have contradicted the denial with a supreme affirmation.

Walt entertained friends by reciting (in falsetto as required) the opening scene of Consuelo, by George Sand. London, 1847

WILLIAM SHAKESPEARE (1564–1616)

The thread of Shakespeare runs through Walt's memories, and others' recollections of Walt: Walt racing along the beach to "declaim Homer or Shakspere to the surf and sea gulls by the hour"; taking long walks around Washington, D.C., with his comrade Pete Doyle: "[Walt] would recite poetry, especially Shakespeare." Walt himself saw Shakespeare "play'd wonderfully well" by the greatest actors of his day, including Junius Brutus Booth, the father of President Lincoln's assassin John Wilkes Booth. Walt deeply admired "old Booth."

While Walt respected Shakespeare's works, he found them anachronistic.

He seems to me of astral genius, first class, entirely fit for feudalism. His contributions, especially to the literature of the passions, are immense, forever dear to humanity—and his name is always to be reverenced in America. But there is much in him ever offensive to democracy. He is not only the tally of feudalism, but I should say Shakspere is incarnated, uncompromising feudalism, in literature.

The Astor Place riot of May 10, 1849, was sparked by the rivalry of two Shakespearean actors: American Edwin Forrest and Englishman William Charles Macready. (Walt praises both in his memoirs; he doesn't mention the riot.) The riot, which left over twenty-two people dead, was not so much a show of artistic conviction as an acting out of hostility toward English people and antagonism between upper class and working class New Yorkers.

Printing

When young Walt stayed in Brooklyn, after his family returned to Long Island in 1833, he was not on his own. He was apprenticed to a printer.

Tyrannic contracts of indenture no longer burdened apprentices, but the foreman, or master, still functioned as a kind of parent, keeping apprentices clothed, housed, and fed, and, in Walt's case, fostering their happiness, education, and moral integrity. The printing industry itself fostered a familial atmosphere, as its technology had not yet been been adapted to large-scale manufactories, as with textiles. Walt had fond memories of his apprentice days.

An old printer in the office, William Hartshorne, a revolutionary character, who had seen Washington, was a special friend of mine, and I had many a talk with him about long past times. The apprentices, including myself, boarded with his grand-daughter. I used occasionally to go out riding with the boss, who was very kind to us boys; Sundays he took us all to a great old rough, fortress-looking stone church, on Joralemon street, near where the Brooklyn city hall now is—(at that time broad fields and country roads everywhere around)....

In 1835, Walt began work as a journeyman compositor in Manhattan. He also wrote articles, and got his first by-line for a piece on old New York, no doubt inspired by his talks with old Mr. Hartshorne.

Walt had barely settled into his job when the Great Fire of 1835 swept lower Manhattan, devastating the financial and publishing sectors. The Panic of 1837, the worst financial crisis so far to hit the United States (worse were to come), slowed rebuilding.

Unemployed, Walt returned to Long Island. There he endured an unhappy five-year stint as a schoolteacher, interrupted by a failed endeavor to run a newspaper with his brother George.

Walt returned to Manhattan in 1841, as the economy began to recover. From then until his death, his working life revolved around words, written and printed.

Great Fire of New York. One of the buildings housed The New York American newspaper. Print, 1836

Composing room, such as Walt might have worked in, with stands holding type cases, upper and lower, and compositors' tools in the foreground

PRE-PRESS WORK

About five years before Walt died, Ottmar Mergenthaler's Linotype machine revolutionized Walt's former trade, with type set by keyboard rather than picked by hand. Until then, innovations in printing centered mostly on the presses themselves. The process of preparing images and text for the press had not changed much for over a century. Images were printed from engravings, and type was set by hand, character by character.

Walt didn't work long in printing itself, but he never completely left it behind. A young compositor with *The Aurora* remembers that when Walt was editor, "Frequently, while I was engaged in sticking type, he would ask me to let him take my case for a little while, and he seemed to enjoy the recreation."

> You shall see hands at work at all the old processes and all the
>   new ones,
> You shall see the various grains and how flour is made and then
>   bread baked by the bakers,
> You shall see the crude ores of California and Nevada passing on
>   and on till they become bullion,
> You shall watch how the printer sets type, and learn what a com-
>   posing-stick is…

— *from "Song of the Exposition"*

A compositor "sticking type" holds a partly loaded compositor (composing) stick, with the type case below. (Walt's stick may have been made of wood.) The stick holds the type picked from the case. The width of the stick's tray can be adjusted, at left, to the column width.

Each compartment in the type case holds a character of a particular face (such as Didot or Roman), size, and variation (eg, regular or italic). Spacers break words or fill out a line shorter than column width. A strip of lead provides "leading," the space between each line of characters. All the characters and spacers have to be packed in tight. In order to print correctly, each character is cast in a mirror image of its true glyph. The compositor works left to right, upside down.

When the print run is finished, the type is cleaned of ink and returned to the type cases.

The illustration below dates from the 18th century, but the work flow in mid-19th century print shops was much the same. The three men illustrate three phases of setting up a page to be printed. From left to right:

STICKING TYPE: The compositor holds his stick in his left hand and selects type with the right. His eye is fixed on the handwritten manuscript fastened to the case, rather than on the type case or stick. He recognizes the bottom of each piece of type by feeling its "nick" or groove.

THE GALLEY: When the stick is full, the compositor will ease the type into the "galley," a metal tray which the compositor is shown holding in his right hand. Careful! One slip and the type will spill; the compositor will end up with a "pie," a jumble of letters. A complete galley holds a full column which, in a book like Walt's, would be a page.

CHASE: Each column is completely filled with characters and spacers, then "tied up," to keep everything together, and arranged as pages. "Furniture"—blocks of wood—is laid in for the margins and "gutters," the space between columns. Complete pages are laid in a "chase," an iron frame, and braced with more furniture. A chase full of pages is called a "form." Here, the compositor levels the pieces of type within the form with a block of wood and hammer.

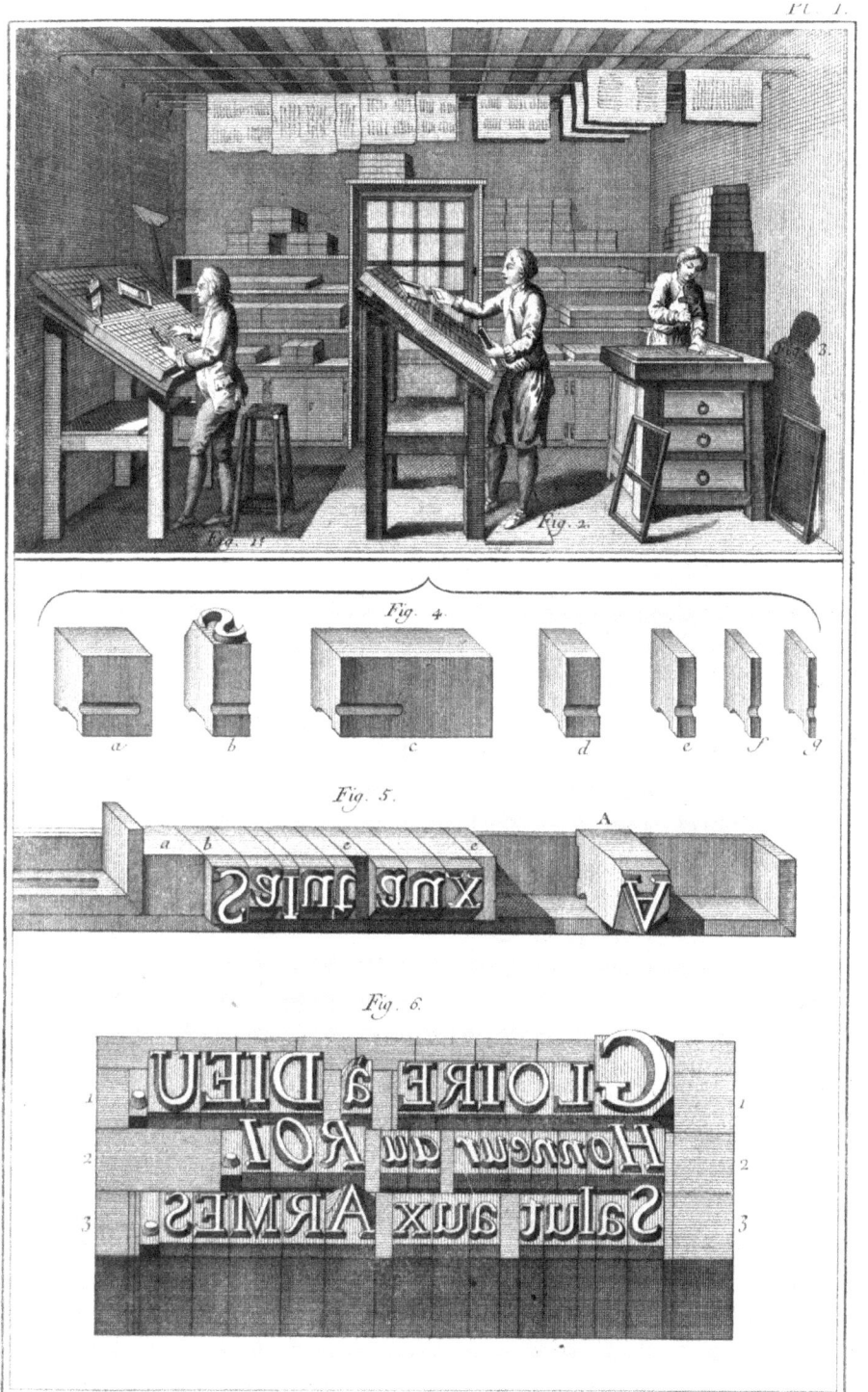

PIECES OF TYPE: Letters and spacers, with a nick at the bottom side of each piece.

THE STICK: The composing stick with a partially set line of characters and spacers (in French).

THREE LINES OF TYPE: The "furniture" at the right holds the margin.

> Why should I be afraid to trust myself to you?
> I am not afraid .... I have been well brought forward by you;
> I love the rich running day, but I do not desert her in whom I lay so long:
> I know not how I came of you, and I know not where I go with you .... but I know I came well and shall go well.
>
> I will stop only a time with the night .... and rise betimes.
>
> I will duly pass the day O my mother and duly return to you;
> Not you will yield forth the dawn again more surely than you will yield forth me again,
> Not the womb yields the babe in its time more surely than I shall be yielded from you in my time.

Leaves of Grass.

> THE bodies of men and women engirth me, and I engirth them,
> They will not let me off nor I them till I go with them and respond to them and love them.
>
> Was it dreamed whether those who corrupted their own live bodies could conceal themselves?
> And whether those who defiled the living were as bad as they who defiled the dead?
>
> The expression of the body of man or woman balks account,
> The male is perfect and that of the female is perfect.
>
> The expression of a wellmade man appears not only in his face,
> It is in his limbs and joints also.... it is curiously in the joints of his hips and wrists,
> It is in his walk .. the carriage of his neck .. the flex of his waist and knees .... dress does not hide him,

Walt ordered the first (1855) edition of Leaves of Grass quite large, with generous margins, an ideal he kept through his life, though not all editions of his book are so. "My idea of a book page is an open one—a wide open one: words broadly spaced, lines with a grin, page free altogether: none huddled." The typeface of the body (the main text) is of the Scotch Roman genre, a fairly new kind of type in Walt's time, elegant and unpretentious. This page shows the opening lines of the poem that would be titled "I Sing the Body Electric."

THE BOOK ARTS

The printers and foremen thought I was crazy, and there were all sorts of supercilious squints (about the typography I ordered, I mean)—but since it has run through the press, they have simmered down. Yesterday the foreman of the press-room … pronounced it, in plain terms, the freshest and handsomest piece of typography that had ever passed through his mill—I like it, I think, first rate—though I think I could improve much upon it now. It is quite 'odd,' of course.

— Walt to his brother Jeff, regarding the 1860 edition of Leaves of Grass

Walt took from his printing days an artisan's attitude toward books. His own books, mostly self-published, never functioned merely as vessels for his words, any more than the body is a mere conveyance for the soul. What we now call print design—the look of type and image on paper—remained paramount in Whitman's interaction with his published works of poetry.

Walt oversaw production of several editions of *Leaves of Grass*, specifying features such as cover design, size, and fonts. His eye for design caused him to direct printers to mix typefaces within lines; for example, if he preferred the ampersand of a particular typeface over that of the main typeface. Sometimes design even won out over his own

Page spread from 1860 edition of Leaves of Grass

words. Noticing that his essay "A Backward Glance" ended at the bottom of a page, he said, "If I had been a little more vigilant I should have cut out five or six lines. I like chapters in books to end short of a page—it pleases my eye better so."

One facet of his design decision caused critics to doubt that his poetry was really poetry. His poems often have very long lines, and each line stretches from left to right margin, breaking only to fit, not for expression. From edition to edition, as the size of *Leaves of Grass* changed, the length of lines changed, too.

> I like to supervise the production of my own books: I have suffered a good deal from publishers, printers—especially printers, damn 'em, God bless 'em! The printer has his rod, which has often fallen on me good and powerful.

Walt's sympathy for working men boosted his illness-sapped energies when he produced the last edition of *Leaves* made in his lifetime.

> I am almost in a hurry, which is remarkable for me. And besides, I have quite a feeling for the printers—for the two you said were laid off: I do not want them to suffer on my account: Ferguson got them for me—I should keep them going.

Books were things, but they were things made by people, and it was the human in all that Walt sought most dearly.

> This printed and bound book—but the printer and the printing-
>   office boy?
> The well-taken photographs—but your wife or friend close and
>   solid in your arms?
> The black ship mail'd with iron, her mighty guns in her turrets—
>   but the pluck of the captain and engineers?
> In the houses the dishes and fare and furniture—but the host and
>   hostess, and the look out of their eyes?
> …
>
> *— from "Song of Myself"*

CHAPTER 5

The Parti-Colored World

(Could but thy flagstones, curbs, façades, tell their inimitable tales;
Thy windows rich, and huge hotels—thy side-walks wide;)
Thou of the endless sliding, mincing, shuffling feet!
Thou, like the parti-colored world itself—like infinite, teeming, mocking life!
Thou visor'd, vast, unspeakable show and lesson!

— *from "Broadway"*

Broadway from Barnum's Museum
Looking North, 1860

Walt lived in Brooklyn, from early childhood to middle age, except for four years in Manhattan and three months in New Orleans. He worked at newspapers, magazines, and print shops in both Brooklyn and Manhattan.

Wherever Walt worked or slept, the streets were his headquarters, his school, his playground, his art gallery, and his social club.

Fulton Street, Brooklyn, looking out from the ferry landing. Fulton Street was a main thoroughfare in Brooklyn and Manhattan, with the ferry line connecting the street over the East River. Circa 1845

> Crowds of men and women attired in the usual costumes! how curious you are to me!
> On the ferry-boats, the hundreds and hundreds that cross, returning home, are more curious to me than you suppose …
>
> — *from "Crossing Brooklyn Ferry"*

In the days when Walt's father tried farming, Walt may have tagged along with him into Manhattan's Fulton General Market, built in 1821. In the circa 1870 photo, the long building is the General Market. At the right is the Fulton Ferry Terminal, built in 1863, after Walt had moved to Washington, D.C. A ferry (at left) approaches. Many masts at Pier 17 can be seen at the right of the image; steam ships would soon crowd out sailing ships.

The Streets of New York

The entire length of Broadway seems to have measured for a new suit of marble and freestone—six and seven story buildings going up...of most magnificent elegance in style.... Indeed public and private buildings are going up in all directions...with Aladdin-like splendor and celerity.

— Gleason's Pictorial, *1852*

From the mid-nineteenth century on, commercial sprawl and the craving to build more magnificent homes nudged the rich uptown, leaving downtown to wholesale and retail establishments, tenements, theaters and galleries, and ateliers later dubbed "sweat shops."

Harper's Magazine, in 1862, summed up the period spanning Walt's years in New York: "Twenty years ago, [Broadway] was a street of three-story red brick houses. Now it is a highway of stone, and marble, and iron buildings."

Walt watched the buildings rise, he surely knew the men who hauled the materials, the laborers, the carpenters and craftsmen.

SHOPPING

When A.T. Stewart opened his splendid dry-goods store on Broadway, in 1846, his merchandise was neatly and novelly arranged by "department," and the term "department store" was coined. Such "commercial palaces" added to the glories of Broadway.

> Looking in at the shop-windows of Broadway the
>   whole forenoon, flatting the flesh of my nose
>   on the thick plate-glass ...

— *from "Song of Myself," 1860 edition*

Walt wasn't much of a shopper, but he loved to window-shop. Through the window panes he imprinted with his nose, he saw enticing arrays of books, ready-made clothes, tools, millinery, lace and other notions, household goods, tobacco and wine, and imported delicacies.

PLATE GLASS here refers not to a large expanse of glass such as we see today in shop fronts. Windows in Walt's day were still divided into individual panes. Plate glass refers to glass made using a technology that eliminated the distortions and flaws that Walt would have seen in the windows of his childhood home.

LEFT: Rowland Hussey Macy opened his first New York store in 1858, on Sixth Avenue between 13th and 14th streets. Macy's department stores eventually spread from coast to coast.
RIGHT: Such was Haughwout's prestige that Mary Todd Lincoln commissioned the firm for a set of hand-painted White House china. The cast-iron external walls actually support the building; in most cast-iron buildings cast-iron facades are fixed to underlying brickwork. The warm beige paint, called "Turkish drab," was reproduced in 1995.

I am the mash'd fireman with breast-bone broken,
Tumbling walls buried me in their debris,
Heat and smoke I inspired, I heard the yelling shouts of my com-
    rades,
I heard the distant click of their picks and shovels,
They have clear'd the beams away, they tenderly lift me forth....
— *from "Song of Myself"*

The Life of a Fireman. Circa 1861

FIREMEN

New York's mid-nineteenth-century firefighters organized in companies called clubs. "Roughs" dominated the clubs, which tended to align with ethnic and political loyalties.

The Americus Engine Company No. 6, called Big 6, helped launch "Boss" Tweed to leadership of Tammany Hall, the Democratic "machine" that controlled New York politics from Walt's time all the way into the early twentieth century.

Ralph Waldo Emerson recalled that Walt brought him to "a noisy fire-engine society." The experience prompted his reflection that Walt's work "belongs yet to the fire clubs, and has not got into the parlors," underlining the perceived contrast between firemen and genteel society.

GANGS

As today, gang members usually grouped by ethnic background and class. Immigrants from Ireland made the majority of gang members in Walt's New York City, and newspaper coverage of gang crime fueled the heavy discrimination faced by Irish-born Americans. Some firemen's clubs blended with gangs.

The Dead Rabbits and the Bowery Boys were the two most notorious gangs. The Dead Rabbits backed New York's Democratic organization, Tammany Hall. The Bowery Boys, touting themselves "Native American," supported the newly formed Republican party. Party bosses employed gangs to sabotage voting in rival precincts and to stuff ballot boxes. In July 1857, a clash between the Dead Rabbits and the Bowery Boys escalated into a riot that left eight dead and roughly fifty hospitalized with injuries.

NATIVE AMERICAN meant, essentially, white and born in the United States, not indigenous to the continent.

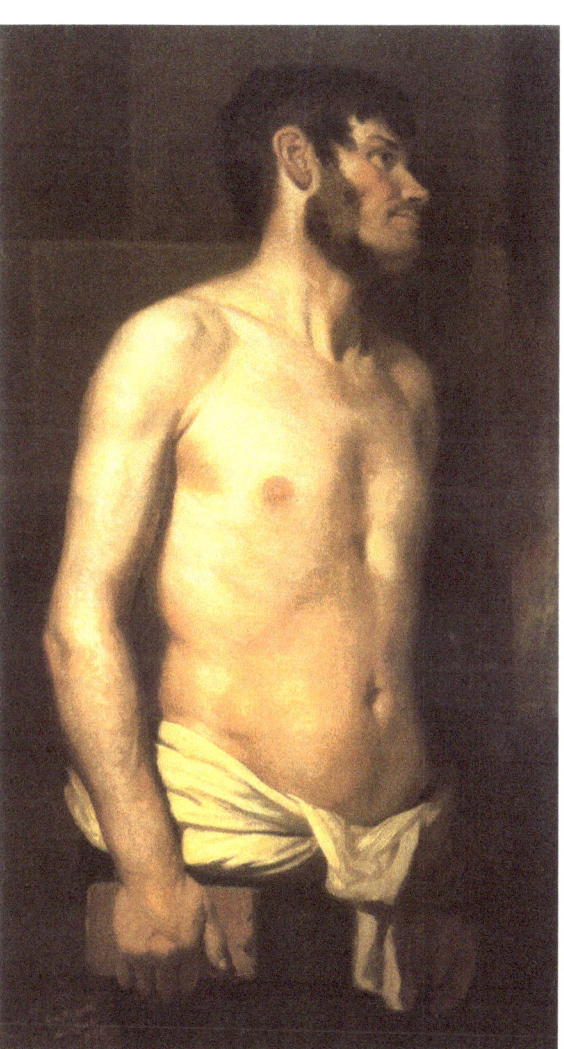

The fireman / gang member "Mose" made the 1848 drama A Glance at New York a huge hit, testifying to popular culture's perenniel fascination with "bad boys."

George Henry Hall's 1858 portrait, Dead Rabbit, shows a young man, posed and semi-nude in a manner reminiscent of portrayals of Christ. He holds a brick; he could be a mason but more likely the brick is a brickbat, to be used as a weapon. Hall (1825-1913) lived in New York City during the 1850s.

At the Broadway Hospital (also called New York Hospital), at Pearl Street and Broadway, Walt visited injured friends who were firemen, coach drivers, and dockworkers, and perhaps gang members injured in fights. His visits foreshadowed his attendance on the wounded during the Civil War. Broadway Hospital. Engraving circa 1869

The prostitute draggles her shawl, her bonnet bobs on her tipsy and pimpled neck;
The crowd laugh at her blackguard oaths, the men jeer and wink to each other;
(Miserable! I do not laugh at your oaths, nor jeer you;)
— *from "To a Common Prostitute"*

PROSTITUTION

Lawyer George Templeton Strong famously called New York City a "whorearchy" for the visibility and numbers of its sexworkers. An 1870 "Gentlemen's Directory," couches the business in arch terms, calling the sexworkers "lady boarders," and the brothels themselves "temples of love." That prostitution was relatively acceptable or at least openly acknowledged is evident in a late nineteenth-century flyer advertising "condumns or preventatives"; the first recommended use is not for birth control but to protect "single young men" from diseases conveyed by "women of a public character."

Walt saw it; he sympathized with the women; he heartily despised its roots, the "miserably poor" wages of working women, and marriage laws that stripped women of property and income, putting them at the mercy of husbands who might be brutal or spendthrift, and leaving widows with no means to feed, warm, and clothe themselves and their children.

An advertisement for "preventatives," condoms, attests to the prevalence of venereal disease, the health dangers to women in pregnancy and childbirth, and poverty, with its threat of "raising subjects for alms houses, poor houses, or workhouses...."

PLAGUE

> Not a cholera patient lies at the last gasp but I also lie at the last gasp,
> My face is ash-color'd, my sinews gnarl, away from me people retreat …
>
> — *from "Song of Myself"*

In the days before medical regulation, any product could be touted as "a certain cure" for cholera and other disorders. Popular remedies like "Dr. C.Y. Girard's Ginger Brandy" probably did more harm than good. The essential treatment for cholera is rehydration, and alcoholic beverages have exactly the opposite effect.

Every summer, city dwellers dreaded outbreaks of yellow fever and cholera. Walt recalled 1832: "the bad cholera year, we (the family) were domiciled in Liberty street—all hands except me moved for several weeks out in the country leaving me alone in the house." Walt was then working as a printer. Maybe he preferred to face an epidemic, rather than farm chores.

Cholera returned with ghastly regularity. An 1848 outbreak killed 642 people in Brooklyn: 1 out of every 155 citizens. The majority of those stricken were German and Irish immigrants living in overcrowded and unsanitary conditions. Access to clean drinking water eventually pushed back cholera in the United States.

Other diseases also posed risk. Malaria, for example, was widespread; Abraham Lincoln was among its sufferers. Though the causes were not understood, treatment by quinine was available from the early nineteenth century.

Measles, pneumonia, typhoid, hepatitis, tuberculosis, and infections of every kind were common afflictions. A vaccination against smallpox had been developed but it was not readily available. The role of sanitation in preventing and treating disease and restricting its spread had been demonstrated scientifically, but was not widely known.

Sounds of the City

> As the fare-collector goes through the train, he gives notice by the jingling of loose change;
> The floor-men are laying the floor, the tinners are tinning the roof, the masons are calling for mortar…
>
> — *from "Song of Myself"*

Today, the roar and growl of motors dominate villages and cities. Until the late nineteenth century, when steam power came into wide use, hand-wielded tools, animals, metal-rimmed wooden wheels, and the human voice dominated.

Let's stroll with Walt down Broadway. We know some of the sounds he heard, from films and from our own experience. Blending them in our imaginations we can immerse ourselves in 1850s New York City.

The Great Fire of 1836 and an influx of immigrants and rural native-born Americans—such as Walt's own family—drove a demand for buildings commercial and residential. Hammers whacked nails into wood, hammer and chisel clinked at stone, tile and brick; barrows of material thumped and rattled along. The crash and bash of demolition competed with the sound of building.

In warm weather, open doors and windows proclaimed trade: blacksmiths hammering at anvils and the hiss of red-hot metal plunged into water, the thump and

Children at work did not faze 19th-century people. The radish vendor may be a farmer's daughter, or she may be a city girl who buys her wares at the seaport, where farmers, including Walt's father, sold their produce, driving their laden wagons onto the ferry.

grumble of printing presses, cobblers tapping together shoes, the clink of glasses from taverns, pianos playing, shop bells tinkling, hostlers tending horses. From amusement gardens came gun shots from shooting arcades, music, and laughter.

Horses clopped and metal-reinforced wagon and carriage wheels bumped over the granite-block paving, freight rattling and clanking. Cart drivers yelled people out of their way. In place of the automobiles' honking horns, bells clanged from streetcars and omnibuses.

The train running into the city would have made plenty of noise, engine chuffing, rails screeching as it made its two turns at Broome Street, bells clanging and steam-whistle shrieking. (Only one train ran into the city during the 1850s. Elevated trains didn't arrive until the late 1860s; subway construction began in the early twentieth century.)

Bells of all kinds sang out. Street vendors enticed with handbells, street cars warned. Near the water, boats hooted and buoys rang, each with a song as distinctive as a human voice. One voice rose faithfully over all: "the tolling tolling bells' perpetual clang": the bells of churches and city towers ringing the hours, mourning deaths, and warning of fire and other disasters—how they must have tolled in the Great Fire of 1836!

Now and then the gurgle of water penetrated the din. Public fountains, fueled by the new Croton Aqueduct, quenched the thirst of pedestrians, their troughs enjoyed by horses and dogs. Another beverage was toted by "bucket men" who rattled along carrying poles hung with growlers—two-quart buckets—of "canned" beer.

Accents have evolved, but the sound of human voices is much the same today as it was then. People laughed, yelled, talked, whistled, sang, and children shouted at play.

Peddlers cried their wares: *Muffins! Hot muffins! Crabs! Crabs alive! Buy any crabs? Here dey are, all alive! Werry nice and fresh! cherries, blackberries, Strawberries, fine ripe strawberries! watermelons, cantaloupes, Peaches, Oh! Here dey go!* Ice cream vendors, tin cans on their shoulders, sang to lure children with music as our trucks do. Firewood and charcoal sold on street corners, the charcoal seller all covered in soot. Scissors and knife sharpeners cried their services to the gritty screech of their grinding wheels. Ragged children cried newspapers and shoe shines, horse tending and clean up. "Recyclers" alerted their clients with distinctive cries. The soap-grease man roved from building to building buying kitchen grease and bones and ash for making soap; the rag man collected rags for paper; the clothes man bought old clothes.

Preachers preached, reformers harangued, and political campaigners made fine airy speeches puffed up with promises. Beggars added their plea. Buskers entertained passersby, as did parades military, political, and religious.

A bucket man with growlers, circa 1890

Entertainment

Walt, along with just about everyone else in his time, pursued entertainment as avidly as we do today. The only "virtual" past-time was reading, from newspapers to magazines to sensational novels to literary efforts. Everything else was live: music, drama, dance, the visual arts, as well as edifying or electrifying lectures and political stump speeches. Circuses, exhibitions, theaters, shooting galleries, urban amusement parks called "gardens," and window-shopping kept nineteenth-century New Yorkers out and about. Anything and everything was up for exploitation when it came to keeping people amazed, amused, sometimes indignant, often enthralled.

The closure of stores and public venues on Sundays made way for promenades, picnics, and sports. Everyone—men, women, boys, and girls—took part in outdoor games, from swimming at the beach to skating at the park. When reformers tried to ban fun on Sunday, nineteenth-century New Yorkers pushed back. Said Walt, "I believe in all that—in baseball, in picnics, in freedom: I believe in the jolly all-round time—with the parsons and the police eliminated."

One 1860 evening of "amusements" listed in the *New York Times* included a circus, a magic act, plays, stand-up comedy, "Ethiopian Entertainments," exhibitions of art and antiquities and "living curiosities"—the last later known as "freak shows."

"Ethiopian Entertainments" meant "black minstrelsy," in which whites impersonated blacks to present what was perceived as African-American life in song, dance, and speech. Frederick Douglass blasted black-face performers as "...the filthy scum of white society, who have stolen from us a complexion denied them by nature, in which to make money, and pander to the corrupt taste of their white fellow citizens."

Amusements this Evening.

NIBLO'S GARDEN—Afternoon and Evening—NIXON'S GRAND CIRCUS.

WINTER GARDEN—PROFESSOR ANDERSON'S MAGICAL SOIREES.

WALLACK'S THEATRE—THE WIFE'S SECRET—THE LOVE CHASE.

BOWERY THEATRE—HERO OF ITALY—WARLOCK OF THE GLEN.

NEW BOWERY THEATRE—SIEGE OF PALMYRA—SUDDEN THOUGHTS.

BARNUM'S MUSEUM—Afternoon and Evening—LIVING CURIOSITIES—WREN JUVENILE COMEDIANS.

HOOLEY & CAMPBELL'S, Niblo's Saloon—ETHIOPIAN ENTERTAINMENTS.

CANAL-STREET—No. 366—WHITLOCK'S FREE GALLERY OF OIL PAINTINGS.

ABBOTT'S EGYPTIAN MUSEUM, No. 659 Broadway—EGYPTIAN ANTIQUITIES.

DUSSELDORF GALLERY—EXHIBITION OF PAINTINGS.

Walt attended "amusements" of all kinds and might have perused this column, from the New York Times, September 1, 1860.

Castle Garden, NY. 1848

GARDENS

"Gardens," such as Castle Garden on the Battery, were somewhat like carnivals, with food and drink, promenades, stages, shooting galleries, and exhibition space. Madison Square Garden in New York descends from the pleasure gardens of Walt's time.

I yet recall the splendid seasons of the Havana musical troupe…the fine band, the cool sea-breezes, the unsurpass'd vocalism…. (The Battery—its past associations—what tales those old trees and walks and sea-walls could tell!)"

— *Specimen Days*

Crystal Palace, circa 1853

CRYSTAL PALACE

Walt was enthralled by the 1853 Exhibition of the Industry of All Nations, housed at present-day Bryant Park, New York City. The iron and glass Crystal Palace displayed countless aspects of human endeavor, from lighthouse lenses to sculpture.

I went a long time (nearly a year)—days and nights—especially the latter—as it was finely lighted, and had a very large and copious exhibition gallery of paintings (shown best at night, I tho't)—hundreds of pictures from Europe, many masterpieces—all an exhaustless study—and, scatter'd thro' the building, sculptures, single figures or groups…curios from everywhere abroad—with woods from all lands of the earth—all sorts of fabrics and products and handiwork from the workers of all nations.

— *Specimen Days*

Winter street scene with sleighs in front of Barnum's Museum, Broadway & Anne Street, Manhattan. 1855

PT BARNUM

P.T. Barnum's Museum furnished attractions fascinating, sensational, grotesque, artistic, amusing—all suitable for families. Spectators could gaze on living human "oddities," exhibits of animals, paintings, historical objects, scenes, and wax figures, and attend live performances.

Today, the human "exhibits" of P.T. Barnum's American Museum would be considered not harmless curiosities, but victims of cruel exploitation. Yet to some of the Museum's performers—misfits in the mainstream world—show business offered prosperity and prestige beyond the hopes of most ordinary citizens.

So…. You want a peek? Here's a ticket for you….

The Lecture Room presented plays and performing artists, such as the famed vocalist Jenny Lind. (Of Lind, Walt said, she "never touched my heart in the least.")

71

TOP LEFT: Chang and Eng were conjoined "siamese twins." They achieved great wealth in their careers, only to lose it by investing in slaves before the Civil War. 1860

TOP RIGHT: "The Quaker Giant and Giantess." 1849

ABOVE: "The Wonderful Albino Family"

LEFT: "General Tom Thumb" was one of Barnum's most famous celebrities. His travels included a visit to the White House, where he met President and Mrs. Lincoln. Circa 1849

RIGHT: In contrast to advertisements that showed a lovely creature half-fish, half-woman, Barnum's "Feejee mermaid" was a mere dried fish, pathetic and grotesque. Yet the crowds poured in to see it.

The Arts

We 'go' heartily for all the rational refinements and rose-colorings of life—such as music, mirth, works of art, genial kindness, and so forth. We wish every mechanic and laboring man and woman in Brooklyn would have some such adornment to his or her abode—however humble that abode may be—a print hung on the wall….

MECHANIC. 1. A person whose occupation is to construct machines, or goods, wares, instruments, furniture, and the like. — Webster, 1832

Walt did not collect art; he energetically supported it, especially as it was offered to the public. He was one of the founders of the Brooklyn Institute, which later became the Brooklyn Museum, a volunteer at a public library, and, as important, a friend and booster to painters, photographers, and other writers, and an enthusiastic patron of lectures, theaters, private galleries, music halls, and exhibitions of all kinds.

Walt called the Brooklyn Institute "decidedly the most interesting feature of Brooklyn life." His praise revolved not only on the displays, but on their availability to all regardless of means. This 1891 photo of the Brooklyn Institute was taken shortly before the buildings were demolished for the Brooklyn Bridge extension.

Broadway housed prominent photographers' galleries, including that of Mathew Brady. The caption of the 1861 print reads, "M.B. Brady's new photographic gallery, corner of Broadway and Tenth Street, New York."

The Egyptian Museum, a private collection at 659 Broadway, housed fragments of ancient pottery, glass, and textiles, as well as human and animal mummies. One of Walt's entries in the guest register adds "20th visit." Walt found in the ancient world, not only of Egypt but of Asia and India, an alternative to the European themes that, he felt, burdened and deadened American art.

The crowd of pictures is typical of art exhibitions of the time. Stereograph of the Picture Gallery in the Upper Main Hall, Smithsonian Building, in 1858, with portraits of Native American by John Mix Stanley and Charles Bird King. The Smithsonian's guidebook listed 152 paintings by Stanley and 139 by King on exhibit in the gallery.

Walt admired and promoted the work of his friend Jesse Talbot. Autumn on the Hudson, painting, circa 1845

THEATER

Walt called the Bowery Theatre, "a little realm, full of little potentates from the stage of the theatre, the saw-dust of the circus, and the arena of the professionally trained fighting-man." The audience was known for its boisterous response to what was happening on stage and amongst themselves. In drama, Walt said, "the heavy tragedy business prevail'd," from melodramas to Shakespeare.

The theater and its patrons reflected the waves of immigrants who lived on Manhattan's Lower East Side. In Walt's time, Irish dominated. By the 1880s the theater was turned over to Germans, in the 1890s, Yiddish, then Italian, then Chinese.

The Park Theatre was "the more stylish and select theatre."

English opera and the old comedies were often given in capital style; the principal foreign stars appear'd here, with Italian opera at wide intervals.... The old Park theatre—what names, reminiscences, the words bring back!...singers, tragedians, comedians. What perfect acting!

Bowery Theatre, 1867

Park Row & Park Theater, 1831. Park Theatre is at right. Further down is the Brick Presbyterian Church. Tammany Hall, headquarters of the Democratic political "machine" in New York, lies in the distance. Across the street is City Hall Park.

The teeming lady comes,
The lustrous orb, Venus contralto, the blooming mother,
Sister of loftiest gods, Alboni's self I hear ...
— from "Proud Music of the Storm"

Walt's idol, contralto Italian opera-singer Marietta Alboni (1826-1894), toured the U.S. in 1852-53. Alboni played male roles en travesti, and female roles. Photograph by Jeremiah Gurney circa 1862.

75

POPULAR MUSIC

The nineteenth century saw an explosion in sheet music for popular songs. Like popular literature, the most successful songs were sentimental and suitable for family entertainment. The Civil War increased the appeal of patriotic songs.

"Plantation" or "minstrel" music, with lyrics in dialect, was hugely popular north and south, before and after the Civil War. Stephen Foster, a white man who never traveled to the South, wrote minstrel songs that endure among the most popular American songs of all time, including "Oh! Susanna," "Camptown Races," and "Dixie." Today's versions usually don't use dialect transcriptions, such as "wid" for "with." (The credit on the sheet music seems to indicate the author of the song is Henry Chadwick, but the credit is intended as: "Arranged for the guitar, by Henry Chadwick.")

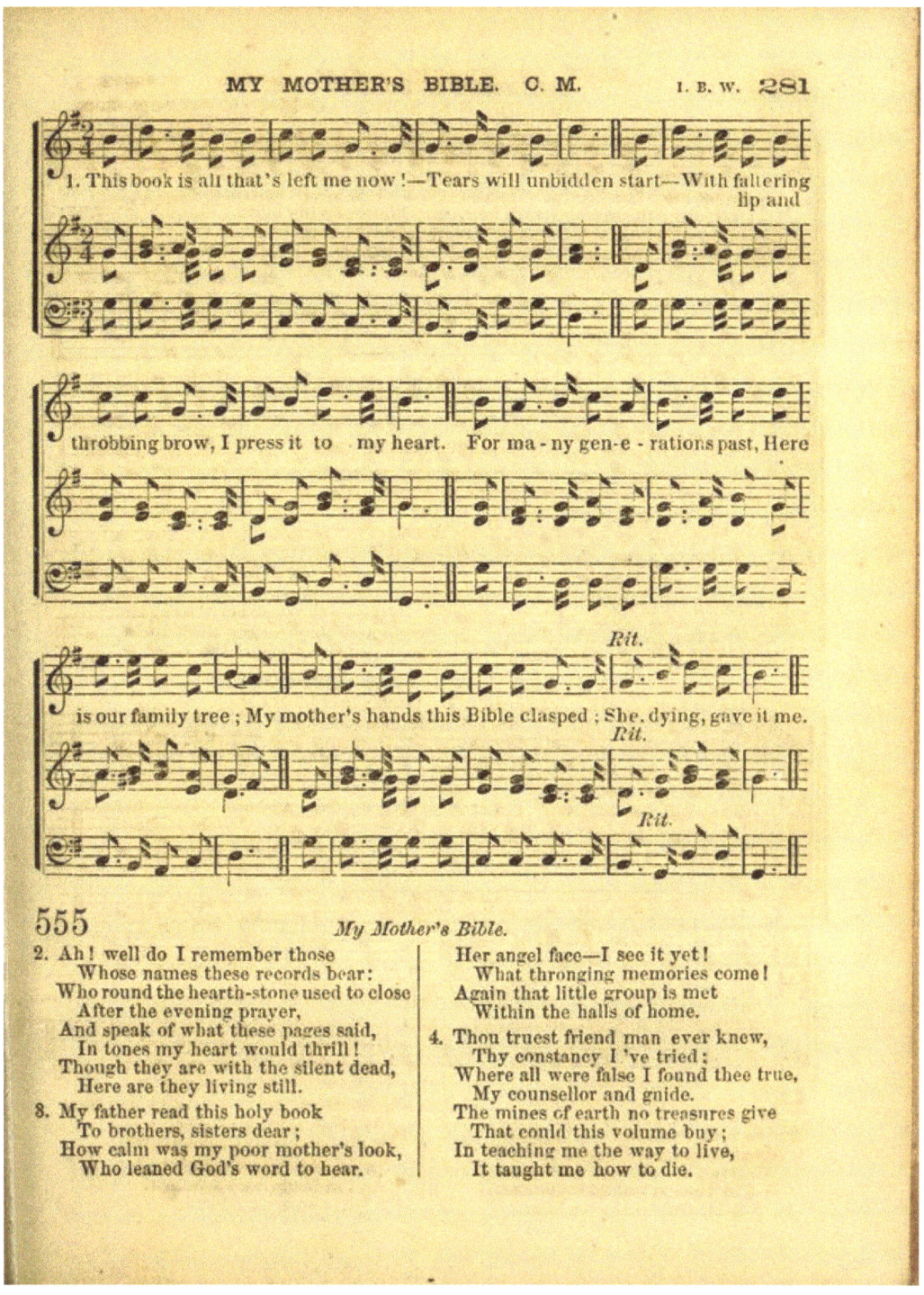

George P. Morris (1802–1864), who published Walt's early prose work in the *Daily Mirror*, was the king of popular lyrics. "My Mother's Bible" and "Woodman, Spare that Tree," are among his poems adapted as song lyrics with thumping great success. A critic wrote of Morris's work, "his lays can bring to the cheek of purity no blush save that of pleasure." Edgar Allan Poe considered him "our best writer of songs." Walt liked Morris's songs, too.

Many songs have the title "My Mother's Bible," but the blockbuster of them all was the one with lyrics by George Pope Morris. Page from Cottage Melodies: A hymn and tune book, for prayer and social meetings and the home circle. 1859

THE ATLANTIC MONTHLY.

A MAGAZINE OF LITERATURE, ART, AND POLITICS.

VOL. IX.—FEBRUARY, 1862.—NO. LII.

BATTLE HYMN OF THE REPUBLIC.

MINE eyes have seen the glory of the coming of the Lord:
He is trampling out the vintage where the grapes of wrath are stored;
He hath loosed the fateful lightning of His terrible swift sword:
    His truth is marching on.

I have seen Him in the watch-fires of a hundred circling camps,
They have builded Him an altar in the evening dews and damps;
I can read His righteous sentence by the dim and flaring lamps:
    His day is marching on.

I have read a fiery gospel writ in burnished rows of steel:
"As ye deal with my contemners, so with you my grace shall deal;
Let the Hero, born of woman, crush the serpent with his heel,
    Since God is marching on."

He has sounded forth the trumpet that shall never call retreat;
He is sifting out the hearts of men before His judgment-seat:
Oh, be swift, my soul, to answer Him! be jubilant, my feet!
    Our God is marching on.

In the beauty of the lilies Christ was born across the sea,
With a glory in his bosom that transfigures you and me:
As he died to make men holy, let us die to make men free,
    While God is marching on.

Entered according to Act of Congress, in the year 1862, by TICKNOR AND FIELDS, in the Clerk's Office of the District Court of the District of Massachusetts.

THE Union song of the Civil War was "The Battle Hymn of the Republic," with lyrics by Julia Ward Howe, set to a tune that some sources give as an "old camp-meeting air." The song, first published in 1862, was later issued as a broadsheet by the Supervisory Committee for Recruiting Colored Regiments. The song foresaw a great turning point in the War: when Northerners began to believe that the Union's mission was not only political but also moral, not only to preserve the United States' union but also to end slavery in the United States.

One of Walt's favorite songs was "A Soldier's Farewell." Which version he liked is unknown; like "My Mother's Bible," the title was used for several songs. This one is by Max Langenschwartz, to the tune of "When this Cruel War Is Over." 1864

Now I am curious what sight can ever be
>   more stately and admirable to me than my mast-
>   hemm'd Manhatta, my river and sun-set, and
>   my scallop-edged waves of flood-tide, the
>   sea-gulls oscillating their bodies, the hay-boat
>   in the twilight, and the belated lighter…
> — *from "Song of Myself," 1856 edition*

This circa 1855 view, "from the steeple of St. Paul's Church, looking east, south, and west," shows what is today's downtown Manhattan. A large building at the lower right carries the banner-sign of one of Walt's favorite places: BRADY'S DAGUERRIAN MINIATURE GALLERY. The crowd of ships' masts at the distant water's edge lends itself to Walt's praise. Brooklyn lies in the distance, at left. Trinity Church, still standing today, is the tallest structure. St. Paul's also still stands, at 209 Broadway.

CHAPTER 6

Letters

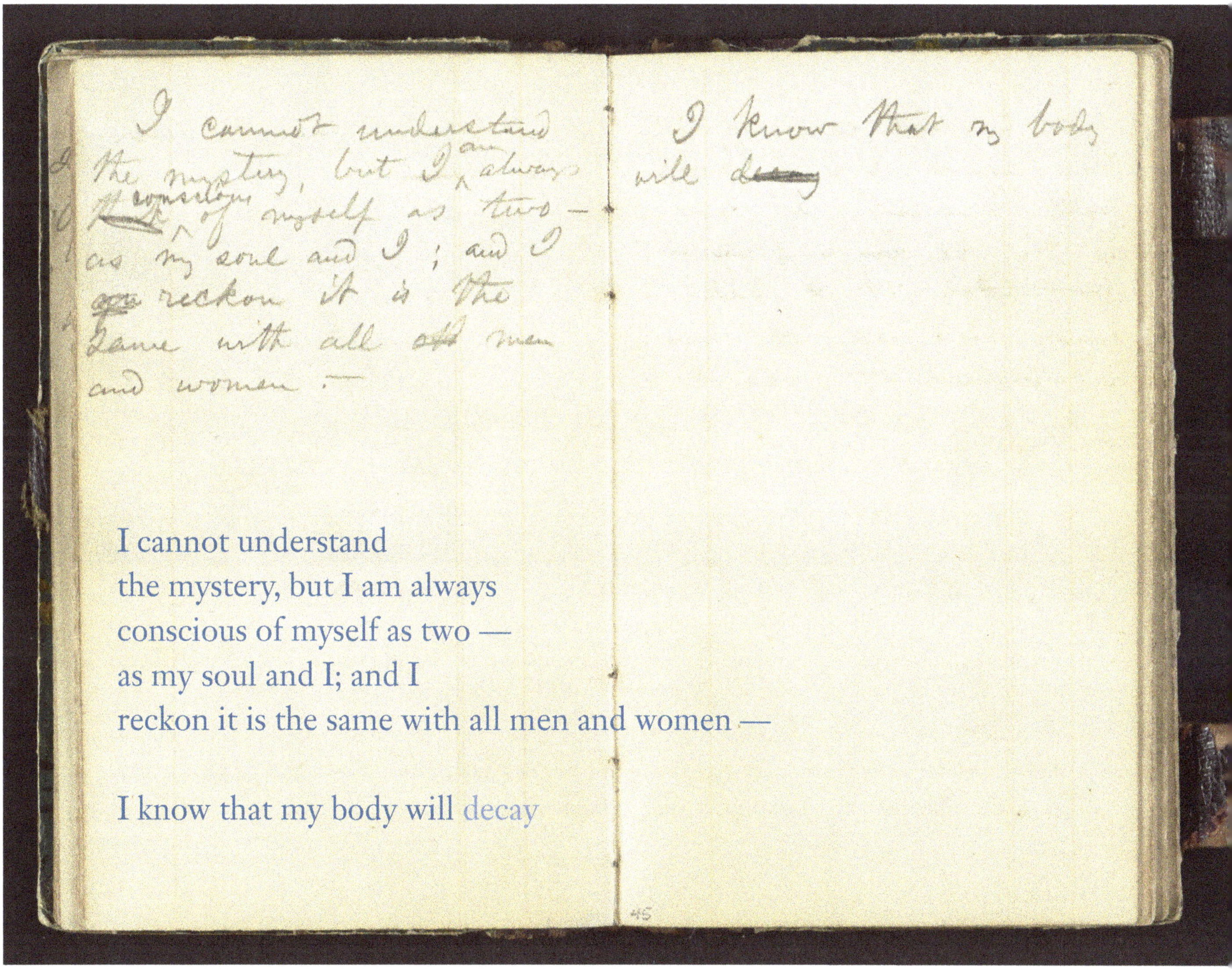

I cannot understand
the mystery, but I am always
conscious of myself as two —
as my soul and I; and I
reckon it is the same with all men and women —

I know that my body will decay

Walt's notebook, 1847

Prose

One of the earliest photographs of Walt shows him around thirty years old, fitted out as a gentleman. In an 1842 issue of Manhattan daily paper, *The Aurora*, Walt poked fun at his own dandy shtick:

We took our cane, (a heavy, dark, beautifully polished, hook ended one,) and our hat, (a plain, neat fashionable one, from Banta's, 130 Chatham street, which we got gratis, on the strength of giving him this puff,) and sauntered forth to have a stroll down Broadway to the Battery…on we went, swinging our stick, (the before mentioned dark and polished one,) in our right hand—and with our left hand tastily thrust in its appropriate pocket, in our frock coat, (a gray one).

A young compositor who worked with Walt during this period remembered that he was "tall and graceful in appearance, neat in attire, and possessed a very pleasing and impressive eye and a cheerful, happy-looking countenance."

Daguerrotype of Walt Whitman, circa 1850

JOURNALISM

Compositors, like Walt in his teens, often moved from print shop to editorial office; both usually shared premises and owners. In the 1840s and 1850s, in his twenties and thirties, Walt shifted the bulk of his professional energy from printing to journalism and editing, with stints of carpentry work with his father.

George P. Morris, a popular songwriter and editor of the *New York Mirror* in the 1830s, published some of Walt's earliest prose works:

I remember with what half-suppress'd excitement I used to watch for the big, fat, red-faced, slow-moving, very old English carrier who distributed the "Mirror" in Brooklyn; and when I got one, opening and cutting the leaves with trembling fingers. How it made my heart double-beat to see my piece on the pretty white paper, in nice type.

American periodicals in the mid-nineteenth century ranged from sensationalistic penny papers, religious papers, and literary magazines, to daily newspapers that mixed crime, scandal, rabidly partisan political coverage, and international and local news with advertisements of every stripe.

In March 1842, when Walt was twenty-two years old, *The Aurora* crowed of having "secured the services of MR. WALTER WHITMAN, favorably known as a bold, energetic and original writer, as their leading editor." Less than a month later, Walt was gone, the publisher now putting him down as "the laziest fellow who ever undertook to edit a city paper."

True, Walt arrived late to the offices and spent long lunches strolling Broadway. But politics generated most of the friction with his employers. A compositor recalled "heated" conferences between "the two grinders of the party 'organ'"—namely Walt and *The Aurora*'s publisher—with Walt refusing to "tone" his articles.

From his next job at *The Evening Tattler*, Walt struck back at *The Aurora*: "There is in this city a trashy, scurrilous, and obscene daily paper, under charge of two as dirty fellows, as ever were able by the force of brass, ignorance of their own ignorance, and a coarse manner of familiarity, to push themselves among gentlemen…." The editors replied (in their paper), "We were fine fellows as long as we consented to pay him for loafing about our office…." Such was the rough and tumble world of journalism.

As an editor, Walt didn't stay at one place long; *The Brooklyn Eagle* was his most enduring gig: about two years, from March 1846 to January 1848, when the *Eagle* fired him for advocating Free Soil and the Wilmot Proviso. Only months later, the *New Orleans Crescent* fired him in a dispute over pay. He left the *Brooklyn Daily Times* in 1859 in another dispute.

Walt's style in reviewing could be described as "no holds barred." He reviewed a play by Park Benjamin, his former employer at *The New World*:

The great Ann Street Bamboozle, Park Benjamin,…one of the most vain, pragmatical nincompoops in creation—sets himself up for a poet! and has lately perpetrated a mass of trash which he calls a comedy!

Walt's editorial jobs and his published articles and essays gave him a presence in the literary world. He also gained a knack for manipulating the media, which he exploited to promote his own work. The hide-thickening from *The Aurora* and other irate journals could only help when the reviews came in for *Leaves of Grass*.

"Free Soil, Free Speech, Free Labor and Free Men" was the motto of the FREE SOIL Party, which opposed permitting slavery in newly acquired U.S. territories and new states. Their stance was shaped more by white labor interests than moral outrage. The former Democratic president Martin Van Buren, for whom Whitman campaigned, was nominated for re-election by the Free Soil party in 1848 (and lost).

The WILMOT PROVISO, introduced by congressman David Wilmot in 1846, proposed to ban slavery in any land gained in the Mexican War, which had begun two months earlier. Reintroduced in various guises, Southern senators ensured it never passed.

Office of the Brooklyn Eagle, where Walt worked for about two years. The bottom floor originally featured an open arcade. Photo was taken circa 1885, after Walt's tenure.

THE BROOKLYN EAGLE,
AND KINGS COUNTY DEMOCRAT.

VOL. 5 —— NO. 81   BROOKLYN, WEDNESDAY, APRIL 1, 1846.   PRICE, TWO CENTS.

The majority of the Brooklyn Eagle, including the front page, is advertisements.

The news begins on page two of the four-page issue. One story tells of a medical student who, on lifting the sheet from a cadaver to be dissected, "uttered a wild, piercing shriek, and fell senseless to the floor." His fellow students gazed horrified on the "delicate form of their recent subject..." et cetera, et cetera. Have you guessed? The body was that of the young student's "betrothed bride."

Walt might have made up the absurdly grotesque story. With no wire services to receive news from around the world, filling a daily paper was no small feat. Only an inch or so down, a quote that, again, Walt might have fabricated, is attributed to a young woman: "A gentleman is a human being, combining a woman's tenderness with a man's courage." Another story, about a young woman who committed suicide by drowning, is headed by a quote from Shakespeare's Hamlet.

FICTION

Parke Godwin and another somebody (who was it?) came to see me about writing it [the novel Franklin Evans]. Their offer of cash payment was so tempting—I was so hard up at the time—that I set to work at once ardently on it (with the help of a bottle of port or what not). In three days of constant work I finished the book. Finished the book? Finished myself. It was damned rot—rot of the worst sort—not insincere, perhaps, but rot, nevertheless: it was not the business for me to be up to. I stopped right there: I never cut a chip off that kind of timber again.

Not Parke Goodwin, but rather the "great Ann Street Bamboozle," Park Benjamin, commissioned Walt to write a Temperance novel (with evidently no hard feelings following Walt's scathing review of his play). Benjamin believed in the cause; he knew it would sell. Walt had published some short stories; they must have impressed Benjamin.

Walt's *Franklin Evans, or The Inebriate*, published in 1842, exemplifies popular nineteenth-century fiction: loaded with long sentences, little homilies, melodrama, violations of the fictive fourth wall, sub-sub-plots, soul-searching questions, and lots of exclamation points!

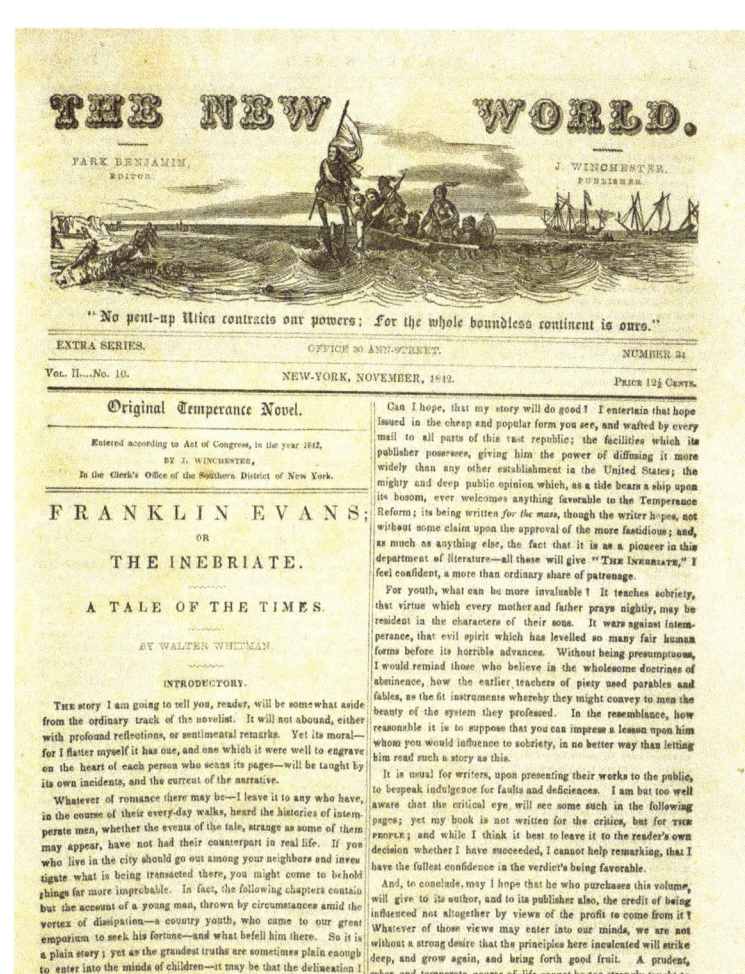

First page of Franklin Evans, printed in The New World. The paper's slogan suits the spirit of the times: "No pent-up Utica contracts our powers; for the whole boundless continent is ours."

Yes, here I had come to seek my fortune! A mere boy, friendless, unprotected, innocent of the ways of the world without wealth, favor, or wisdom here I stood at the entrance of the mighty labyrinth, and with hardly any consciousness of the temptations, doubts, and dangers that awaited me there…. How many had entered on the race, as now I was entering, and in the course of years, faint, tired, and sick at heart, had drawn themselves out aside the track, seeking no further bliss than to die. To die! The word is too hard a one for the lip of youth and hope. Let us rather think of those who, bravely stemming the tide, and bearing up nobly against all opposition, have proudly come off victorious waving in their hands, at last, the symbol of triumph and glory.

What should be my fate? Should I be one of the fortunate few?…What probability was there that amid the countless multitude, all striving for the few prizes which Fortune had to bestow, my inexperienced arms should get the better of a million others?…

— *From Franklin Evans, or The Inebriate*

85

Literary Scene

Even in the convivial environment of Pfaff's beer cellar, Walt claimed, "My own greatest pleasure...was to look on—to see, talk little, absorb." An unknown companion sketched Walt in Walt's notebook, circa 1860, probably at Pfaff's beer cellar.

PUBLICATION OF LEAVES OF GRASS will be covered in more depth in Chapter 10: Poetry

Walt later described the decade of his life before the Civil War as one of "stagnation." After his wartime vocation of nursing thousands of wounded and ill men, it's easy to see why, looking back, he felt that way. Yet in that period, he contributed scores of articles to periodicals, wrote and published a novel as well as some short stories, traveled for the first time outside New York, published in 1855 the first edition of *Leaves of Grass,* and in 1856 and 1860 issued new editions of *Leaves* that included more poems. He established a literary presence not only in his published work, but in his social life.

THE BOHEMIANS AT PFAFF'S

Pfaff's chop house and beer cellar, at 647 Broadway, was Walt's favorite hangout from 1859 to 1862. A 1903 memoir, *Literary New York*, describes Pfaff's as "a hole beneath the surface of the street, ill-lighted, ill-ventilated, ill-kept"—a true haunt of Bohemians:

> They were gifted men with great power of intellect, who spoke without fear and without favor and whose every word expressed a thought. They were real men and they made the world a real place, a place without affectation, without pretence, without show, without need of applause, and without undue cringing to mere conventional forms....

Walt relished carousing at Pfaff's with actors, painters, other writers, and publishers of brave and short-lived literary magazines. He did admit, it "smelt atrociously," and his unpublished note-poem on Pfaff's has a sardonic ring:

Henry Clapp, the "king of the Pfaffian Bohemians" and a friend of Walt's, ran the weekly literary magazine *Saturday Press*, which sometimes lionized, sometimes parodied Walt, and published several of his poems, including the first version of "Out of the Cradle Endlessly Rocking."

> The vault at Pfaffs where the drinkers and laughers meet to eat and drink and carouse,
> While on the walk immediately overhead, pass the myriad feet of Broadway
> As the dead in their graves, are underfoot hidden
> And the living pass over them, reeking not of them,
> Laugh on laughters [sic]! Drink on drinkers!
> Bandy the jests! Toss the theme from one to another!
> Beam up—brighten up bright eyes of beautiful young men!
> Eat what you, having ordered, are pleased to see placed before you—after the work of
> the day, now with appetite, eat,
> Drink wine—drink beer—raise your voice.

The free-spirited poet and actress Adah Isaacs Menken (1835–1868) was one of Walt's friends at Pfaff's. Menken, nicknamed The Naked Lady, stayed in the news with erotic photos, a stage role in which she wore a body suit that simulated male nudity, cross-dressing, numerous love affairs and divorces, and genuine dramatic talent. Her devoted fans included celebrated British writers Arthur Conan Doyle and Charles Dickens. Walt remembered her as among those who publicly supported his poetry when most critics were dragging it through the mud. Napoleon Sarony, who took these photographs circa 1866, also photographed Walt.

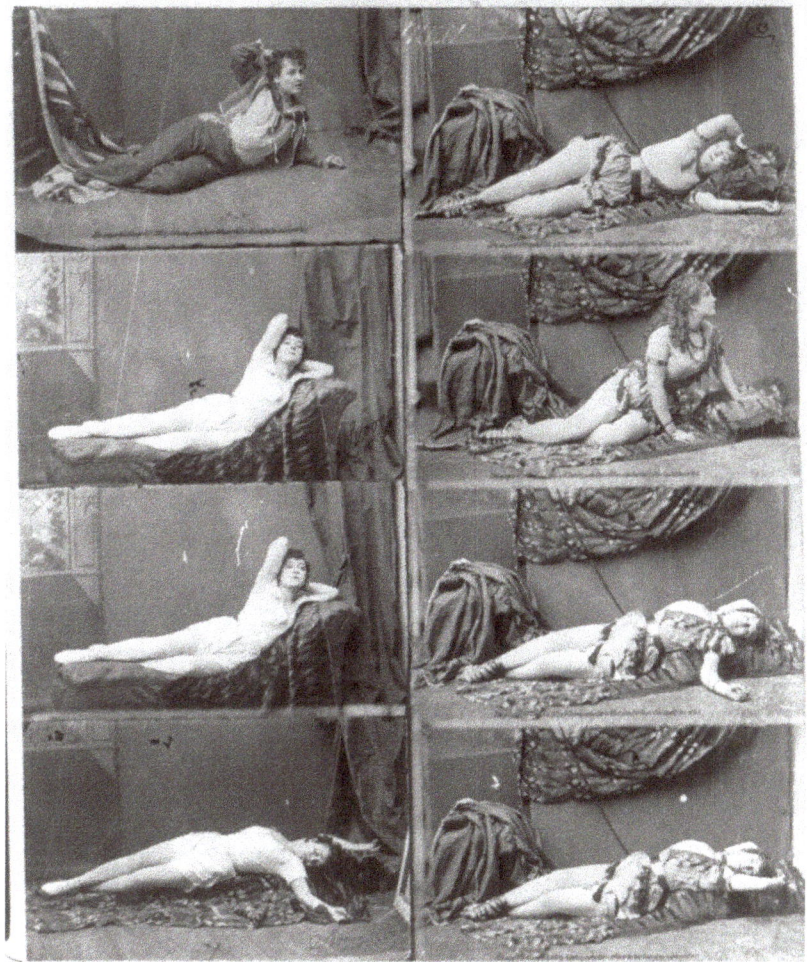

A SALON

Anne Charlotte Lynch Botta (1815–1891) was an accomplished poet, essayist, and sculptor, but her legacy lies in the literary salon she hosted in her home. Among those who attended were immortals Edgar Allan Poe, Ralph Waldo Emerson, Herman Melville, and Walt Whitman.

Walt's address to her in letters, "My dear Madam," indicates they weren't close friends, but they stayed in touch. In the 1870s, Botta published Walt's poems in the literary magazine *Galaxy*, and she included him in her influential 1889 *Handbook of Universal Literature:*

Walt Whitman (b. 1819) writes with great force, originality, and sympathy with all forms of struggle and suffering, but with utter contempt for conventionalities and for the acknowledged limits of true art.

Edgar Allan Poe described Anne Charlotte Lynch Botta: "In person she is rather above the usual height, somewhat slender, with dark hair and eyes— the whole countenance at times full of intelligent expression. Her demeanor is dignified, graceful, and noticeable for repose."

Writers of Walt's Time

I believe we [Americans] have: believe that Emerson (Emerson without a doubt) with Bryant, Whittier, Longfellow—perhaps also some of the Southern writers—writers of single poems—deserved to be ranked high…

The books sampled in this section met success in the nineteenth century. Some are by writers Walt loved throughout his life; some are by writers he didn't like at all; some are examples of a type of book Walt would have run across. The images are from editions published during Walt's life; he may have held a volume of the same edition in his hand.

The painting Kindred Spirits, by Asher Brown Durand, portrays the renowned poet William Cullen Bryant (left) and his friend the painter Thomas Cole (holding painting supplies). The painting was made after Cole's unexpected death in early 1848. The men overlook a gorge in the Catskills of New York.

EMILY DICKINSON (1830–1886)

Walt's only contemporary whose work approaches his in originality and beauty is Emily Dickinson.

Dickinson was born in Amherst, Massachusetts, on December 10, 1830, her father a lawyer, her mother a studious woman especially interested in science. Emily herself received and enjoyed a full education. Like her contemporary Henry David Thoreau, a close observation of and engagement with nature inspired her spiritual life and her poetry. Her shyness, as well as her mother's illness and her father's demands, tied her to home. Though reclusive, a few close friends and her nieces and nephews visited her.

Only a few handfuls of Dickinson's thousands of poems were published during her life. The encouragement of abolitionist and literary critic Thomas Wentworth Higginson was a lifeline to her. He wrote in the preface to the first edition of her poems, 1890:

Emily Dickinson, circa 1847

...She habitually concealed her mind, like her person, from all but a very few friends; and it was with great difficulty that she was persuaded to print, during her lifetime, three or four poems. Yet she wrote verses in great abundance; and though curiously indifferent to all conventional rules, had yet a rigorous literary standard of her own, and often altered a word many times to suit an ear which had its own tenacious fastidiousness.

A point in common she had with Whitman was a powerful physical charisma, though Higginson found Dickinson's disconcerting. "[I was never] with any one who drained my nerve power so much," he said. "Without touching her, she drew from me. I am glad not to live near her."

Dickinson died, probably of Bright's Disease, at age fifty-five. Knowing that she was near the end, she sent a message to her cousins, "Little Cousins, Called Back. Emily." Her coffin, at her request was "carried through fields of buttercups" to her family's plot in the graveyard.

Comparing Walt and Emily is irresistible: two poets who towered over the others of their generation, two poets who could not be more different from each other.

She: reclusive, proper; scarcely published in her life; interior, metaphysical, abstract; garden flowers, death driving a carriage through a small-town graveyard…

He: outgoing, outrageous; well-published; earthy, oratorical; oceans and woods, roughs driving streetcars down Broadway, battlefields strewn with the dead…

Because I could not stop for Death –
He kindly stopped for me –
The Carriage held but just Ourselves –
And Immortality.
We slowly drove – He knew no haste
And I had put away
My labor and my leisure too,
For His Civility –
We passed the School, where Children strove
At Recess – in the Ring –
We passed the Fields of Gazing Grain –
We passed the Setting Sun –
Or rather – He passed us –
The Dews drew quivering and chill –
For only Gossamer, my Gown –
My Tippet – only Tulle –
We paused before a House that seemed
A Swelling of the Ground –
The Roof was scarcely visible –
The Cornice – in the Ground –
Since then – 'tis Centuries – and yet
Feels shorter than the Day
I first surmised the Horses' Heads
Were toward Eternity –

196 JUNE.

> The oriole should build and tell
> His love-tale, close beside my cell;
>   The idle butterfly
> Should rest him there, and there be heard
> The housewife-bee and humming-bird.
>
> And what if cheerful shouts, at noon,
>   Come from the village sent,
> Or songs of maids, beneath the moon,
>   With fairy laughter blent?
> And what if, in the evening light,
> Betrothed lovers walk in sight
>   Of my low monument?
> I would the lovely scene around
> Might know no sadder sight nor sound.
>
> I know, I know I should not see
>   The season's glorious show,
> Nor would its brightness shine for me,
>   Nor its wild music flow;
> But if, around my place of sleep,
> The friends I love should come to weep,
>   They might not haste to go.
> Soft airs, and song, and light, and bloom,
> Should keep them lingering by my tomb.
>
> These to their softened hearts should bear
>   The thought of what has been,
> And speak of one who cannot share
>   The gladness of the scene;

From "June," in Poems, by William Cullen Bryant. 1842

(right) William Cullen Bryant. 1843

WILLIAM CULLEN BRYANT (1794–1878)

During the 1840s, when Walt was most active as a journalist, he and Bryant took long walks around Brooklyn together. Later Bryant raised some hard feelings when he left Walt's poetry out of his anthologies, but the two men remained friends. Bryant published several of Walt's poems in his prestigious newspaper, *The New York Evening Post*.

A feature in Bryant which is never to be under-weighed is the marvelous purity of his work in verse. It was severe—oh! so severe!—never a waste word—the last superfluity struck off: a clear nameless beauty pervading and overarching all the work of his pen.

NATHANIEL HAWTHORNE (1804–1864)

In contrast to his fellow novelist Herman Melville, Nathaniel Hawthorne was respected and esteemed as a writer throughout his career, though he struggled for his success in the beginning and came in for his share of negative and mixed reviews. His most well-known works today are the novels *The Scarlet Letter* and *The House of the Seven Gables*. The moralistic tone of Hawthorne's work and its sentimentality can seem old-fashioned today, yet his psychological insights of human society and of individuals, not to mention his great stories, keep his work alive.

Nathaniel Hawthorne. Painting by Charles Osgood. 1840. Hawthorne was as shy as he was handsome.

Hester Prynne, who bore a child by a man other than her estranged husband, was sentenced by the elders of her Puritan village to wear the "Scarlet Letter" whenever she ventured out of her home. Here, the letter is revealed for the first time to the harsh gaze of the public. From the first edition, published in 1850 by Ticknor, Reed, and Fields of Boston

HENRY WADSWORTH LONGFELLOW (1807–1882)

In his youth, Walt esteemed Longfellow, but when struggling to find his own voice during the 1850s and 1860s, he rejected Longfellow's "beautiful words" as irrelevant, especially as their nation plunged into division and tumult. Whitman's scorn and perhaps jealousy of a poet who was generally reckoned as greater than himself eventually mellowed back to respect. "Hiawatha," "Geraldine," and "The Wreck of the Hesperis" are Longfellow's most well-known poems.

> HIAWATHA AND THE PEARL-FEATHER.   89
>
> ### IX.
>
> ### Hiawatha and the Pearl-Feather.
>
> On the shores of Gitche Gumee,
> Of the shining Big-Sea-Water,
> Stood Nokomis, the old woman,
> Pointing with her finger westward,
> O'er the water pointing westward,
> To the purple clouds of sunset.
>
>   Fiercely the red sun descending
> Burned his way along the heavens,
> Set the sky on fire behind him,
> As war-parties, when retreating,
> Burn the prairies on their war-trail;
> And the moon, the night-sun, eastward,
> Suddenly starting from his ambush,
> Followed fast those bloody footprints,
> Followed in that fiery war-trail,
> With its glare upon his features.
>   And Nokomis, the old woman,

From "The Song of Hiawatha," by Henry Wadsworth Longfellow. "Gitche Gumee" is Lake Superior. London. 1856

Henry Wadsworth Longfellow, circa 1850

THE HUSKERS. 37

There wrought the busy harvesters; and many a creaking wain
Bore slowly to the long barn-floor its load of husk and grain;
Till broad and red, as when he rose, the sun sank down, at last,
And like a merry guest's farewell, the day in brightness passed.

And lo! as through the western pines, on meadow, stream and pond,
Flamed the red radiance of a sky, set all afire beyond,
Slowly o'er the Eastern sea-bluffs a milder glory shone,
And the sunset and the moonrise were mingled into one!

As thus into the quiet night the twilight lapsed away,
And deeper in the brightening moon the tranquil shadows lay;
From many a brown old farm-house, and hamlet without name,
Their milking and their home-tasks done, the merry huskers came.

John Greenleaf Whittier, circa 1860

From "The Huskers." Songs of Labor and Other Poems. Boston, 1850

JOHN GREENLEAF WHITTIER (1807–1892)

Poet, Quaker, and staunch abolitionist, John Greenleaf Whittier allegedly found passages of *Leaves* so offensive he threw his 1855 edition into the fire. Later, Walt's nursing work during the War as well as his poetic tribute to Lincoln earned Whittier's respect. Whittier chipped in for a buggy after Walt's stroke made walking difficult. "The Huskers," with its long verse lines and laboring men and women, foreshadows Walt's own poems.

Edgar Allan Poe, 1848

From The Poetical Works of Edgar Allan Poe. James Hannay, ed. London: Charles Griffin and Company, 1852.

EDGAR ALLAN POE (1809–1849)

Walt met Edgar Allan Poe in 1845 and had "a distinct and pleasing remembrance" of him. He admired Poe's work, with reservations.

Toward the last I had among much else look'd over Edgar Poe's poems—of which I was not an admirer, tho' I always saw that beyond their limited range of melody (like perpetual chimes of music bells, ringing from lower b flat up to g) they were melodious expressions, and perhaps never excell'd ones, of certain pronounc'd phases of human morbidity.

The two writers had a common enemy in literary critic Rufus Wilmot Griswald. It was Griswald who, after Poe's death, portrayed the poet as a wastrel and drunkard, and Griswald who wrote an exceptionally vicious review of *Leaves of Grass*. Griswald is now known as the defamer of Poe. The works of Edgar Allan Poe and Walt Whitman live.

Late in life, Walt wrote a Poesque impression of Poe and his work:

In a dream I once had, I saw a vessel on the sea, at midnight, in a storm. It was no great full-rigg'd ship, nor majestic steamer, steering firmly through the gale, but seem'd one of those superb little schooner yachts I had often seen lying anchor'd, rocking so jauntily, in the waters around New York, or up Long Island sound—now flying uncontroll'd with torn sails and broken spars through the wild sleet and winds and waves of the night. On the deck was a slender, slight, beautiful figure, a dim man, apparently enjoying all the terror, the murk, and the dislocation of which he was the centre and the victim. That figure of my lurid dream might stand for Edgar Poe, his spirit, his fortunes, and his poems—themselves all lurid dreams.

ANNABEL LEE.

"So that her highborn kinsmen came
And bore her away from me."

ANNABEL LEE.

I.

It was many and many a year ago,
  In a kingdom by the sea,
That a maiden there lived whom you may know
  By the name of ANNABEL LEE;
And this maiden she lived with no other thought
  Than to love and be loved by me.

II.

I was a child, and *she* was a child,
  In this kingdom by the sea;
But we loved with a love that was more than love,
  I and my ANNABEL LEE;
With a love that the wingèd seraphs of heaven
  Coveted her and me.

III.

And this was the reason that, long ago,
  In this kingdom by the sea,
A wind blew out of a cloud, chilling
  My beautiful ANNABEL LEE;
So that her highborn kinsmen* came
  And bore her away from me,
To shut her up in a sepulchre
  In this kingdom by the sea.

* Viz., the angels,—a graceful fancy.—ED.

ALFRED, LORD TENNYSON (1809–1892)

Alfred, Lord Tennyson, ranked among the most prominent English-language poets of the nineteenth century. He was appointed Poet Laureate of Great Britain and Ireland by Queen Victoria. Quotes from Tennyson's poetry endure today:

> Nature, red in tooth and claw...
> Tis better to have loved and lost
> Than never to have loved at all...
>
> — *from In Memoriam*

> Theirs not to reason why,
> Theirs but to do and die...
>
> — *from "The Charge of the Light Brigade"*

Though in 1855 Walt derided Tennyson as a "bard of ennui and of the aristocracy," he later enjoyed a friendly correspondence with him and grew to respect Tennyson's work. Of him, Walt said:

He has all that in him, the eligibility for all that—for title, place, deference, hauteur—but in the great deeps behind, below, the great spirit pervading all, something more, something truly human, lasting, unerringly true.

Tennyson invited Walt to be his guest at his home in England, but Walt was never to journey overseas.

Alfred, Lord Tennyson, circa 1870

CXXVIII.

Dear friend, far off, my lost desire,
    So far, so near in woe and weal;
    O loved the most, when most I feel
There is a lower and a higher;

Known and unknown; human, divine;
    Sweet human hand and lips and eye;
    Dear heavenly friend that canst not die
Mine, mine, for ever, ever mine;

Strange friend, past, present, and to be;
    Loved deeplier, darklier understood;
    Behold, I dream a dream of good,
And mingle all the world with thee.

From "In Memoriam A.H.H." The poem was dedicated to Tennyson's friend Arthur Henry Hallam, who died in 1833, at only twenty-two years old. Its tribute to passionate male friendship would have resonated with Walt.

Herman Melville, circa 1860

HERMAN MELVILLE (1819–1891)

Herman Melville is surely among the most perplexing, brilliant, and demanding American writers. His novel *Moby Dick*, whose villain is a crusty old whale and its hero a crazed, peg-legged sea captain, has tormented and enthralled readers since its publication in 1851. It regularly features in lists of books most hated and books most loved. After some flashes of success, though, Melville's fiction, including *Moby Dick*, fell into obscurity amidst rumors that its author had gone insane.

In 1866 Melville came back with a volume of poetry on the Civil War, *Battle Pieces and Aspects of War*. Its reception was mixed; the book never made its publication costs. Fortunately Melville's poetry, together with his fiction, especially *Moby Dick*, the story "Bartleby the Scrivener," and the unfinished novella *Billy Budd*, were revived in the twentieth century.

The first sentence of Moby Dick is one of the most famous in English-language fiction. The novel's tone is as various as the shades of the sea itself, but a current of humor runs through all but the grimmest passages.

This page is from the first edition, published in 1851 by Harper & Brothers, New York.

CHAPTER I.

LOOMINGS.

CALL me Ishmael. Some years ago—never mind how long precisely—having little or no money in my purse, and nothing particular to interest me on shore, I thought I would sail about a little and see the watery part of the world. It is a way I have of driving off the spleen, and regulating the circulation. Whenever I find myself growing grim about the mouth; whenever it is a damp, drizzly November in my soul; whenever I find myself involuntarily pausing before coffin warehouses, and bringing up the rear of every funeral I meet; and especially whenever my hypos get such an upper hand of me, that it requires a strong moral principle to prevent me from deliberately stepping into the street, and methodically knocking people's hats off—then, I account it high time to get to sea as soon as I can. This is my substitute for pistol and ball. With a philosophical flourish Cato throws himself upon his sword; I quietly take to the ship. There is nothing surprising in this. If they but knew it, almost all men in their degree, some time or other, cherish very nearly the same feelings towards the ocean with me.

There now is your insular city of the Manhattoes, belted round by wharves as Indian isles by coral reefs—commerce surrounds it with her surf. Right and left, the streets take you waterward. Its extreme down-town is the battery, where that noble mole is washed by waves, and cooled by breezes, which a few hours previous were out of sight of land. Look at the crowds of water-gazers there.

Circumambulate the city of a dreamy Sabbath afternoon. Go from Corlears Hook to Coenties Slip, and from thence, by

LOUISA MAY ALCOTT (1832–1888)

Louisa May Alcott's writing career was shaped by the too-often opposing forces of idealism and the need to make money. Her father Amos Bronson Alcott was a man of strong principles: an ardent abolitionist, a women's rights advocate, an educator of the kind Walt believed in, rejecting corporal punishment in favor of drawing out the best in his students. He was one of the founders of the Transcendental movement. A variety of idealistic enterprises, from schools to communes, failed to provide his wife and daughters material security.

Louisa absorbed her father's ideals and ideas, but wrote pot-boilers and worked a variety of jobs to support the family. Like Walt, she went to D.C. to nurse soldiers in the Civil War. She never met Walt there, however, as she soon contracted typhoid and returned home to convalesce.

Publication in *The Atlantic* and other periodicals brought Alcott some success, but the novel *Little Women* proved to be her breakthrough work. From its publication in 1868, *Little Women*'s popularity has never flagged.

The book's "little women," the four March sisters, together with their mother, hold the home front while their father serves the Union as an Army chaplain. *Little Women*'s virtuous and harmonious home in Concord, Massachusetts, could have been a planet away from the Whitman family's tempestuous and often sordid life in Brooklyn.

Walt had a warm acquaintance with the Alcotts and refers to "old Mr. Alcott" in an 1868 letter to his mother: "he compliments me highly, & speaks of Mr. Emerson too & his friendliness to me." Mr. Alcott, with Henry Thoreau, had visited Walt in Brooklyn shortly after publication of the first edition of *Leaves of Grass*.

Walt probably read Louisa May Alcott's 1863 memoir *Hospital Sketches*. The two met at least once, in 1881, at Ralph Waldo Emerson's; she forty-nine, he sixty-two, Mr. Emerson seventy-eight and suffering dementia. Whether or not this was their only or their first meeting, they were almost certainly aware of each other's works through the years.

Louisa May Alcott. 1870. Photo by George Kendall Warren.

Page 10 of the first edition of Little Women introduces Jo, the protagonist. Jo, a writer and a tomboy reflects Louisa May Alcott herself. Alcott shared Jo's frustration at the limitations of being a woman.

MARK TWAIN (1835 – 1910)

Mark Twain, pen-name of Samuel Langhorne Clemens, was engaged in many enterprises, but is most known for his novels *Adventures of Tom Sawyer* and *Adventures of Huckleberry Finn*, both set in the antebellum South and written after the Civil War, and *The Prince and the Pauper*.

Ironically, during Twain's life, *Tom Sawyer* and *Huckleberry Finn* were banned for language; now they're often deleted from school curricula for what is perceived as racial stereotyping. Twain himself was an ardent abolitionist, and spoke out against racism in colonial settings and in America.

Both Walt and Twain worked (not together) as printers, publishers, journalists; they were both published in their friend Henry Clapp's short-lived *Saturday Press*. Both could be soaringly idealistic and caustically cynical. Their most important literary work diverged into prose and poetry, yet in it they tried to capture, in their ways, what they considered a quintessentially American spirit. As a publisher in the late 1880s, Twain issued a volume of *Selected Poems, by Walt Whitman*.

About Twain, Walt told his friend Horace Traubel in 1885, "I think he mainly misses fire: I think his life misses fire: he might have been something: he comes near to being something: but he never arrives." At that time, he described Twain as "friendly, but not warm: not exactly against me: not for me either." A few years later, though, his attitude toward Twain had grown considerably more friendly. On several occasions, Twain chipped in with others to help Walt financially.

Twain's 1889 public letter to Walt, a tribute for Walt's 70th birthday, focuses not a bit on Walt's work but on the technological and social progress that unfolded during Walt's life, and he bids his elder to stay alive for another 30 years, to see "marvel upon marvels, added to those whose nativity you have witnessed." Some scholars believe that Twain didn't mention Walt's work in his letter because he was uneasy at what Boston authorities had ruled as "obscene" in Walt's poetry. In fact, private papers by Twain indicate he deeply admired Walt's "noble work," as he called it, and found "the Whitman controversy" hypocritical, given the bawdy scenes in books deemed classics. His playful exhortation to Walt, to live a full century, expressed their shared enthusiasm for the work of human hands and ingenuity.

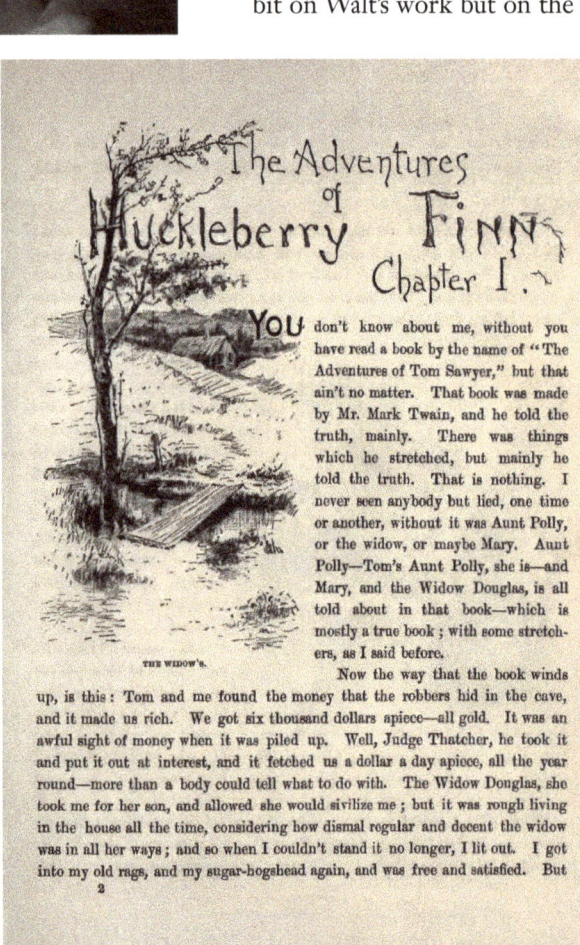

Above left: Mark Twain, circa 1871. The original photo shows Twain seated with two other men; this is cropped. Photo attributed to Mathew Brady. Brady-Handy Collection, Library of Congress.

First page of Adventures of Huckleberry Finn. Charles L. Webster and Co.: New York, 1885.

FAMOUS...IN THEIR TIME

Then, as now, writers could be wildly popular—for a while. Most lapsed into obscurity, remembered today only by literary historians.

Ned Buntline (1821/23-1886) was the penname of Edward Zane Carroll Judson. Like other writers of the time, he worked variously as a publisher, journalist, and writer. He became most famous for his dime novels, paperback adventure fiction set in exotic locales, including the American West, and eccentric characters with fantastic nicknames like Death Notch Dick and Buffalo Bill. Buffalo Bill became the stage name for real-life Bill Cody, "king of the scouts." Decades after Buntline's death, his Wild West adventures continued going strong. This cover is from a circa 1910 edition of one of the Buffalo Bill novels. It's likely Walt read Buntline's novels, but he called Buntline's promotional activities, humorously, "tremendous puff."

FITZ HUGH LUDLOW
(1836–1870)
Ludlow met Walt at Pfaff's. His 1857 book The Hasheesh Eater made him a best-selling author at twenty-one years old, much as Confessions of an English Opium Eater made Thomas de Quincy an overnight success in 1821.
From The Hasheesh Eater, by Fitz Hugh Ludlow. New York, 1857

VIII.
Vos non vobis—wherein the Pythagorean is a By-stander.

The judgment that must be passed upon the hasheesh life in retrospect is widely different from the one which I formed during its progress. Now the drug, with all its revelation of interior mysteries, its glimpses of supernatural beauty and sublimity, appears as the very witch-plant of hell, the weed of madness. At the time of its daily use, I forgave it for all its pangs, for its cruel exercise of authority, its resistless fascination, and its usurpation of the place of all other excitement, at the intercession of the divine forms which it created for my soul, and which, though growing rarer and rarer, when they were present retained their glory until the last. Moreover, through many ecstasies and many pains, I still supposed that I was only making experiments, and that, too, in the most wonderful field of mind which could be opened for investigation, and with an agent so deluding in its influence that the soul only became aware that the strength of a giant was needed to escape when its locks were shorn.

In accordance with these facts, I did not suppose that I was imperiling any friend of mine by giving him an opportunity to make the same experiment which he beheld producing in me phenomena so astonishing to a mind in love with research. Several of

much to be a little sentimental at the time, and feel tempted to indulge to some small extent even here—but I forbear; and shall adhere closely to matters more in keeping with my subject.

I think, to be precise, the time was the last, the very last of April, and I recollect well that even at that early season, by availing myself with sedulous application, of those times when I was fain to quit the vehicle through fear of the perilous mud-holes, or still more perilous half-bridged marshes, I picked upwards of twenty varieties of wild-flowers—some of them of rare and delicate beauty;—and sure I am, that if I had succeeded in inspiring my companion with one spark of my own floral enthusiasm, our hundred miles of travel would have occupied a week's time.

The wild-flowers of Michigan deserve a poet of their own. Shelley who sang so quaintly of 'the pied wind-flowers and the tulip tall,' would have found many a fanciful comparison and deep-drawn meaning for the thousand gems of the road-side. Charles Lamb could have written charming volumes about the humblest among them. Bulwer would find means to associate the common three-leaved white lily so closely with the Past, the Present, and the Future—the Wind, the Stars, and the Tripod of Delphos, that all future botanists, and eke all future philosophers, might fail to unravel the 'linked sweetness.' We must have a poet of our own.

Since I have casually alluded to a Michigan mud-hole, I may as well enter into a detailed memoir on the subject, for the benefit of future travellers, who, flying over the soil on railroads, may look slightingly back upon the achievements of their predecessors. In the 'settlements,' a mud-hole is considered as apt to occasion an unpleasant jolt—a break-

CAROLINE KIRKLAND (1801–1864)
A prominent writer and editor, Kirkland probably knew Walt from Charlotte Lynch Botta's salons. Her satirical book on frontier life in Michigan sold well, as did her stories. Walt would certainly have concurred with the line, "We must have a poet of our own." He praised her, as co-editor of Union Magazine, for publishing "among the best, freshest, and most charming specimens of American literature." From A New Home—Who'll Follow? or, Glimpses of Western Life, by Caroline Kirkland. New York, 1855

JOHN NEAL (1793-1876)
Given Walt's voracious appetite for fiction, he most likely read John Neal's novels, which were popular in the 1820s. In the 1840s, John Neal published two of Walt's early poems in the magazine Brother Jonathan.
Excerpt from Randolph, by John Neal. 1823

(JOHN TO SARAH—ENCLOSED.)

O, Sarah, what a brother I have. How little I have known him. The gay, unthinking young man—he is a hero. And Juliet too, what shall I say of her? Is it not strange that I never suspected the depth and devotion of Frank's attachment to her? He would never confess it; and his general hilarity, his free bearing, before all women, deceived me. I thought, and we all thought, that he was invulnerable. Yes—that man loved her;—that man was worthy of her. What solemnity, what feeling! Indeed cousin, the tears, the steadiness of such men, men that are always cheerful and careless——oh, they have weight, and substance in them, like the smile of a man that smiles but seldom. I have seen men shed tears—tears like sweat—tears like molten lead—but never did I see such tears, as escaped from the eye-balls of my poor brother, when I handed her note to him.

"Are you prepared,"—said I——as soon as I could speak;—for, when I entered the room, he was standing with his collar open——a——no, no——I cannot tell thee——pay no regard to what I have said, but listen—

"Are you *prepared*, brother?" said I.

He shuddered.

I reached him the billet, saying emphatically, *"Be prepared for the worst."*

"I am," said he, in a voice that went to my heart. I thought that I should never be able to speak again. At this moment, he shut his eyes, two or three times, quickly; a dark spasm passed over his face——, and a few drops, a very few, fell upon his naked arm. He started—shook them off as if the skies had rained blood upon him;—sat down;—read the note;—and, without uttering a single word, wrote a brief reply, which he read to me. I wondered at his composure. Once, only once, he faltered, like one suffocating, as he read it to me; but he instantly overcame it, and went on, in a stern, deep voice, like one reading his own death warrant—aloud—to his mortal enemy.——O what a heart he has!—so proud, so mighty. Why, really, it was our notion, because he was never melancholy, never absent, abstracted, or thoughtful, and

FERN GLEN. 279

He holds little Nelly closer to his heart;—the wide earth contains nothing for him so precious as the love of that sweet child. Uncle Peter thanks God there is no trace, on lip, or cheek, or brow, of him who won the mother's love but to break her heart. But no more reveries, if you please, Uncle Peter! Curious eyes have been peeping through that vine-clad bower, at the "good things" spread upon that rustic table. Strawberries, red and tempting as childhood's lip; cakes, that only Uncle Peter could conjure up; sugar-plums and candy, from Betty Prim's thread-and-needle store; sweet milk from steady old Brindle; crispy little crackers for cunning little mouths, and a bunch of wood violets for each little plate.

And now the dimpled hands are reverently folded, and laughing eyes grow serious, for good old Uncle Peter cannot forget to thank "Our Father" for daily bread and for the sweet solace of childhood's love. And soon the table is cleared, as if scoured by a party of squirrels; and what cannot be eaten is stowed away in little pockets, for future use. They all gather round Uncle Peter, and every story he tells is "prime," and better than the one that went before. There are no captious critics in his audience, you may be sure! Little Nelly is nestled in his arms; the dimple in her rosy cheek has ceased to play; the long lashes lay wearily over the violet eyes, and the silver locks of age mingle lovingly with childhood's sunny

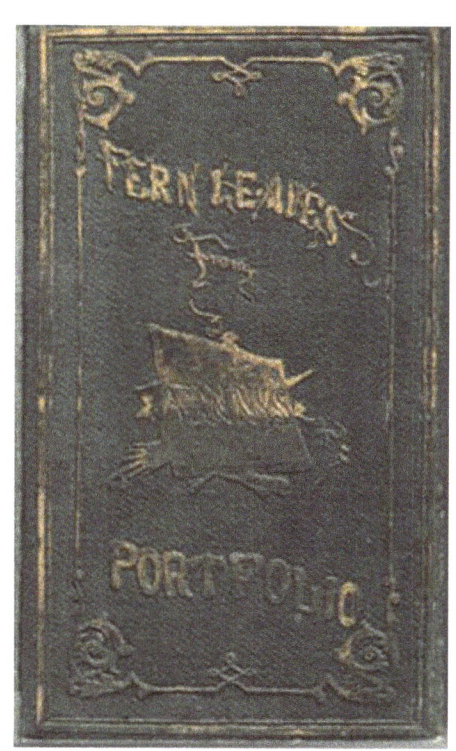

FANNY FERN (1811–1872) Fanny Fern, pen name of Sara Willis Parton, succeeded in every genre she put her pen to: poetry, novels, short stories, and essays. America's first woman newspaper columnist, Fern was an early and ardent supporter of Leaves of Grass, writing in 1856, "Walt Whitman, the effeminate world needed thee. The timidest soul whose wings ever drooped with discouragement, could not choose but rise on thy strong pinions."

The title and botanical-themed lettering on the cover of her 1853 book Fern Leaves likely inspired the cover of Walt's 1855 Leaves. Sentimental, melodramatic, and moralistic, Fern Leaves achieved Walt's own ambition, finding a place on many mid-nineteenth-century American parlor tables. Cover and page of Fern Leaves from Fanny's Portfolio, 1853

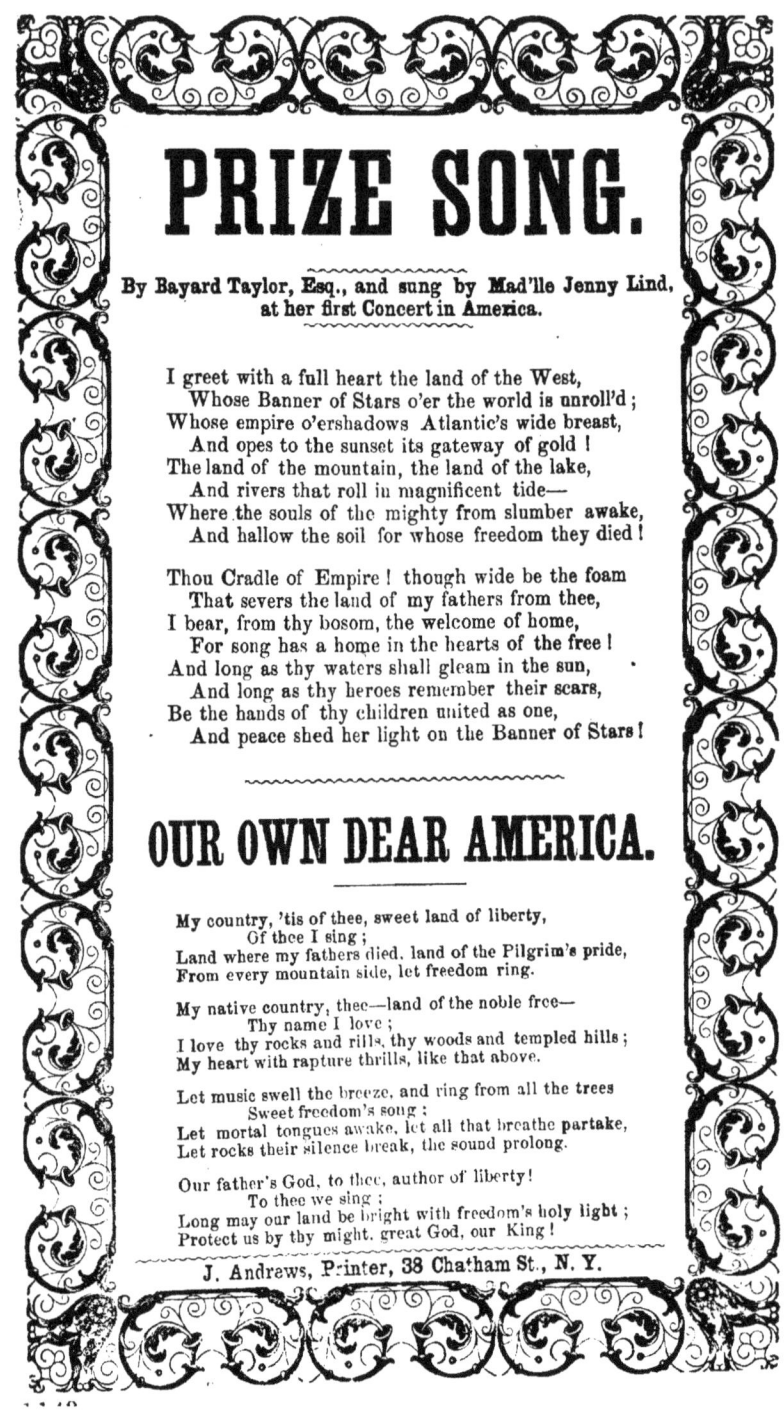

BAYARD TAYLOR (1825-1878) Bayard Taylor and Walt may have met at Pfaff's and Charlotte Lynch Botta's salon. During the 1860s, Taylor wrote to Whitman of "your deep and tender reverence for Man—your unwearied, affectionate, practical fraternity," and visited Walt in D.C., though later the two men fell out. Taylor enjoyed great success as a travel writer and middling success as a poet. His poem, "Our Own Dear America," won a contest sponsored by P.T. Barnum, with a cash prize and the additional honor that Jenny Lind, the world-famous soprano, would perform it at her first concert in the United States. Taylor idolized Lind, but gloomily foresaw that the prize would be his only shot at fame, writing a friend, "Is that damned song to be the only thing that will save my name from oblivion?"

The Transcendentalists

Centered in Concord, Massachusetts, the Transcendentalists led an influential philosophical and artistic movement that rejected handed down conventions and espoused self-realization. In some respects, they descended from Free Thinkers, with a kind of spiritual intuition displacing reason in the quest for truth. Among Walt's contemporaries, the Transcendentalists most influenced him. They in turn were among the first to recognize Walt's originality and stature.

The Transcendentalists included Amos Bronson Alcott, philosopher and father of *Little Women* author Louisa May Alcott, poets and essayists Ralph Waldo Emerson and Henry David Thoreau, feminist essayist Margaret Fuller, and from a physical and

Asher Brown Durand's "sublime landscape," in the style of the Hudson River school, bears out Transcendental philosophy. Light-washed, almost unnaturally vivid, bearing a hushed potency both mystic and awesome, here nature transcends the senses to impart an inarticulate, undeniable truth to the receptive soul. Of Durand, Walt wrote, "all he does is good." The Catskills, by Asher Brown Durand, 1858

philosophical distance, poets Emily Dickinson and Walt Whitman. Others in their orbit were novelists Nathaniel Hawthorne and Herman Melville.

These Transcendalists [sic] are not a sect, and have no creed. No two individuals of them think alike, except on the point that the highest truths are perceived by a faculty transcending the understanding, and not dependent on the senses for its knowledge.

— *The Aurora, 1842*

Walt never quite settled on how he felt about about the literary establishment in Concord—or rather, how he thought they felt about him. In 1888, his confidant Horace Traubel recorded a conversation between himself and Walt:

I said to W.: "You seem to think you have enemies at Concord." "Enemies? I may not call them that: maybe not that: but suspectors, certainly—people who would rather not than rather." He smiled a bit over it. "But we will not make overmuch of these matters: after all they come along, have a place, but are not the chief thing."

RALPH WALDO EMERSON (1803–1882)

Ralph Waldo Emerson, circa 1850

Ralph Waldo Emerson, considered the head of the Transcendentalists, was and remains a giant of American literature and thought. The poet, essayist, and philosopher instigated the "American Renaissance," a period stretching from the 1830s to the 1880s, during which American artists and thinkers struggled to break free of forms and conventions handed down from Europe.

In his 1844 essay, "The Poet," Emerson charged American artists and thinkers to shape an American view and voice:

We will walk on our own feet; we will work with our own hands; we will speak our own minds.

Readers of poetry see the factory-village, and the railway, and fancy that the poetry of the landscape is broken up by these; for these works of art are not yet consecrated in their readings; but the poet sees them fall within the great Order not less than the bee-hive, or the spider's geometrical web....

The pairing of the birds is an idyl, not tedious as our idyls are; a tempest is a rough ode, without falsehood or rant: a summer, with its harvest sown, reaped, and stored, is an epic song, subordinating how many admirably executed parts....

The poet turns the world to glass, and shows us all things in their right series and procession.

— *from Emerson, "The Poet"*

"The Poet" reads like a Bible of Walt's literary aspirations. Years later, Walt would say of his own work:

I have always been best pleased with what seems most to disregard literariness: the artistic, the formal, the traditional aesthetic, the savor of mere words, jingles, sound—I have always eschewed: language itself as language I have discounted—would have rejected it altogether but that it serves the purpose of vehicle, is a

necessity—our mode of communication. But my aim has been, to so subordinate that, no one could know it existed—as in fine plate glass one sees the objects beyond and does not realize the glass between. My determination being to make the story of man, his physiological, emotional, spiritual, self, tell its own story, unhindered by artificial agencies.

A poet reveals truth, both Walt and Emerson believed, and does not shape it with words and ideas, however beautifully arranged. External appearances are not used as static symbols but as living windows to universal truth.

[The poet] is the true and only doctor; he knows and tells; he is the only teller of news, for he was present and privy to the appearance which he describes. He is a beholder of ideas, and an utterer of the necessary and causal.

— *from Emerson, "The Poet"*

The material of the poet, that "fine plate glass," was not to be found in past philosophies or art works. The poet's everyday life yields insight.

Wherever snow falls, or water flows, or birds fly, wherever day and night meet in twilight, wherever the blue heaven is hung by clouds, or sown with stars, wherever are forms with transparent boundaries, wherever are outlets into celestial space, wherever is danger, and awe, and love, there is Beauty, plenteous as rain, shed for

Walt's love of Jean-François Millet's paintings sheds light on what he saw as the artist's job: "Millet has the right idea: anything done according to its own nature is beautiful." Of all painters, Walt felt that Millet most captured the elemental forces of both people and nature. In contrast with the luminosity pursued by the Hudson River School, Walt saw in Millet's work "a sublime murkiness and original pent fury." The Potato Harvest, by Jean-François Millet, 1855

107

thee, and though thou shouldest walk the world over, thou shalt not be able to find a condition inopportune or ignoble.

— *from Emerson, "The Poet"*

Walt's poetry jumps right in to the "inopportune or ignoble":

The pedler sweats with his pack on his back, (the purchaser higgling about the odd cent;)
The bride unrumples her white dress, the minute-hand of the clock moves slowly,
The opium-eater reclines with rigid head and just-opened lips…

— *from "Song of Myself"*

Walt's mix of conditions gave Emerson doubts—respectful doubts. Emerson was among the first to recognize Walt's *Leaves of Grass* as a breakthrough work. On reading the first edition of *Leaves*, Emerson wrote Walt:

I find [Leaves of Grass] the most extraordinary piece of wit and wisdom that America has yet contributed…. I give you joy of your free brave thought. I have great joy in it. I find incomparable things said incomparably well, as they must be. I find the courage of treatment, which so delights us, & which large perception only can inspire. I greet you at the beginning of a great career….

Others criticized Walt for using the letter to promote his book, and Emerson himself was taken by surprise, but didn't take it amiss. The two men visited each other in New York and Boston several times.

On one visit, Emerson tried to persuade Walt to tone down the sexual content of his poems. He knew that its popularity would grow—if only it didn't contain verses that many would condemn as obscene. Emerson was right, and Walt knew it, but he refused Emerson's advice. Emerson might have known, too, that Walt was righter. Emerson said himself, in "The Poet":

The world is full of renunciations and apprenticeships, and this is thine: thou must pass for a fool and a churl for a long season.

Of Emerson, Walt said, "He was a far-fetching force, a star of the first, the very first, magnitude."

Emerson bought this house in 1835, shortly after getting married. There he raised his family, composed his most renowned essays and poetry, and hosted many influential Transcendentalist thinkers and writers, including young Louisa May Alcott. When Walt visited, Emerson was elderly and no longer mentally acute, but Walt treasured being in Emerson's presence.

HENRY DAVID THOREAU (1817–1862)

Henry David Thoreau, another star of the Transcendentalist movement, did not have Emerson's stature during his life, but he is more widely read today, all over the world, than Emerson or any other American Transcendentalist. His essay "Civil Disobedience," a call to follow conscience above law, has inspired activists from Mahatma Gandhi to Martin Luther King, Jr., and his memoir *On Walden Pond* has sent many a young and old person back to nature to connect with a more authentic life.

Henry David Thoreau, daguerrotype by Benjamin D. Maxham, made in 1856, the year he met Walt Whitman

This page spread from the first edition of Walden; or, Life in the Woods (now more well-known simply as Walden), includes a passage widely quoted to this day, "I went to the woods because I wished to live deliberately...."

---

98   WALDEN.

tion, only one in a hundred millions to a poetic or divine life. To be awake is to be alive. I have never yet met a man who was quite awake. How could I have looked him in the face?

We must learn to reawaken and keep ourselves awake, not by mechanical aids, but by an infinite expectation of the dawn, which does not forsake us in our soundest sleep. I know of no more encouraging fact than the unquestionable ability of man to elevate his life by a conscious endeavor. It is something to be able to paint a particular picture, or to carve a statue, and so to make a few objects beautiful; but it is far more glorious to carve and paint the very atmosphere and medium through which we look, which morally we can do. To affect the quality of the day, that is the highest of arts. Every man is tasked to make his life, even in its details, worthy of the contemplation of his most elevated and critical hour. If we refused, or rather used up, such paltry information as we get, the oracles would distinctly inform us how this might be done.

I went to the woods because I wished to live deliberately, to front only the essential facts of life, and see if I could not learn what it had to teach, and not, when I came to die, discover that I had not lived. I did not wish to live what was not life, living is so dear; nor did I wish to practise resignation, unless it was quite necessary. I wanted to live deep and suck out all the marrow of life, to live so sturdily and Spartan-like as to put to rout all that was not life, to cut a broad swath and shave close, to drive life into a corner, and reduce it to its lowest terms, and, if it proved to be mean, why then to get the whole and genuine meanness of it, and publish its meanness to the world; or if it were sublime, to

---

WHAT I LIVED FOR.   99

know it by experience, and be able to give a true account of it in my next excursion. For most men, it appears to me, are in a strange uncertainty about it, whether it is of the devil or of God, and have *somewhat hastily* concluded that it is the chief end of man here to "glorify God and enjoy him forever."

Still we live meanly, like ants; though the fable tells us that we were long ago changed into men; like pygmies we fight with cranes; it is error upon error, and clout upon clout, and our best virtue has for its occasion a superfluous and evitable wretchedness. Our life is frittered away by detail. An honest man has hardly need to count more than his ten fingers, or in extreme cases he may add his ten toes, and lump the rest. Simplicity, simplicity, simplicity! I say, let your affairs be as two or three, and not a hundred or a thousand; instead of a million count half a dozen, and keep your accounts on your thumb nail. In the midst of this chopping sea of civilized life, such are the clouds and storms and quicksands and thousand-and-one items to be allowed for, that a man has to live, if he would not founder and go to the bottom and not make his port at all, by dead reckoning, and he must be a great calculator indeed who succeeds. Simplify, simplify. Instead of three meals a day, if it be necessary eat but one; instead of a hundred dishes, five; and reduce other things in proportion. Our life is like a German Confederacy, made up of petty states, with its boundary forever fluctuating, so that even a German cannot tell you how it is bounded at any moment. The nation itself, with all its so called internal improvements, which, by the way, are all external and superficial, is just such an unwieldy and overgrown establishment, cluttered with furniture and tripped up by

Walt and Thoreau met several times in the 1850s, in New York. Years later, Walt paid Thoreau the highest praise:

Thoreau was a surprising fellow—he is not easily grasped—is elusive: yet he is one of the native forces—stands for a fact, a movement, an upheaval: Thoreau belongs to America, to the transcendental, to the protesters…. One thing about Thoreau keeps him very near to me: I refer to his lawlessness—his dissent—his going his own absolute road let hell blaze all it chooses.

Like Emerson, Thoreau, too, found Walt's poetry too earthy, and he, too, recognized that *Leaves of Grass* was new and important:

He is a great fellow. There are two or three pieces in the book which are disagreeable, at least, simply sensual…. But even on this side he has spoken more truth than any modern I know…. On the whole it is to me very brave and American. We ought to rejoice greatly in him. He occasionally suggests something a little more than human…. To be sure I sometimes feel a little imposed on. By his heartiness and broad generalities he puts me into a liberal frame of mind prepared to see wonders—as it were sets me upon a hill or in the midst of a plain—stirs me well up and then—throws in a thousand of brick.

TOWARD LEAVES OF GRASS

I was simmering, simmering, simmering; Emerson brought me to a boil.

As Walt told his friend John Townsend Trowbridge, he was working as a carpenter, living with his mother, when he first encountered Emerson's work, the work that would finally coalesce within him and be expressed as *Leaves of Grass*.

This was in 1854; he was then thirty-five years old…. He lived at home with his mother; going to his work in the morning and returning at night, carrying his dinner pail like any common laborer. Along with his pail he usually carried a book, between which and his solitary meal he would divide his nooning. Once the book chanced to be a volume of Emerson; and from that time he took with him no other writer. His half-formed purpose, his vague aspirations, all that had lain smouldering so long within him, waiting to be fired, rushed into flame at the touch of those electric words, the words that burn in the prose-poem Nature, and in the essays on Spiritual Laws, The Over-Soul, Self-Reliance…. He freely admitted that he could never have written his poems if he had not first "come to himself," and that Emerson helped him to "find himself." I asked if he thought he would have come to himself without that help. He said, "Yes, but it would have taken longer." And he used this characteristic expression: "I was simmering, simmering, simmering; Emerson brought me to a boil."

CHAPTER 7

Comrades, Friends, Spouse

From Walt's notebooks, 1857–59. "To a new personal admirer" evolved into "Whoever You Are Holding Me in Hand," one of the poems in the "Calamus" cluster in Leaves of Grass.

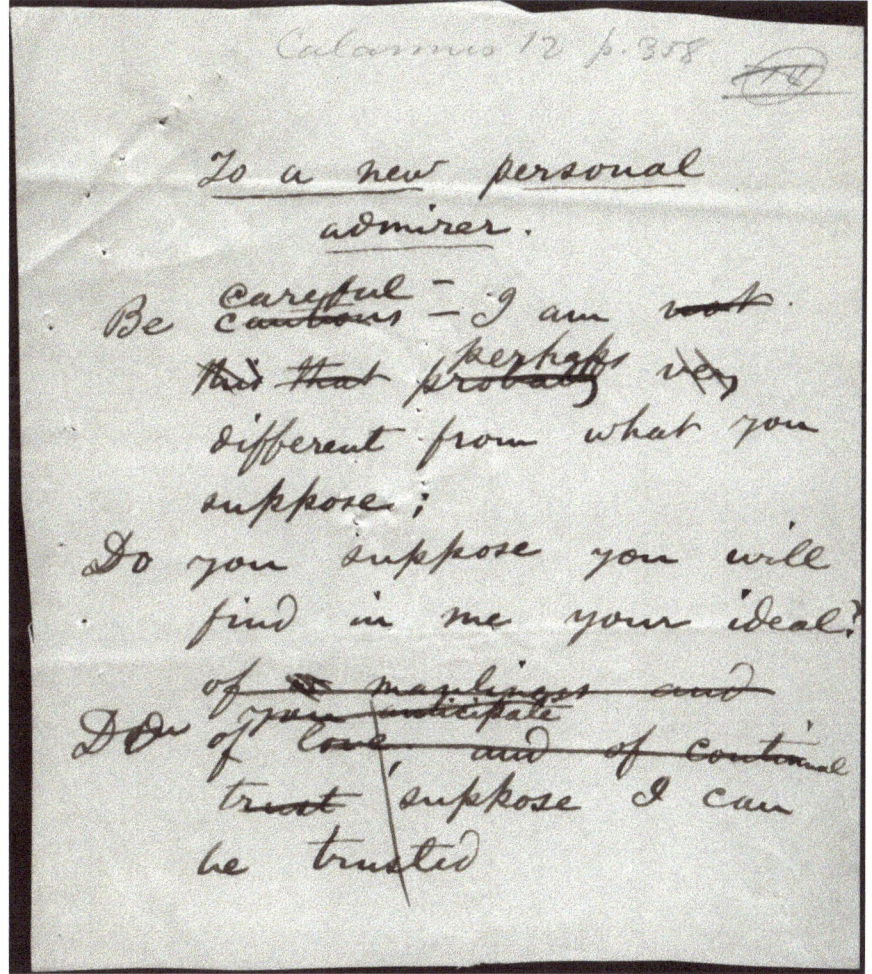

Be careful—I am
perhaps
different from what you
suppose;
Do you suppose you will
find in me your ideal?

Comrades

Why be there men I meet, and others I know, that while they are with me, the sunlight of Paradise expands my blood—that when I walk with an arm of theirs about my neck, my soul scoots and courses like an unleashed dog—that when they leave me the pennants of my joy sink flat and lank in the deadest calm.

— *from Walt Whitman's notebook*

Walt described comradeship—"adhesiveness," to use the phrenological term—as both parallel to and in contrast with romantic love between men and women, or "amativeness."

Many will say it is a dream, and will not follow my inferences: but I confidently expect a time when there will be seen, running like a half-hid warp through all the myriad audible and visible worldly interests of America, threads of manly friendship, fond and loving, pure and sweet, strong and life-long, carried to degrees hitherto unknown—not only giving tone to individual character, and making it unprecedently emotional, muscular, heroic, and refined, but having the deepest relations to general politics. I say democracy infers such loving comradeship, as its most inevitable twin or counterpart, without which it will be incomplete, in vain, and incapable of perpetuating itself.

"'Calamus' is a common word here. It is the very large & aromatic grass, or rush, growing about water-ponds in the valleys…. The recherché or ethereal sense of the term, as used in my book, arises probably from the actual Calamus presenting the biggest & hardiest kind of spears of grass—and their fresh, aquatic, pungent bouquet." The hidden, phallic seed-form of the plant, also called sweet flag, gives itself as a symbol of male sexuality.

(O here I last saw him that tenderly loves me, and returns again never to separate from me,
And this, O this shall henceforth be the token of comrades, this calamus-root shall,
Interchange it youths with each other! let none render it back!)
…
I will give of it, but only to them that love as I myself am capable of loving.

— *from "These I Singing in Spring"*

The Calamus cluster of poems in *Leaves of Grass* is often read today as a testimonial to erotic love between men. In Walt's time, however, it would not have occurred to most readers to read homosexuality into any published work. Homosexual activity, in the mind of the average citizen, ranged from criminal to unspeakable to unimaginable. Gay culture was discerned and tolerated mainly by artists and gay people. *Little Women* author Louisa May Alcott confessed to her friend and fellow journalist Louise Chandler Moulton to having fallen in love with "so many pretty girls," but never with a man. Alcott's candor points to a paradox of the nineteenth century that can be hard to grasp today. Same-sex romantic love was embraced, even idealized, with physical warmth and contact perfectly acceptable, as long as the relationship didn't cross into sexual intimacy. Lincoln scholar Doris Kearns Goodwin gives an example: "At one point I found a letter where Stanton writes to Chase [both members of Lincoln's cabinet], 'Ever since our pleasant intercourse last summer there is no one in my mind more, waking or sleeping. I dream of being with you. I want to hold your hand by the fire and tell you I love you.' And no one ever suggested those men were gay."

Nor did Walt suffer for these lines:

> …two simple men I saw to-day, on the pier, in the
>   midst of the crowd, parting the parting of dear friends,
> The one to remain hung on the other's neck, and passionately
>   kiss'd him,
> While the one to depart, tightly prest the one to remain in his arms.
> — from "What Think You I Take My Pen in Hand?"

In the nineteenth century, censure of *Leaves of Grass* focused not on the Calamus cluster, but rather on the heterosexual Children of Adam cluster. Sensuality in the Calamus poems is tender and diffused, perhaps encoded. The Children of Adam sequence explores sex aggressively, explicitly: "quivering jelly of love, white-blow and delirious juice" in "I Sing the Body Electric," versus kisses and hugs and, in "Live Oak with Moss," "the measureless ocean of love within him."

When J.A. Symonds, an English friend and admirer, asked Walt whether his "conception of Comradeship" might include "semi-sexual emotions and actions which no doubt do occur between men," Walt slapped him down. "I am fain to hope," Walt replied, "the pages themselves are not to be even mention'd for such gratuitous and quite at the time undream'd & unreck'd [unreckoned] possibility of morbid inferences—wh'[ich] are disavow'd by me & seem damnable.…" In the same letter, Whitman claimed to have fathered six children, as if that would prove he did not have a same-sex orientation. (Walt's response didn't damage Symonds' esteem for Walt.)

The interpretations wrapped around Walt's sexuality seem overly determined by the wishes or bias of the person interpreting, and by his or her milieu. Walt's own cloud of words in correspondence and conversations doesn't clear the ambiguity. His poetry must speak—be careful to listen closely.

> Here to put your lips upon mine I permit you,
> With the comrade's long-dwelling kiss or the new husband's kiss,
> For I am the new husband and I am the comrade.
>
> Or if you will, thrusting me beneath your clothing,
> Where I may feel the throbs of your heart or rest upon your
>   hip,
> Carry me when you go forth over land or sea;
> For thus merely touching you is enough, is best,
> And thus touching you would I silently sleep and be carried
>   eternally.
>
> But these leaves conning you con at peril,
> For these leaves and me you will not understand,
> They will elude you at first and still more afterward, I will
>   certainly elude you,
> Even while you should think you had unquestionably caught me,
>   behold!
> Already you see I have escaped from you.
> — from "Whoever You Are Holding Me Now in Hand"

TWO WORLDS

Walt's relationship with PETE DOYLE was the most enduring of his life; more on Pete in Chapter 12: Washington, D.C.

Walt's male friends inhabited two different worlds, as he himself did: the world of working men, and the world of professionals, what we now call "blue collar" and "white collar." Class divisions, in Walt's time, were even deeper than they are today. Gaps in education were wide, with children of the working class receiving little formal education.

"All the omnibus drivers knew him," Walt's friend Pete Doyle, himself a transportation worker, commented after the two visited New York City together. Walt fondly remembered "my old pilot friends" on the ferries:

And the ferry men—little they know how much they have been to me, day and night—how many spells of listlessness, ennui, debility, they and their hardy ways have dispell'd.

Walt found in working men freedom from intellectual contention and pretension, but their beloved company could not completely fulfill him. A more educated set of friends, including publishing professionals and physicians, offered stimulating conversation and support for his work.

Two men named Fred illustrate the two opposite types of Walt's male friends.

FRED VAUGHAN

No pictures of Fred Vaughan are known. The picture here, though dated 1901, gives an impression of how Fred would have looked on his job of driving a stagecoach.

During the 1850s, Walt briefly shared an apartment in Manhattan with a stagecoach driver, Fred Vaughan. So intense was their relationship that years after it ended, Walt exhorted himself to exercise more self-control in a similar relationship, writing: "Remember Fred Vaughan!" The comradeship was sweet and true while it lasted. In 1860, Fred wrote to Walt:

I heard [Ralph Waldo Emerson] lecture.... I think he has that in him which makes men capable of strong friendships.—This theme he also touched on, and said that a man whose heart was filled with a warm, ever enduring not to be shaken by anything Friendship was one to be set on one side apart from other men, and almost to be worshipped as a saint.—There Walt, how do you like that? What do you think of them setting you & myself, and one or two others we know up in some public place, with an immense placard on our breast, reading Sincere Friends!!!

FRED GRAY

Frederick Schiller Gray's name was attached to the "Fred Gray Association," a clique of young men who frequented Pfaff's beer cellar in the 1850s, along with artists, writers, actors, journalists and other Bohemian types, including Walt.

In contrast to Walt's working class chums, members of the Fred Gray Association were well-educated and well-to-do. Several were associated with the New York Hospital, where Fred's father, a physician, had worked and where Walt visited working friends injured on the job.

When Walt met Fred, Fred had enlisted in the Union army but was not yet deployed. Once Gray left for the War, his career duties in the army and, later, his work as a physician along with family cares prevented the two men from spending much time together. Their correspondence dwindled over the years but their mutual affection did not.

Walt treasured throughout his life a book that Fred gave him, *Prose Writers of Germany*. He read the book and made it an album of his friendship with Fred, with pictures and notes of their occasional meetings pasted and written within its covers.

Such mergings of friendship and inspiration run throughout *Leaves of Grass*.

Friends

"Gray, aide de camp, 3d Sept '62." Fred Gray gave Walt this carte de visite, which Walt kept in the book Fred gave him, Prose Writers of Germany.

Leaves of Grass is essentially a woman's book: the women do not know it, but every now and then a woman shows that she knows it: it speaks out the necessities, its cry is the cry of the right and wrong of the woman sex—of the woman first of all, of the facts of creation first of all—of the feminine: speaks out loud: warns, encourages, persuades, points the way.

Walt never wavered in his conviction—far from universal in his time (far from universal in our time)—that women and men possess equal worth and potential. He extolled and cultivated in himself qualities perceived to be feminine: gentleness, receptivity, tenderness.

America's full potential could be realized, he believed, only when women become full, equal, and active partners in public and private life.

Democracy, in silence, biding its time, ponders its own ideals, not of literature and art only—not of men only, but of women. The idea of the women of America, (extricated from this daze, this fossil and unhealthy air which hangs about the word lady,) develop'd, raised to become the robust equals, workers, and, it may be, even practical and political deciders with the men—greater than man, we may admit, through their divine maternity, always their towering, emblematical attribute—but great, at any rate, as man, in all departments; or, rather, capable of being so, soon as they realize it, and can bring themselves to give up toys and fictions, and launch forth, as men do, amid real, independent, stormy life.

Walt's ideal woman possessed her own feminine and fully realized sexuality, with desires as imperative as those of men. In a time before reliable birth control, that usually meant a woman with children; and maternity was bound into Walt's ideal woman.

To the movement for the eligibility and entrance of women amid new spheres of business, politics, and the suffrage, the current prurient, conventional treatment of sex is the main formidable obstacle.

ABBY PRICE (1814–1878)

Walt's views do not always fit comfortably in a feminist framework. As with abolitionism, in the realm of women's rights Whitman kept his views philosophical, not activist. Still, he was keenly interested in women's rights and and was close friends with Abby Hills Price, a feminist activist and essayist. When distance separated them, Walt longed for her company and conversation.

Scholar Sherry Ceniza illustrates the exchange of ideas and expression shared by Walt and Abby Price, quoting Price's exhortation:

> [Woman] needs to have her whole nature developed and strengthened by exercise; her attention directed to a larger circle of wants than those of her own household. She needs fully to apprehend the condition of the world; in fact, to realize the actual of the life she wishes her children to fill. This she cannot do, without some experience in its struggles and its triumphs.

Whitman called to women to do just what Price proposed, "to realize the actual of life":

> Whoever you are, come forth! or man or woman come forth!
> You must not stay sleeping and dallying there in the house,
>   though you built it, or though it has been built for you.
>
> Out of the dark confinement! out from behind the screen!
> It is useless to protest, I know all and expose it....
>
> — *from "Song of the Open Road"*

Abby Hills Price, circa 1875

ANNE GILCHRIST (1828–1885)

One of Walt's most ardent admirers was Anne Gilchrist, a widow with three children and a member of the literary world in England. On her husband's death, she completed the biography of William Blake he had begun; it remains a foundational work today.

Gilchrist's essay, "A Woman's Estimate of Walt Whitman," drawn from her letters to Walt, addresses him directly:

> You argued rightly that my confidence would not be betrayed by any of the poems in this book. None of them troubled me even for a moment; because I saw at a glance that it was not, as men had supposed, the heights brought down to the depths, but the depths lifted up level with the sunlit heights, that they might become clear and sunlit, too.... Do they really think that God is ashamed of what he has made and appointed? And, if not, surely it is somewhat superfluous that they should undertake to be so for him.

Walt later told a close friend:

> You can imagine what such a thing as her Estimate meant to me at that time. Almost everybody was against me—the papers, the preachers, the literary gentlemen—nearly everybody with only here and there a dissenting voice—when it looked on the surface as if my enterprise was bound to fail—bound to fail. Then this letter—these letters: this wonderful woman. Such things stagger a man—leave him without words to say.

The first of "these letters" from Anne included a proposal of marriage. In their ensuing correspondence, sometimes he held her off, sometimes he held her close. When she declared her intention to move from England to America in order to be near him, he fluttered, "I do not approve your American trans-settlement—I see so many things here, you have yet no idea of—the American social & almost every other kind of crudeness, meagreness, (at least in appearance)—Don't do any thing toward such a move, nor resolve on it, nor indeed make any move at all in it, without further advice from me."

Anne Gilchrist, circa 1870

After exchanging letters with Walt for six years, Anne moved to America, settling for two years across the Delaware River in Philadelphia, an easy commute from Camden, then Walt's home. She lived in New England for another year.

Some literary historians have given in to depicting Anne as a lovesick buffoon, her relationship with Walt a failure, but nothing could be further from the truth. Despite his physical reserve, they came to enjoy a deep, warm, and mutually fulfilling friendship. The company of her and her three children comforted Walt and offered him a familial second home during a period of ill health and financial instability.

I have that sort of feeling about her which cannot easily be spoken of—put into words—indeed, the sort of feeling that words will not fit: love (strong personal love, too), reverence, respect—you see, it won't go into words: all the words are weak and formal.

Walt's poem "Going Somewhere" refers to Gilchrist as his "noblest woman-friend."

GOING SOMEWHERE
My science-friend, my noblest woman-friend,
(Now buried in an English grave—and this a memory-leaf
    for her dear sake,)
Ended our talk—"The sum, concluding all we know of old or
    modern learning, intuitions deep,
"Of all Geologies—Histories—of all Astronomy—of Evolution,
    Metaphysics all,
"Is, that we all are onward, onward, speeding slowly, surely
    bettering,
"Life, life an endless march, an endless army, (no halt, but it is
    duly over,)
"The world, the race, the soul—in space and time the universes,
"All bound as is befitting each—all surely going somewhere."

Spouse

As with so much about Walt, his relationships pose a paradox. In some respects, he related to women more deeply; in some respects, he related to men more intensely. Of marriage, Walt told a friend, "I suppose the chief reason why I never married must have been an overmastering passion for entire freedom, unconstraint; I had an instinct against forming ties that would bind me." This may seem like a misdirection to conceal homosexuality. Yet Walt could have married and had children, as many gay men have done through the ages.

Does Walt's poetry transcend or evade his sexual orientation?

We who follow, carrying the baggage of our own longings and preconceptions, will never know for sure. We may need simply to trust that we know of Walt what he wanted to tell us, no more, no less.

Walt maintained a mystery about himself, part cultivated, part innate. The English artist Edward Carpenter, who visited Walt in his age, said, "I was aware of a certain radiant power in him, a large benign effluence and inclusiveness, as of the sun, which filled out the place where he was—yet with something of reserve and sadness in it too, and a sense of remoteness and inaccessibility." Even his brother George admitted, "He was like us—and yet he was different from us, too."

Maybe Walt's spouse was *Leaves of Grass,* and his reserve fidelity to it. Once written, his life revolved around the work. Whatever else occupied him, he continued to revise and gather inspiration for additions. His friends, especially in later life, tended to take roles of disciples, praising and promoting *Leaves*. As failing health pulled him toward death, his most urgent concern was to complete a final edition.

Or maybe, truly, Walt's spouse is you and me, we who read and love his poems.

Old man. Photo by George Hodan

TO A STRANGER.
PASSING stranger! you do not know how longingly I look upon
    you,
You must be he I was seeking, or she I was seeking, (it comes to
    me as of a dream,)
I have somewhere surely lived a life of joy with you,
All is recall'd as we flit by each other, fluid, affectionate, chaste,
    matured,
You grew up with me, were a boy with me or a girl with me,
I ate with you and slept with you, your body has become not yours
    only nor left my body mine only,
You give me the pleasure of your eyes, face, flesh, as we pass, you
    take of my beard, breast, hands, in return,
I am not to speak to you, I am to think of you when I sit alone
    or wake at night alone,
I am to wait, I do not doubt I am to meet you again,
I am to see to it that I do not lose you.

CHAPTER 8

Voyager

If I rested 'Leaves of Grass' on the usual claims—if I did not feel that the deepest moral, social, political purposes of America are the underlying endeavors at least of my pages: that the geography and hydrography of this continent, the Prairies, the St. Lawrence, Ohio, the Carolinas, Texas, Missouri are their real veins and current concrete—I should not dare to have them put in type, and printed, and offer'd for sale.

Map of North America, circa 1880, with Walt's red-ink annotations of his travels, including his wartime journey to Fredericksburg, Virginia

Steamboat race, art circa 1859 attributed to Weingärtner. Inside the pilot house, illustration circa 1850

Transports

Pullman sleeper car, circa 1870

In Walt's early childhood, goods and people moved by the power of humans and draft animals or by the whims of winds, currents, and tides. Walt's parents witnessed the beginning of the age of steam, but the age of sails and draft animals did not fade to an end until the early twentieth century, when engines took over.

Early and mid nineteenth-century transportation relied on waterways much as we rely on highways today. Ferries carried workers to offices and factories, farmers to market—horses, carts, and all— and families to church. Ships under steam and sail conveyed everyone from children going to school to pioneers heading West, along with cargo of all kinds. Animals hauled people and freight inland and to the waterside. In cities, horse-drawn streetcars were used into the twentieth century.

The sprawl of railroads accelerated after the Civil War. Trains moved products bred, harvested, mined, quarried, and manufactured with an efficiency that defied earlier modes of transportation. Farmers, merchants, and manufacturers gained access to vast new markets. The fortunes of individuals and entire towns rose and fell according to the favors of the iron horse and the men who owned it.

In the 1840s, Walt traveled to New Orleans by riverboats, steam- and sail-powered, with coaches for shorter legs of the journey. In the 1870s, when he laid eyes on the Rockies, he arrived by train, with his own comfortable sleeping berth.

The tracks embedded in the street for the horsecar, or horse-drawn trolley, were an innovation that allowed the horses to draw heavier loads more smoothly and safely. Horsecar, 4th Avenue near 10th Street, New York City, circa 1865

Before the Brooklyn Bridge spanned the East River in 1883, only ships and boats crossed between Manhattan and Brooklyn, strengthening cooperation as well as fueling fierce rivalry between the two then-independent cities. An 1853 hand-colored lithograph shows a variety of vessels plying the East River; the view is from Manhattan toward Brooklyn.

Walt's commute across the East River between Brooklyn and Manhattan inspired one of his greatest poems, "Crossing Brooklyn Ferry." The back of this 1890 photo is inscribed, "To Walt Whitman with best wishes from J. Johnston, Bolton, England."

I too many and many a time cross'd the river of old,
Watched the Twelfth-month sea-gulls, saw them high in the air floating with motionless wings, oscillating their bodies,
Saw how the glistening yellow lit up parts of their bodies and left the rest in strong shadow,
Saw the slow-wheeling circles and the gradual edging toward the south,
Saw the reflection of the summer sky in the water,
Had my eyes dazzled by the shimmering track of beams,
Look'd at the fine centrifugal spokes of light round the shape of my head in the sunlit water,
Look'd on the haze on the hills southward and south-westward,
Look'd on the vapor as it flew in fleeces tinged with violet,
Look'd toward the lower bay to notice the vessels arriving,
Saw their approach, saw aboard those that were near me,
Saw the white sails of schooners and sloops, saw the ships at anchor,
The sailors at work in the rigging or out astride the spars,
The round masts, the swinging motion of the hulls, the slender serpentine pennants,
The large and small steamers in motion, the pilots in their pilot-houses,
The white wake left by the passage, the quick tremulous whirl of the wheels…

— *from "Crossing Brooklyn Ferry"*

New Orleans

After leaving his job at the *Brooklyn Eagle* newspaper in 1848, Walt went with his brother Jeff to New Orleans, their first trip outside of New York. Walt was twenty-eight, Jeff fifteen. Working as editor for the *New Orleans Crescent* newspaper, Walt wrote "light-hearted sketches of colorful types he saw about town." The *Crescent* advertised slave auctions, but Walt did not publish any pieces on slavery during his tenure there.

His antipathy toward slavery did not harden him against the southern states. Lively, exotic, diverse New Orleans endeared the South to Walt. He believed that the Union derived its strength in large part from regional diversity and inclusiveness.

Jeff did not thrive in New Orleans. His physical and emotional malaise, as well as a dispute Walt had with the *Crescent*'s owners, sent the brothers back to New York in little more than three months. Brief as was his sojourn there, in old age, Walt named New Orleans, with Brooklyn and Washington, D.C., as "my cities of romance…the cities of things begun."

Miss Dusky Grisette is the young 'lady' who takes her stand of evenings upon the pavement opposite the St. Charles Hotel, for the praiseworthy purpose of selling a few flowers by retail, showing off her own charms meanwhile, in a wholesale manner. She drives a thriving trade when the evenings are pleasant. Her neat basket of choice bouquets sits by her side, and she has a smile and a wink for every one of the passers-by who have a wink and a smile for her….

— *New Orleans Crescent, March 1848*

Often, of a Sunday morning, we have heard the melodious, guttural voice of Timothy Goujon, in that place in the city of New Orleans where men and women do, at this especial hour of the week, "most congregate," namely, in the Market-place. There have we seen and heard the sentimental Goujon trill forth harmonious ditty in accents somewhat like the following, though it would require a mixture of the French horn and the bassoon to grunt out the strain with any degree of exactness, especially the chorus: "Ah-h-h-h-h-h-h-h-h-h a bonne marche—so cheep as navair vas—toutes frais—var fresh. Ah-h-h un veritable collection—jentlemens and plack folks. Ah-h-h come and puyde veritable poisson de la mer—de bonne huitres—Ah-h-h-h-h-h-h-h!"

— *New Orleans Crescent, April 1848*

New Orleans French Market. 1880 photo by William Henry Jackson

One of my choice amusements during my stay in New Orleans was going down to the old French Market, especially of a Sunday morning. The show was a varied and curious one; among the rest, the Indian and negro hucksters with their wares. For there were always fine specimens of Indians, both men and women, young and old. I remember I nearly always on these occasions got a large cup of delicious coffee with a biscuit, for my break-fast, from the immense shining copper kettle of a great Creole mulatto woman (I believe she weigh'd 230 pounds.) I never have had such coffee since.

— *Specimen Days*

The 1840s view shows the Mississippi river with steamboats, sailing ships and small craft, and the area from the Faubourg St. Marie through the Vieux Carre, with the spires of St. Louis Cathedral at Jackson Square visible right of center.

Sundays I sometimes went forenoons to the old Catholic Cathedral in the French quarter. I used to walk a good deal in this arrondissement….

— *from "November Boughs"*

The Mexican War ended shortly after Walt and Jeff arrived in New Orleans. Many veterans passed through the city on their way home.

Following a brilliant campaign…we were returning after our victory.… I remember the crowds of soldiers, the gay young officers, going or coming, the receipt of important news, the many discussions, the returning wounded, and so on.

Although this picture was taken in 1859, the young soldiers returning from the Mexican War would have resembled this one. The soldier's military unit, Battery K, 1st U.S. Artillery, fought in Mexico. The unit, like all of the U.S. Army, would be fragmented by the Civil War. One of Battery K's most famous Mexican War veterans was Confederate General "Stonewall" Jackson.

A slave at auction!
I help the auctioneer…the sloven does not half know his business.
Gentlemen look on this curious creature,
Whatever the bids of the bidders they cannot be high enough for him.…

— from the poem later titled, "I Sing the Body Electric," in Leaves of Grass, 1855 edition.

SLAVE BLOCK, OLD ST. LOUIS HOTEL, NEW ORLEANS, LA.

Photo of the slave blocks at the St. Louis Hotel, New Orleans. The names of the auctioneers appear above the arches. Photo circa 1906

I used to wander a midday hour or two now and then for amusement on the crowded and bustling levees, on the banks of the river. The diagonally wedg'd-in boats, the stevedores, the piles of cotton and other merchandise, the carts, mules, negroes, etc., afforded never-ending studies and sights to me. I made acquaintances among the captains, boatmen, or other characters, and often had long talks with them—sometimes finding a real rough diamond among my chance encounters.
— *Specimen Days*

New Orleans wharf. 1875

Draft manuscript of part of "Live Oak with Moss."

Walt in New Orleans, aged 29. Gray is just touching his hair and beard; he hasn't yet adopted his more casual, less conventional fashion and still wears a tie and waistcoat, and a pressed white shirt. 1848

LIVE OAK, WITH MOSS

Walt's poem set in New Orleans, "Live Oak, with Moss" is part of a group of poems by Whitman that scholar Herschel Parker names "a brave sexual manifesto" of gay love.

> Publish my name and hang up
>   my picture as that of the
>   tenderest lover,
> The friend, the lover's portrait, of
>   whom his friend, his lover,
>   was fondest,
> Who was not proud of his songs,
>   but of the measureless ocean
>   of love within him—and
>   freely poured it forth.
>
> …
>
> Whose happiest days were these, far
>   away through fields, in woods, on hills, he
>   and another, wandering hand in
>   hand, the twain, apart from
>   other men.…

— *from draft manuscript*

Voyages

Walt never traveled overseas, but he saw a good deal of the United States and a bit of Canada. His voyages to and from New Orleans took him the length of the Mississippi, over Lake Huron and Lake Erie and along the Hudson River. His stops included St. Louis, Chicago, Milwaukee, Cleveland, Buffalo, and Albany.

After Jeff settled in St. Louis, Walt stayed with him several times. He also visited Boston and Concord, Massachusetts, where his friend Ralph Waldo Emerson lived. In 1879 he traveled as far west as Denver. He longed to go further, but his body just wasn't up for it.

Our voyage up the Mississippi was after the same sort as the voyage, some months before, down it. The shores of this great river are very monotonous and dull—one continuous and rank flat, with the exception of a meagre stretch of bluff, about the neighborhood of Natchez, Memphis, etc.

— *from Specimen Days*

The Sidewheeler 'The City of St. Paul' on the Mississippi River, Dubuque, Iowa. Painting by Alfred Thompson Bricher, 1872

VIEW ON THE HUDSON: WEST POINT.

The delicious tender summer day, just warm enough—the constantly changing but ever beautiful panorama on both sides of the river—(went up near a hundred miles)—the high straight walls of the stony Palisades—beautiful Yonkers, and beautiful Irvington—the never-ending hills, mostly in rounded lines, swathed with verdure,—the distant turns, like great shoulders in blue veils—the frequent gray and brown of the tall-rising rocks—the river itself, now narrowing, now expanding—the white sails of the many sloops, yachts, &c., some near, some in the distance—the rapid succession of handsome villages and cities, (our boat is a swift traveler, and makes few stops)—the Race—picturesque West Point, and indeed all along—the costly and often turreted mansions forever showing in some cheery light color, through the woods—make up the scene.

I was delighted with the appearance of the towns along Wisconsin…. They say the country back is beautiful and rich. (It seems to me that if we should ever remove from Long Island, Wisconsin would be the proper place to come to.) The towns have a remarkable appearance of good living, without any penury or want. The country is so good naturally, and labor is in such demand.

TOP: View on the Hudson - West Point, circa 1870
Photo near Sheboygan, Wisconsin, 2012

… up the blue waters of Lake Michigan…

Photo of Lake Michigan, in Wisconsin, 2012

Walt saw enough misery in his life to appreciate prosperity wherever he found it. Yet his description clearly shows: Cleveland did not have much dash. City of Cleveland, Ohio in 1872

The streets are unusually wide, and the buildings appear to be substantial and comfortable. We went down through Main Street and found, some distance along, several squares of ground very prettily planted with trees and looking attractive enough.

It was 10 o'clock A. M. when we got in Chicago, too late for the steamer; so we went to an excellent public house, the 'American Temperance,' and I spent the time that day and till next morning, looking around Chicago.

That's all he wrote, of Chicago, at least. Sadly, we'll never know what Walt saw, when "looking around Chicago." We do know that the Chicago he saw in the 1840s was utterly different from the Chicago of thirty years later, after the devastating fire of 1871. Lithograph, "Chicago as It Was," circa 1860.

129

[St. Louis'] American electricity goes well with its German phlegm. Fourth, Fifth and Third streets are store-streets, showy, modern, metropolitan, with hurrying crowds, vehicles, horse-cars, hubbub, plenty of people, rich goods, plate-glass windows, iron fronts often five or six stories high. You can purchase anything in St. Louis.

Between Pueblo and Bent's fort, southward, in a clear afternoon sun-spell I catch exceptionally good glimpses of the Spanish peaks.... We pass Fort Lyon—lots of adobe houses—limitless pasturage, appropriately fleck'd with those herds of cattle—in due time the declining sun in the west—a sky of limpid pearl over all—and so evening on the great plains. A calm, pensive, boundless landscape—the perpendicular rocks of the north Arkansas, hued in twilight—a thin line of violet on the southwestern horizon—the palpable coolness and slight aroma—a belated cowboy with some unruly member of his herd…and around all the indescribable chiaroscuro and sentiment, (profounder than anything at sea,) athwart these endless wilds.

Lithograph, View of Front Street, St. Louis. 1840, by John Caspar Wild

Study for Spanish Peaks, Southern Colorado. Painting by Samuel Colman, circa 1870

So much for my feeling toward the Queen city of the plains and peaks, where she sits in her delicious rare atmosphere, over 5000 feet above sea-level, irrigated by mountain streams, one way looking east over the prairies for a thousand miles, and having the other, westward, in constant view by day, draped in their violet haze, mountain tops innumerable. Yes, I fell in love with Denver, and even felt a wish to spend my declining and dying days there.

I have been accompanied on my whole journey from Barnegat to Pike's Peak by a pleasant floricultural friend, or rather millions of friends—nothing more or less than a hardy little yellow five petal'd September and October wild flower…. This trip it follow'd me regularly, with its slender stem and eyes of gold, from Cape May to the Kaw valley, and so through the cañons and to these plains. In Missouri I saw immense fields all bright with it. Toward western Illinois I woke up one morning in the sleeper and the first thing when I drew the curtain of my berth and look'd out was its pretty countenance and bending neck.

Denver, 1898—about twenty years after Walt visited, yet the view remains. Hand-tinted photograph by William Henry Jackson, circa 1898

Photo shows an eight-petalled variety of Coreopsis: Coreopsis verticillata.

131

Atlantic Ocean off Ocracoke Island, North Carolina. 2010

The attractions, fascinations there are in sea and shore! How one dwells on their simplicity, even vacuity! What is it in us, arous'd by those indirections and directions? That spread of waves and gray-white beach, salt, monotonous, senseless—such an entire absence of art, books, talk, elegance—so indescribably comforting, even this winter day—grim, yet so delicate-looking, so spiritual—striking emotional, impalpable depths, subtler than all the poems, paintings, music, I have ever read, seen, heard.

CHAPTER 9

America

In thee America, the soul, its destinies,
Thou globe of globes! thou wonder nebulous!

— *from "Thou Mother with Thy Equal Brood"*

U.S. flag with 34 stars, 1861. Kansas was admitted to the Union as a free state on January 29, 1861, making it the 34th state. Months later, the Union fractured into North and South.

One Nation

> The Americans of all nations at any time upon the earth have probably the fullest poetical nature. The United States themselves are essentially the greatest poem.
>
> — *from introduction to 1855* Leaves of Grass

If *Leaves of Grass* has another hero besides Walt himself, it is the United States of America. Walt's prose and poetry are framed by the United States, filled in by the United States, animated by its land, its features and resources, its politics, and its people. While he looks to future readers, his present is the earthy, robust, sometimes grotesque life of nineteenth-century America, with its violent convulsions of war and expansion, exuberant national egoism, boisterous innovations, tumult and pain and joy.

Walt's life began in the Jacksonian Era, stretched through the Civil War and Reconstruction, and ended in the Gilded Age. Not yet one hundred years as a country, Walt's America was still (is still) creating itself, making and remaking its legends, its history, its story. Walt reveled in its pioneer rawness, its brash innovation unfettered by feudalism, its creative spark unshadowed by cultural convention. Nothing overseas, he believed, could possibly measure up to anything American.

Like the peoples who left the Old World to find new opportunity in America, Walt found—demanded—new opportunity for poetry in America. He deliberately discarded old forms, allusions, and tropes, and consciously shed the overburden of the past.

Nineteenth-century America was pulling away from her own past, too—slave-supported agriculture and manufacturing, artisan labor, a seemingly unlimited frontier—and moving toward her future—ethnic diversity, abolition, wage labor and manufacturing, and American settlers, government, schools, and churches occupying the land from coast to coast. The process nearly tore the nation apart forever.

1835. United States. Before the Mexican War, much of what is now the Southwest United States was colonized by Spain.

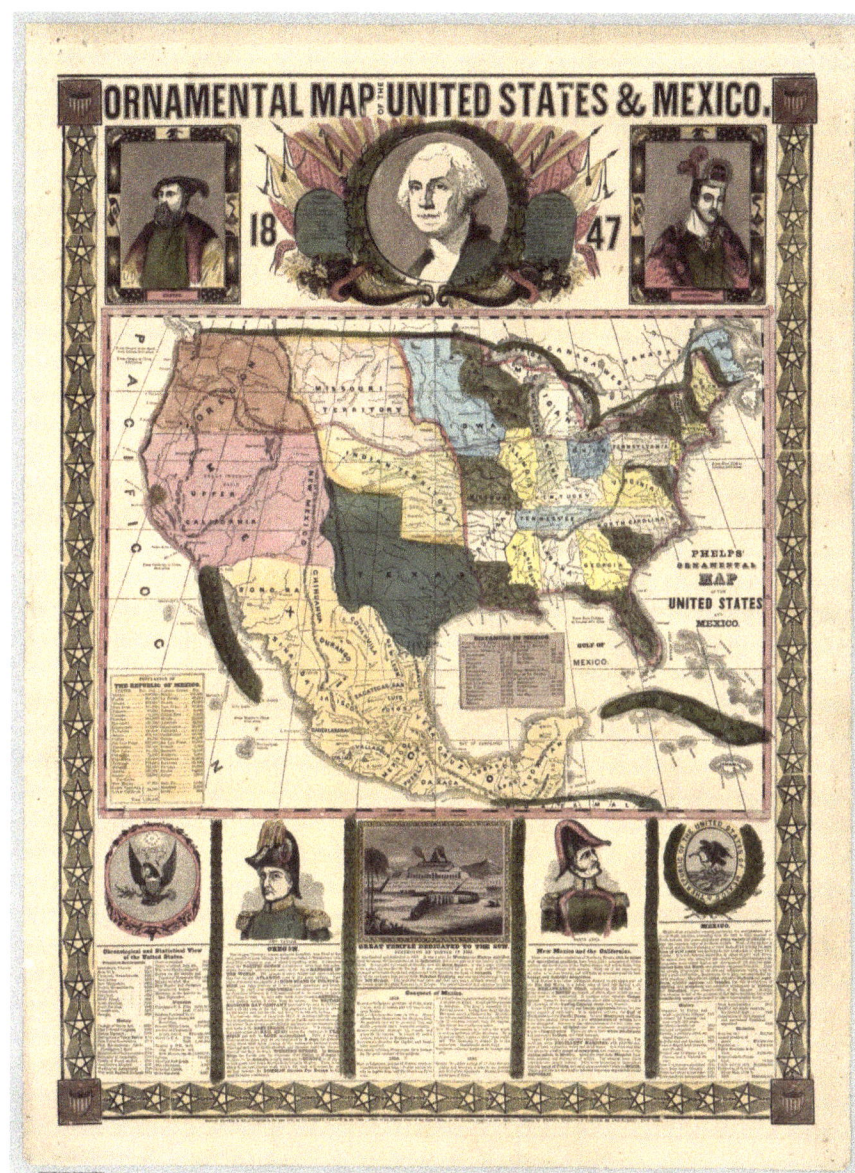

TOP: 1847. Ornamental Map Of The United States & Mexico. The map was published during the Mexican War, which ended in 1848. The text under the picture of Mexican commander Santa Anna predicts (part correctly), of "New Mexico and the Californias": "These countries are destined to become important acquisitions to our republic."

1860. Map of the United States and Territories. The outline of the continental U.S.A., except Alaska, is complete. The question of slave state or "free soil" would threaten to re-shape the U.S. not more than a year after this map was published.

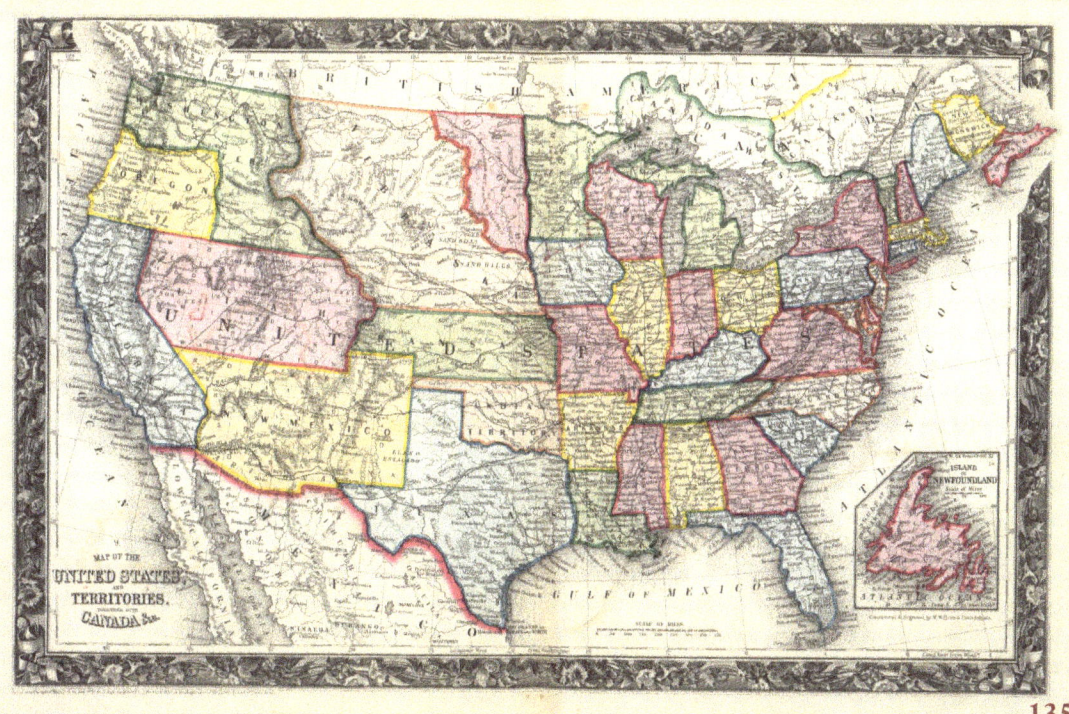

POLITICS

My father was always a Democrat—a Democrat of the old school.

Andrew Jackson, a Democrat "of the old school" and namesake of one of Walter Whitman's sons, served as U.S. president from 1829 to 1837, Walt's late childhood and adolescence. A populist, Jackson advocated for family farmers like Walt's ancestors and artisans like his father.

Jackson's darkest legacy is the removal, by treaty, legislation, and force, of Native Americans from their ancestral lands in the eastern U.S. to the territorial West, an exodus that came to be known as The Trail of Tears. Over 4,000 of the 15,000 people forced to take the trail died enroute of hunger, disease, and exhaustion. Jackson's Farewell Address of 1837 justified the removal in terms that the average citizen of the time accepted, believed, found comfortable.

Andrew Jackson. 1824 portrait by Thomas Sully

The States which had so long been retarded in their improvement by the Indian tribes residing in the midst of them are at length relieved from the evil, and this unhappy race—the original dwellers in our land—are now placed in a situation where we may well hope that they will share in the blessings of civilization and be saved from that degradation and destruction to which they were rapidly hastening while they remained in the States; and while the safety and comfort of our own citizens have been greatly promoted by their removal, the philanthropist will rejoice that the remnant of that ill-fated race has been at length placed beyond the reach of injury or oppression, and that the paternal care of the General Government will hereafter watch over them and protect them.

Like Thomas Jefferson, Jackson foresaw that the issue of slavery could, probably would, fracture the country. He criticized the North for aggressive abolitionism and the South for belligerent opposition to import tariffs, which favored Northern manufacturing.

What have you to gain by division and dissension? Delude not yourselves with the belief that a breach once made may be afterwards repaired. If the Union is once severed, the line of separation will grow wider and wider, and the controversies which are now debated and settled in the halls of legislation will then be tried in fields of battle and determined by the sword....

The Whig party opposed the Democrats. A new Republican party would be formed later; its first president was Abraham Lincoln.

Walt campaigned for the Democratic Party in the 1830s and '40s, and ground several party organs—Democratic-backed newspapers. The vicious personal attacks of political campaigning didn't faze him. When he stumped for the party, he slung filth with gusto.

Eventually, though, corruption and horse-trading, including repeated concessions to slavery interests, turned Walt against politics. He particularly despised the presidents Millard Fillmore (1850–1853), Franklin Pierce (1853–1857), and James Buchanan (1857–1861):

> Who are they as bats and night-dogs askant in the capitol?
> What a filthy Presidentiad! (O South, your torrid suns! O North, your arctic freezings!)
> Are those really Congressmen? are those the great Judges? is that the President?
>
> — *from "To the States, To Identify the 16th, 17th, or 18th Presidentiad"*

Abraham Lincoln would be Walt's next, last, and greatest political love.

The Society of St. Tammany, known as Tammany Hall, was the heart of the Democratic political "machine" in New York City. Originally founded to resist an aristocratic form of government in the United States, Tammany Hall became a kind of aristocracy of its own, gaining influence by supporting under-represented working class and immigrant people, and then placing its operatives in important government positions. Walt, whose working class roots bonded him with working men, naturally found a home at Tammany Hall (and he wrote his temperance novel there).

Tammany Hall's most famous leader, William Magear "Boss" Tweed (1823-1878), rose from the ranks of the firefighters to be a power in New York politics through the mid-19th century. Tobacco label showing Boss Tweed seated

INDUSTRY

> Over the fields of the West those crawling monsters,
> The human-divine inventions, the labor-saving implements;
> Beholdest moving in every direction imbued as with life the revolving hay-rakes,
> The steam-power reaping-machines and the horse-power machines,
> The engines, thrashers of grain and cleaners of grain, well separating the straw, the nimble work of the patent pitchfork,
> Beholdest the newer saw-mill, the southern cotton-gin, and the rice-cleanser....
>
> — *from "The Return of the Heroes," 1881 edition*

A rolling wave of innovations enhanced productivity in the early nineteenth century: to name a few, Robert McCormick's reaper, Eli Whitney's cotton gin, Richard March Hoe's rotary printing press. Steam power boosted mass production, and railroads provided the means to transport large quantities of goods, manufactured and agricultural, farther and faster.

The circa 1830 advent of the balloon frame in building construction gives an example of the decline of artisans—and insight on why Walt's father never was able to get out of debt. Timber framing, Walter Whitman's technique of building, uses large timbers that cannot be supported by nails and hence are joined. A balloon-framed building is supported by multiple smaller timbers. Because the load is distributed, balloon frames do not depend on massive timbers. The studs (vertical) and joists (horizontal) can be nailed together rather than joined. The process lent itself to a more "as-

Sketch from 1845 patent of an improved grain reaper by Cyrus Hall McCormick. The horse-drawn reaper outmoded scythes and sickles for harvesting grain.

137

sembly-line" labor dynamic with fewer skilled workers needed. Materials were cheaper, since studs and joists could be milled offsite to uniform dimensions for any number of buildings, and nails were no longer hand-wrought but "cut" by machine. This and other efficiencies widened the gap between workers and capitalists.

In the South, economic downturns forced small farmers succumbing to sell their land; the wealthy class gobbled them up. Plantation-style agriculture gained ascendancy, and the lines of slavery hardened.

FINANCIAL PANICS & REGIONALISM

Fast economic growth and the government's sale of western land fueled speculation and over-extension of credit, leading to the Panic of 1819, the year Walt was born. The Panic of 1837 followed much the same pattern; a promising decade went sour as speculation combined with unskillful government policies set off a severe depression that lasted until 1842.

The Panic of 1857 came when rapid growth in U.S. manufacturing collided with lowered import tariffs on manufactured goods. The North, which had a stronger manufacturing sector, favored high tariffs. Fewer imports meant less competition. The South, however, resented high tariffs, which forced them to buy more expensive, northern-made goods, and which cramped foreign markets for Southern produce, including flour and cotton. During the Panic, however, the South stood steady with cotton which England, for example, needed for the cornerstone of its economy, the textile industry.

The deep fracture in the country is plain to see. When one half of the country prospered, the other half was doomed to struggle.

"The Times" uses a Fourth of July celebration to illustrate the belief that bankers and speculators, not hard working, sober citizens, now ruled the United States. 1837 lithograph by Edward Clay

A changing "us"

Racism and sexism still flow steady and strong in American society, politics, and domestic life. Yet the extent to which bigotry was accepted and entrenched, north, south, east, and west, in the nineteenth-century is difficult to grasp today.

Ethnologists analyzed cultural norms and cast their findings in a way so as to bolster white male supremacy. Reputable men of science defended slavery, the Indian Wars, repressive marriage laws, wage inequity, anti-Semitism, and anti-immigration policies.

Changing demographics, borders, and economic conditions pressured the status quo that defined who was "American." A flow, a current of social movements, also began coming together. Some took a long time to bear any kind of fruit; some ripen still today.

RELIGION

Faith communities were the strongest, most coherent drivers of social change in nineteenth-century America. Christianity especially permeated and drove every aspect of life. Protestant denominations dominated, but faced powerful rivals. Immigrant Irish and German Catholics, marginalized by mainstream American Christians, boosted Tammany Hall Democrats. Jews were vulnerable to persecution and prejudice. Hinduism, Buddhism, and Islam were known only through news items in far away lands, except among scholars and philosophers. Paradoxically, nineteenth-century America gave rise to new religious movements and denominations. For example, the Church of the Latter Day Saints took root in the 1820s, its movement West driven by persecution back East. The "Second Great Awakening" saw a rise in revival-type meetings. Baptist and Methodist congregations took root and grew as missionaries visited far-flung pioneer communities starving for spiritual guidance. Radical thinkers founded utopian communities.

Christian ministers defended or condemned from the pulpit slavery, sexism, and the appropriation of Native American lands. The Underground Railroad, which helped slaves escape to the North, was organized largely within Christian faith groups. Christianity fueled the Temperance movement, desperately needed in a hard-drinking time, when a family went hungry if Father drank his wages.

Walt did not adhere to any sect, but he wrote newspaper "reviews" of church services around town. The human drama, not religious fervor, drew him to rousing revivals. At the Sands Street Methodist Church, he enjoyed spotting some "pretty girls," and observed, "The galleries of the church were often sprinkled with the mischievous ones that come to ridicule and make sport; but even here the arrows of prayer and pleading sometimes took effect."

A star attraction among New England preachers was abolitionist Henry Ward Beecher (1813–1887), pastor of Brooklyn's Plymouth Congregationalist Church. "He hit me so hard," Walt said, "fascinated me to such a degree that I was afterwards willing to go far out of my way to hear him talk." Beecher's showmanship was not lost on Walt: "We may well doubt whether his is not making people Beecherites instead of Christians."

From his pulpit, Beecher espoused the great causes of his day and of his faith: temperance, women's suffrage, evolutionism, scholarly biblical analysis, and abolitionism. Beecher was active in political circles, first with the Free Soil movement and later with the Republican party. He brought many to the cause of abolitionism, as did his sister Harriet Beecher Stowe, author of the novel *Uncle Tom's Cabin*. From his pulpit, he conducted mock "slave auctions" and raised money for "Beecher's Bibles," rifles sent to abolitionist militants.

Henry Ward Beecher, circa 1855–60.

Plymouth Church, Brooklyn. Although the photograph was taken in 1934, it shows the church much as it would have been when Walt attended, with the out-thrust stage specified by Henry Ward Beecher. By nineteenth-century standards, it was a mega-church.

NATIVISM AND IMMIGRATION

As Walt reached adulthood, the United States struggled to assimilate its biggest wave of European immigrants so far. Germans and Irish made up about two-thirds of the immigrants. Most Irish left their homeland for economic reasons. A first wave of Germans, in the early to mid seventeenth century, also sought relief from poverty. In the mid-nineteenth century, many Germans arrived in America fleeing political oppression after unrest that culminated in 1848 with a failed revolution.

Many "native born" (the term used for white people born in the United States) feared job competition and a threat to American identity. They suspected that the loyalties of Roman Catholic Irish and German immigrants lay with the pope rather than with the United States. The "Know Nothing," or Native American party, formed a rallying point for anti-immigrant sentiment. The "Know Nothing" party opposed slavery mainly on the premise that slave labor depressed wages and created unfair job competition.

Lincoln summed up his feelings on the Native American Party:

I am not a Know-Nothing — that is certain. How could I be? How can any one who abhors the oppression of negroes, be in favor of degrading classes of white people? Our progress in degeneracy appears to me to be pretty rapid. As a nation, we began

An 1854 paper of the "Know Nothing" party

Before 1855, "dull-faced immigrants," as Walt described new arrivals in "I Sing the Body Electric," disembarked from their long, gruelling sea voyage at the southeast end of Manhattan, close to where Walt would have boarded or disembarked from the ferry. The newcomer's first look at New York was not the Statue of Liberty, which rose in the 1880s, but rather the crowd of ships and boats. In 1855, the state of New York converted nearby Castle Garden, which had been an entertainment center, to an immigration intake center. Ellis Island opened in 1892 after the Federal government took over immigration. Painting, In the Land of Promise, Castle Garden, by Charles Frederic Ulrich, 1884

by declaring that 'all men are created equal.' We now practically read it 'all men are created equal, except negroes.' When the Know-Nothings get control, it will read 'all men are created equal, except negroes and foreigners and Catholics.

Women's Rights

The first women's rights convention in the United States gathered at Seneca Falls, New York, in 1848. Its goals, expressed in "The Declaration of Sentiments," were framed by feminist and abolitionist activists Elizabeth Cady Stanton (1815–1902) and Lucretia Mott (1793–1860). The convention focused on the influence of women in society, marriage laws, educational opportunities for girls and women, and suffrage. Women activists often focused on abolitionism and temperance as well as women's rights.

Susan B. Anthony (1820–1906) worked throughout her adult life for women's suffrage, and saw women get the vote in several states. She did not live to see women vote on a national level. As with any cause, many put in hard work, a few are recognized; as Susan B. Anthony herself said, "There have been others [suffragists] also just as true and devoted to the cause — I wish I could name every one — but with such women consecrating their lives, failure is impossible!"

The Civil War slowed the political momentum of the women's movement, despite efforts of feminists including African-American orator, writer, and abolitionist Frederick Douglass, who believed that suffrage should extend not only to black men, but to all women.

The War also brought women into new spheres of public life. A surprising number of women—at least 250—served in the military disguised as men. Many more became nurses, an occupation not always considered suitable for "the fair sex," with its physical demands and raw exposure to men's bodies. Women and girls collected money and goods, from quilts to underwear to food, for husbands, sweethearts, brothers, sons, and strangers. They ran farms and households, and worked outside the home in factories, including arms plants.

The Fifteenth Amendment to the U.S. Constitution, passed in 1870, said, "The right of citizens of the United States to vote shall not be denied or abridged by the United States or by any State on account of race, color, or previous condition of servitude." Despite women's contributions to the Union during the War, they were not considered citizens. Still, the natural force of feminism continued, and in 1920 the U.S. Constitution guaranteed voting rights to all adult citizens, including women.

TOP: Elizabeth Cady Stanton (seated) and Susan B. Anthony worked together for decades on women's rights, and were active and renowned abolitionists. Photo between 1880 and 1902.

Of Lucretia Mott, Walt said, "I knew her just a little: she was a gracious, superb character." Photo circa 1860–80

Slavery

> I hear the wheeze of the slave-coffle, as the slaves march on, as the husky gangs pass on by twos and threes, fastened together with wrist-chains and ankle-chains…
>
> — *from* Leaves of Grass, *1856 edition*

Slavery festered in the nation's body, a congenital wound that gaped wider as the years passed. The Southern states wanted to expand slavery. The Northern states, some of which had not yet abolished slavery, wanted to contain slavery. Westward expansion repeatedly challenged the status quo with the question of whether each new state or territory should be slave or free. One compromise after another fell to sectionalism. The entire nation felt the effects of slavery; Walt would not have seen a "slave-coffle" in 1856, except through media.

Walt steadfastly opposed slavery for its cruelty and degradations, but his political concerns lay with white labor. "The young men of the free States

Harriet Beecher Stowe's novel Uncle Tom's Cabin is considered, today, a catalogue of stereotypes, including "Uncle Tom" himself, a long-suffering, faithful slave. Yet when the book broke sales records in the 1850s, it popularized the abolitionist cause by putting slavery in human terms and showing its devastating impact on families and society, white and black. Henry Ward Beecher was Stowe's brother.

Dishes upstairs, "negro sales" downstairs. The cigar manufactory next door probably employed slaves. Atlanta, Georgia. Photograph by George Bernard, September – November 1864

Slave cells, Alexandria, Virginia. Walt may have viewed this photo, displayed at Mathew Brady's gallery in New York City.

must not be shut out from the new domain (where slavery does not now exist) by the introduction of an institution which will render their honorable industry no longer respectable."

Walt and many other Americans believed that slavery would naturally, peacefully wither away. Gradual emancipation seemed to be working in the North; it had worked in New York. He opposed any movement that threatened to dismember the Union, and like most mid-century Americans, he considered abolitionists divisive radicals. What he did not seem to grasp was the depth of attachment the South had to slavery, culturally and economically. Slaves supported the ruling class with labor and with the literal market value of their bodies. As the voice of abolitionism gained force, the divide between North and South grew deeper, harder, grimmer.

Most people of Walt's time were certain: all men and women are not created equal. Walt's poetry leaped ahead of his time, and at times ahead of himself: affectionate, inclusive, respectful, even worshipful of men and women, girls and boys, of different races and nationalities.

FREDERICK DOUGLASS (1818–1895)

Frederick Douglass, circa 1856.

Frederick Douglass, who escaped slavery in 1838, dedicated his freedom to the abolitionist movement. His autobiography, *The Narrative of the Life of a Slave*, gained him fame, and his oratory gained him influence. Walt heard him speak at the 1848 Free Soil convention in Buffalo, New York, and described his voice as "loud, clear and sonorous." Walt did not comment on the content of Douglass's writings or speeches, but he remained aware of Douglass, as did many other Americans. In March 1865, he noted that President and Mrs. Lincoln received at the White House "Frederick Douglass, who had initially been barred by guards from entering the White House because he was African-American."

Addressing a Fourth of July gathering in 1852, Douglass said:

What, to the American slave, is your 4th of July? I answer: a day that reveals to him, more than all other days in the year, the gross injustice and cruelty to which he is the constant victim. To him, your celebration is a sham; your boasted liberty, an unholy license; your national greatness, swelling vanity; your sounds of rejoicing are empty and heartless; your denunciations of tyrants, brass fronted impudence; your shouts of liberty and equality, hollow mockery; your prayers and hymns, your sermons and thanksgivings, with all your religious parade, and solemnity, are, to him, mere bombast, fraud, deception, impiety, and hypocrisy — a thin veil to cover up crimes which would disgrace a nation of savages.

JOHN BROWN (1800–1859)

No one person in the time leading up to the Civil War inspired as much terror and hate, admiration and awe, as John Brown. A radical abolitionist, Brown believed himself to be the instrument of a God made wrathful by slavery.

Brown gained notoriety in "Bleeding Kansas," by taking part in the violent struggle to bring the territory into the Union as slave or free state. In May 1856, pro-slavers raided Lawrence, Kansas, destroying several buildings, including two abolitionist printing houses. Although the only death was of one of the raiders, the action incensed John Brown and his partisans. A few days later, Brown and his sons and two other men slaughtered five pro-slavery Kansans.

Three years later, in July 1859, Brown raided Harper's Ferry with the plan to seize a Federal arsenal and instigate a slave rebellion. Fellow abolitionist and former slave Harriet Tubman helped recruit men for the raid. The raid failed, and federal troops captured Brown, who was executed in December 1859.

To abolitionists, John Brown towered as a hero and a martyr. To most citizens, especially Southerners, Brown was a fanatic murderer.

John Brown in 1859, the year he led the raid at Harper's Ferry.

HARRIET TUBMAN (CIRCA 1822–1913)

Like Frederick Douglass, Harriet Tubman escaped slavery. To describe her life as an incredible adventure from beginning to end is not to exaggerate or to diminish its moral dimensions. Having attained her own freedom, she dived back into slave territory to rescue dozens of enslaved people through the Underground Railroad, a network of men and women who provided direction, supplies, and shelter to escaping slaves. She and Susan B. Anthony worked together to help enslaved people escape; they continued working together, after Emancipation, in the cause of women's rights.

I had reasoned this out in my mind; there was one of two things I had a right to, liberty, or death; if I could not have one, I would have the other; for no man should take me alive; I should fight for my liberty as long as my strength lasted, and when the time came for me to go, the Lord would let them take me.

— *Harriet Tubman, from* Harriet, The Moses of Her People *1886*

Harriet Tubman. 1911

American Progress, print after 1872 painting by John Gast. An allegorical figure of America leads pioneers westward, as they travel on foot, in a stagecoach, conestoga wagon, and by railroads, where they encounter Native Americans and herds of bison.

Westward

The east and the west are mine, and the north
    and the south are mine.
I am larger than I thought!
I did not know I held so much goodness!…

— *from* Leaves of Grass, *1860 edition*

During Walt's life, expansion of the United States mostly pressed westward and came through acquisitions such as the 1803 Louisiana Purchase and the 1819 Florida Purchase; through wars, especially the Mexican War and the Indian Wars; and through treaties with Native American and European powers.

In essays and poetry, Walt idealized the West. Its soil, he believed, bred a hardier, more honest species of American, one who would overcome the corrupt East Coast establishment to give the nation a fresh start. His hero Abraham Lincoln was a Western man, Kentucky and Illinois then considered the West.

As a voracious reader of newspapers and magazines, Walt could not have been oblivious to the grueling hardship suffered by settlers, the mutual depredations of American settlers and Native Americans, or the rapaciousness of national expansion. Yet like other artists and writers, he veiled the gritty realities of frontier life with a vision of rugged yet tranquil self-sufficiency.

Walt's late-life journey westward confirmed his enthusiasm: "Pete this is a wonderful country out here," he wrote his friend, "& no one knows how big it is till he launches out in the midst of it…."

THE MEXICAN WAR

The Mexican War, lasting from 1846 to 1848, won for the United States nearly all of what would later be the states of Arizona, Nevada, New Mexico, Texas, and Utah, and parts of Colorado, Kansas, Oklahoma, and Wyoming. The southern part of the nation now reached from the Atlantic to the Pacific.

Expansion of the southern territories of the United States opened the prospect of slavery from coast to coast. The Mexican War also nourished ambitions for a generation of military officers, including West Pointers U.S. Grant and R.E. Lee.

Ulysses S. Grant resigned from the army a few years after the Mexican War, only to fail at one business venture after another, including farming his in-laws' property with the help of slave labor. Robert E. Lee, who detested running his in-laws' plantation, stayed in the army, but chafed at military assignments that offered little hope of promotion. Thirteen years later, the Civil War would bestow fame and high rank upon them and others.

Walt not only fiercely supported war with Mexico, he advocated the annexation of "the main bulk of that republic." He disclaimed a "lust of power and territory": "We

In 1823, when Walt was four years old, the eastern states had contours familiar today. Most of the Southwest was a possession of Spain; the Pacific Northwest was British. Cartographer John Melish. 1823.

147

Robert E. Lee, circa 1846. A hero of the Mexican War, when his home state of Virginia seceded from the Union in 1861, Lee turned in his Union blue coat for Confederate gray.

A crowd gathers on the porch of the American Hotel, enthralled by news of the Mexican War. The somber black witnesses perhaps reflect common knowledge: the expansion of the southern United States through acquisition of the Southwest threatened to extend slavery coast to coast. War News from Mexico. Painting by Richard Caton Woodville, 1848.

pant to see our country and its rule far-reaching, only inasmuch as it will take off the shackles that prevent men the even chance of being happy and good...."

Walt later saw the Mexican War as a wrong. During the Civil War he reflected:

There is certainly not one government in Europe but is now watching the war in this country with the ardent prayer that the United States may be effectually split, crippled, and dismember'd by it.... I think indeed it is to-day the real, heartfelt wish of all the nations of the world, with the single exception of Mexico—Mexico, the only one to whom we have ever really done wrong, and now the only one who prays for us and for our triumph, with genuine prayer.

THE INDIAN WARS

The wars with Native American nations crept east to west, fueled by craving for land and minerals. As Americans occupied traditional Native American grounds, hostilities erupted. Land was reserved for Indians, but white settlers repeatedly encroached. Violent raids fueled hatred and fear.

As with the Mexican War, many U.S. Army veterans of the Indian Wars later achieved high rank in the Civil War. Many Civil War veterans continued their military careers fighting Indians.

Walt treasured the heritage of America's native peoples. His views wobbled from negative or romanticized stereotypes to honest attempts at understanding. A passage in "Song of Myself" presents a tableau of "the marriage of the trapper in the open air in the far west, the bride was a red girl." As Whitman scholar Ed Folsom observes, the scene "has been read as suggestive of the white domination of the Native, but also indicative of the possibility of a joining of the races and all they represented in nineteenth-century America."

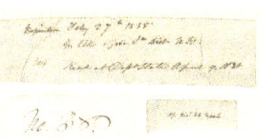

Walt kept in his room a print of Osceola of Florida, by George Catlin. Catlin (1796–1892) was an American artist whose paintings and drawings of Native Americans form his most important legacy. Walt advocated the purchase of Catlin's work by the U.S. Government. 1838 lithograph by George Catlin, from his original painting

Generals Wesley Merritt, Philip Sheridan, George Crook, James William Forsyth, and George Armstrong Custer pose around a table examining a document, presumably a map. All of them fought in the Civil War as well as the Indian Wars. Most famously (or infamously), in the Indian Wars, Forsyth commanded the 7th Cavalry at the Wounded Knee Massacre (December 1890), and Custer was killed at the Battle of Little Big Horn (June 1876). 1865 photo by Alexander Gardner; print by Moses P. Rice.

Roots of Leaves

By the mid-1850s, Walt turned his energies to poetry that would be accessible, relevant and inspiring to Americans of every kind. His purpose was not to expose inequities. He made his poetry a mold into which he poured what he saw as the best, raw, authentically American qualities to make an ideal form. His aim was to shape his nation, to bring America to realize her full potential, an ideal not abstract, but rooted in ordinary life and ordinary people untrammeled by dogmas and customs.

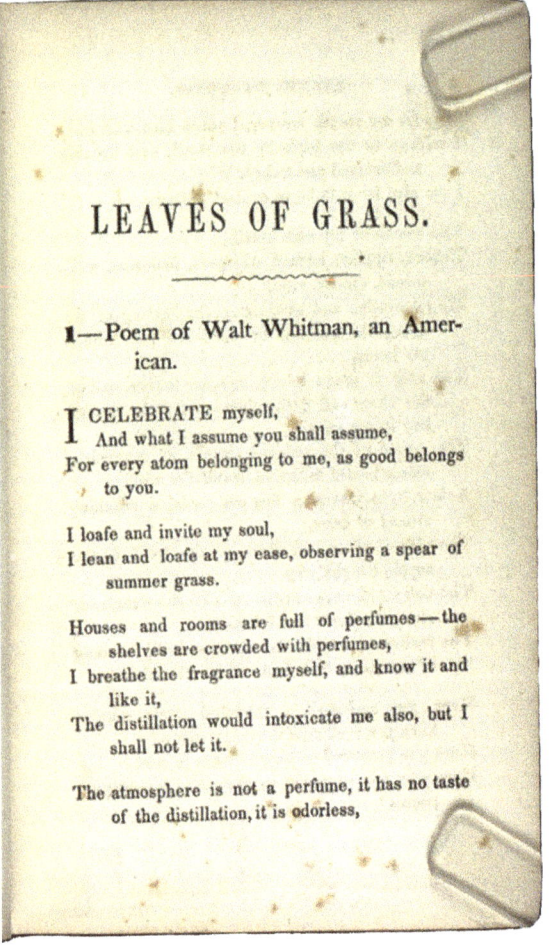

In the 1856 Leaves of Grass, the poem later titled "Song of Myself" is "Poem of Walt Whitman, an American."

...
O I see now that this America is only you and me,
Its power, weapons, testimony, are you and me,
Its roughs, beards, haughtiness, ruggedness, are you and me,
Its ample geography, the sierras, the prairies, Mississippi, Huron, Colorado, Boston, Toronto, Releigh, Nashville, Havana, are you and me
Its settlements, wars, the organic compact, peace, Washington, the Federal Constitution, are you and me,
Its young men's manners, speech, dress, friendships, are you and me,
Its crimes, lies, thefts, defections, slavery, are you and me,
Its Congress is you and me, the officers, capitols, armies, ships, are you and me,
Its endless gestations of new States are you and me,
Its inventions, science, schools, are you and me,
Its deserts, forests, clearings, log-houses, hunters, are you and me,
The perpetual arrivals of immigrants are you and me,
Natural and artificial are you and me,
Freedom, language, poems, employments, are you and me,
Failures, successes, births, deaths, are you and me,
Past, present, future, are only you and me.

I swear I dare not shirk any part of myself,
Not America, nor any part of America...

from "Poem of Many in One," 1856 Leaves of Grass

CHAPTER 10

THE NEW WORLD.

PARK BENJAMIN, EDITOR.

J. WINCHESTER, PUBLISHER.

Poetry

"No pent-up Utica contracts our powers; for the whole bounded continent is ours."

QUARTO EDITION. OFFICE 30 ANN STREET. $3 PER ANNUM.

VOLUME III......No. 21. NEW YORK, SATURDAY, NOVEMBER 20, 1841. WHOLE NUMBER 77.

> On earth are many sights of wo,
> And many sounds of agony,
> And many a sorrow-wither'd cheek,
> And many a pain-dulled eye.
>
> The wretched weep, the poor complain,
> And luckless love pines on unknown;
> And faintly from the midnight couch
> Sounds out the sick-child's moan.
>
> Each has his grief—old age fears death;
> The young man's ills are pride, desire,
> And heart-sickness; and in his breast
> The heat of passion's fire.
>
> And he who runs the race of fame,
> Oft feels within a feverish dread,
> Lest others snatch the laurel crown
> He bears upon his head.
>
> —from "Each Has His Grief," 1841

PREVIOUS PAGE: The byline of Walt's poem is "W.W."; the story features the byline Walter Whitman. Walt used various bylines: Walter Whitman, W., W.W., W. Whitman, even Paumanok. By the late 1850s, his byline was consistently Walt Whitman. "Wo," in the first line, may be a typo or a poetic urge. The New World, 20 November 1841

Coming to Poetry

As a journalist, Walt turned up the gritty side of life. What people expected a poet to do, however, was to make sense of life, and of death, to dignify them, to give them meaning.

Death poems abounded in Walt's time, as did death itself, coming with disease, accidents, childbirth, human violence, overwork, starvation, exposure, and sometimes old age. Whether pathetic or dignified, and however tawdry the circumstances, poems rewarded the good, at their demise, with a passage to heaven.

Several poems by Walt, published before *Leaves of Grass*, fit expectations; they were well-received.

> So, welcome, death; whene'er the time
> That the dread summons must be met,
> I'll yield without one pang of awe,
> Or sigh, or vain regret;
>
> But like unto a wearied child,
> That over field and wood all day
> Has ranged and struggled, and at last,
> Worn out with toil and play—
>
> Goes up at evening to his home,
> And throws him, sleepy, tired, and sore,
> Upon his bed, and rests him there,
> His pain and trouble o'er.

— *from "We Shall All Rest at Last"*

Had Walt continued writing in the style that first brought him publication, he might eventually have achieved what he longed for, a place on every American parlor table. He would also be among countless other parlor poets whose work is forgotten by all except a handful of literary scholars.

COMING TO LEAVES

In the 1840s, Walt applied himself to a systematic study of poetry, clipping and annotating essays and articles by critics. He also began keeping "notebooks," what we call journals today. Some of the notebooks were bought already bound, others Walt made with paper fastened together with a pin or ribbon. The notebooks recorded ideas, observations, mundane information as well as inspirations and scraps of original verse.

As Walt's commitment to poetry grew, his standards became exacting, even narrow. Rather than continuing to use conventional poeticisms, he did his utmost to shed them, even as his vision of what was worthy to consider broadened.

> I believe a leaf of grass is no less than the journeywork of the stars,
> And the pismire is equally perfect, and a grain of sand, and the egg of the wren,
> And the tree-toad is a chef-d'oeuvre for the highest,
> And the running blackberry would adorn the parlors of heaven,
> And the narrowest hinge in my hand puts to scorn all machinery,

And the cow crunching with depressed head surpasses any statue,
And a mouse is miracle enough to stagger sextillions of infidels,
And I could come every afternoon of my life to look at the farmer's girl boiling her
    iron tea-kettle and baking shortcake.

— *from* Leaves of Grass, *1855*

Walt refused to force a cow, or a mouse, or a farmgirl to express other than their innate nature, their own divinity. He counted himself among the "new breed of poets":

They shall not deign to defend immortality or God or the perfection of things or liberty or the exquisite beauty and reality of the soul.

Many found Walt's poetry defiantly coarse. But while it may have been designed to provoke cultural sensibilities, Walt didn't seek to disgust or shock anyone.

What I tell I tell for precisely what it is.

What had been conventional and predictable in his poetry twisted and turned, coiled inward, coiled outward—renewed itself—rose into a form free-spirited, invigorating, physical, soul-refreshing.

The body of work that would be collected as *Leaves of Grass* came into being.

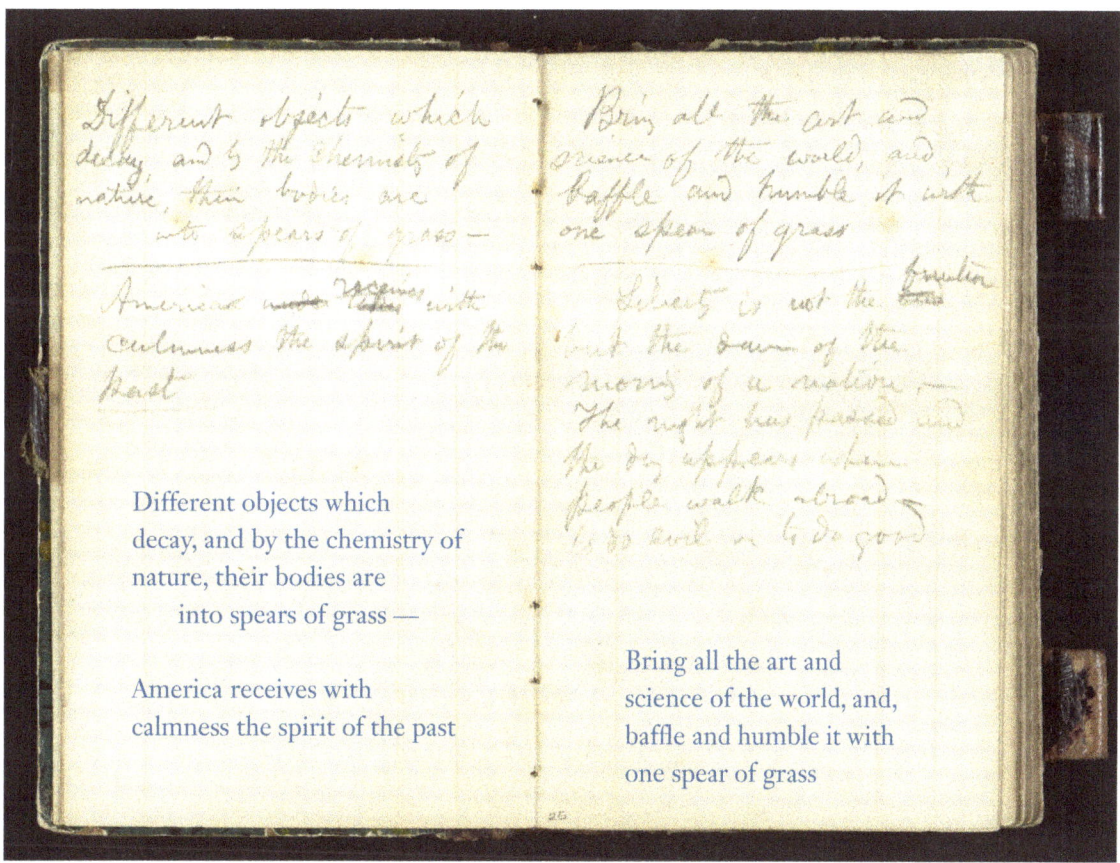

Different objects which
decay, and by the chemistry of
nature, their bodies are
    into spears of grass —

America receives with
calmness the spirit of the past

Bring all the art and
science of the world, and,
baffle and humble it with
one spear of grass

Two pages from Walt Whitman's notebook, 1847 (#80).

Liberty is not the fruition
but the dawn of the
morning of a nation —
The night has passed and
the day appears when
people walk abroad
to do evil or to do good

153

Leaves of Grass.

I CELEBRATE myself,
And what I assume you shall assume,
For every atom belonging to me as good belongs to you.

I loafe and invite my soul,
I lean and loafe at my ease .... observing a spear of summer grass.

Houses and rooms are full of perfumes .... the shelves are crowded with perfumes,
I breathe the fragrance myself, and know it and like it,
The distillation would intoxicate me also, but I shall not let it.

The atmosphere is not a perfume .... it has no taste of the distillation .... it is odorless,
It is for my mouth forever .... I am in love with it,
I will go to the bank by the wood and become undisguised and naked,
I am mad for it to be in contact with me.

The smoke of my own breath,
Echos, ripples, and buzzed whispers .... loveroot, silkthread, crotch and vine.
My respiration and inspiration .... the beating of my heart .... the passing of blood and air through my lungs,
The sniff of green leaves and dry leaves, and of the shore and darkcolored searocks, and of hay in the barn,
The sound of the belched words of my voice .... words loosed to the eddies of the wind,
A few light kisses .... a few embraces .... a reaching around of arms,
The play of shine and shade on the trees as the supple boughs wag,
The delight alone or in the rush of the streets, or along the fields and hillsides,
The feeling of health .... the full-noon trill .... the song of me rising from bed and meeting the sun.

Leaves of Grass

The year 1855 held for Walt tremendous ups and tremendous downs. Walt lived with his family in Brooklyn, working as printer, writer, bookseller, and carpenter. On July 6, the first edition of *Leaves*, self-published, was announced for sale. A week later, on July 11, Walt's father died. Later that month, he received an empowering endorsement in the form of a letter from the person whose praise probably meant the most to him, Ralph Waldo Emerson:

I am not blind to the worth of the wonderful gift of "Leaves of Grass." I find it the most extraordinary piece of wit & wisdom that America has yet contributed. I am very happy in reading it, as great power makes us happy.... I give you joy of your free and brave thought. I have great joy in it.... I greet you at the beginning of a great career...

PREVIOUS PAGE: From first edition of Leaves of Grass, 1855

Letter from Ralph Waldo Emerson, on publication of Leaves of Grass, 1855 (Letter is matted by Library of Congress)

Emerson's acclamation did not sell the book. Too soon, Walt could not avoid the harsh reality that many another writer has faced, before and since: his work was not destined to reach a wide audience. But Emerson's praise, the encouragement of friends, and, over the years, a growing following, and most important, his own faith in his work kept *Leaves* alive.

The 1855 edition—the first edition—contains twelve poems, untitled. The first, later titled "Song of Myself," is titled "Song of Walt Whitman, an American." The rest of the poems are delineated not by titles but by a double line and typography: the first letter a drop cap and the rest of the first word in caps. The 1856 edition contains twice as many poems, and they're titled, though not always with the titles familiar today. For example, the poem later called "I Sing the Body Electric" was "Song of the Body."

Over the years, Walt added new poems and revised already published poems. Beginning with the 1860 edition, he formed and reformed thematic "clusters" of poems. For example, "Drum Taps," both the title of a poem and a cluster, revolved around the Civil War. Not only the content, but the format itself mutated from edition to edition, changing in size, layout, and typography.

FOLLOWING PAGE: Front cover and spine (angled) of first edition of Leaves of Grass, 1855. The image is slightly reduced from the original size of 8 1/8 inches by 11 1/8 inches, the largest size of all the editions printed in Walt's lifetime. To compare, this book you are reading (With Walt Whitman: Himself) measures 8 1/2 by 11 inches; the 1855 Leaves would have been slightly taller and narrower.

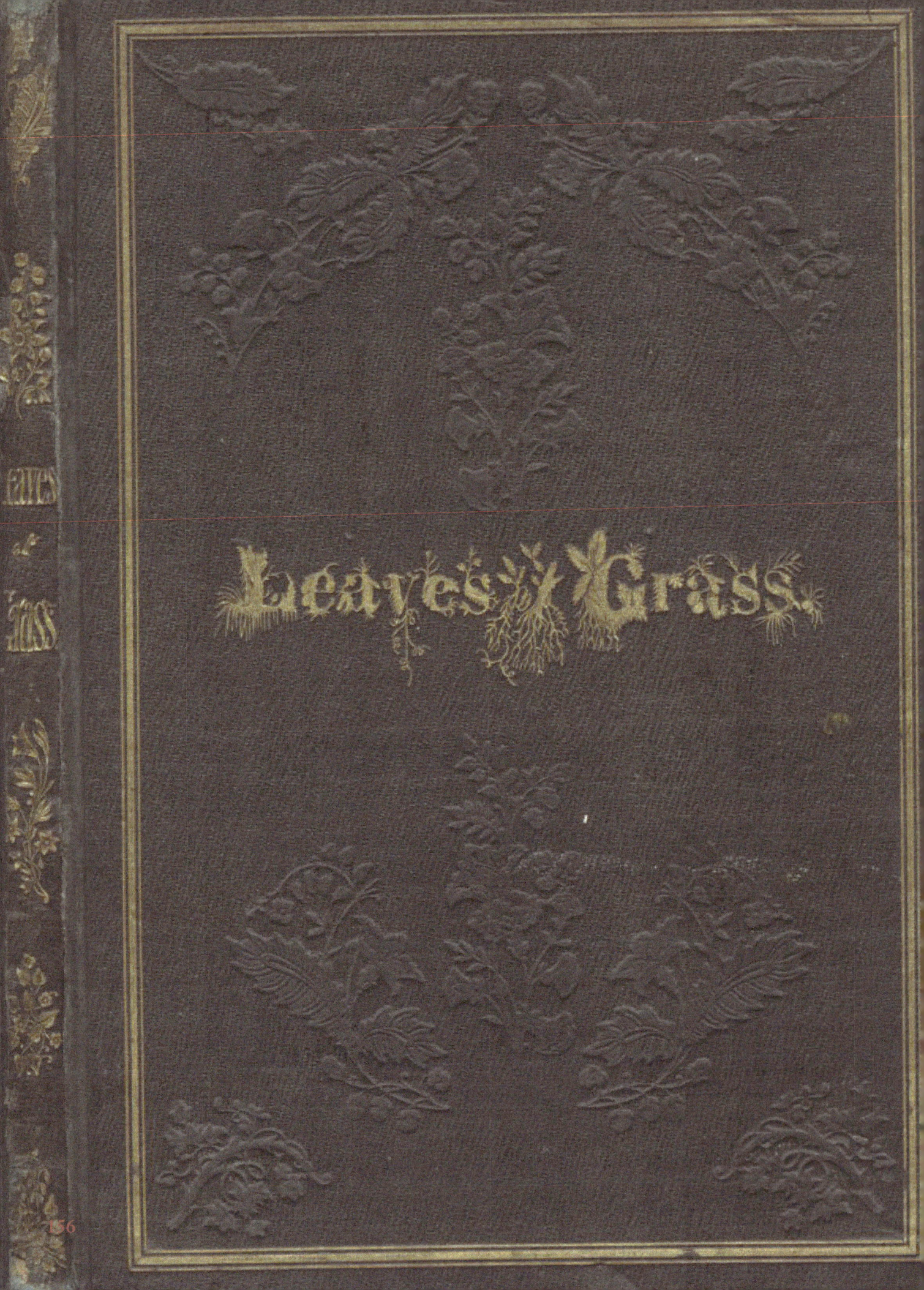

CHAPTER 11

The Civil War

… my book and the war are one,
Merged in its spirit I and mine, as the contest hinged on thee,
As a wheel on its axis turns, this book unwitting to itself,
Around the idea of thee….

— *from "To Thee, Old Cause"*

Of this photo, Walt said: "The picture [of me] is by some criticised very severely indeed but I hope you will not dislike it, for I confess to myself a perhaps capricious fondness for it, as my own portrait, over some scores that have been made or taken at one time or another."
It's hard to fathom what there is to criticize in this beautiful portrait. The shapeless hat? The shadow falling over the eyes? Maybe some found it revealed too nakedly the sadness, the weariness, the pain, that Walt experienced in nursing thousands of men during the Civil War.

Photograph attributed to William Kurtz or Mathew Brady.

PREVIOUS PAGE: Catalpa tree, "within ten yards" of the Chatham house, near Fredericksburg, Virginia. When Walt arrived there in December 1862, the mansion had been requisitioned for use as a hospital. This same tree, alive at the time, witnessed with Walt "the marrow of the tragedy concentrated in those Hospitals." Its roots bathed in the anguish the poet beheld, no wonder its form holds such tortured beauty.

The American Civil War—the War of the Rebellion, as it came to be called in U.S. government documents, or the Four Year War, as Walt eventually called it—stretched from April 1861 to April 1865. Its cause is much debated, but whatever may be said about states' rights, the instigating issue was slavery.

The slave-holding states (including Delaware) resented even a hint of restrictions on slavery. Southern states feared especially that as free states entered the Union, anti-slavery interests would gain majority power in the government and abolish slavery.

Abraham Lincoln stated he would not interfere with slavery as it existed in the United States, but he and his political party, the newly formed Republicans, were associated with abolition and opposed slavery's expansion. On his election as president, southern states began to secede from the United States, forming the Confederate States.

In April 1861, Confederates fired upon a Federal installation—Fort Sumter in South Carolina—and the War began. The War effectively ended with the surrender of Confederate General Robert E. Lee and the Union occupation of the Confederate capital, Richmond, Virginia, in April 1865.

Less than two weeks after the surrender, the assassination of President Lincoln plunged the triumphant Union into mourning.

In December 1865, the Thirteenth Amendment to the Constitution of the United States was ratified.

The dead in this war—there they lie, strewing the fields and woods and valleys and battle-fields of the south—Virginia, the Peninsula—Malvern hill and Fair Oaks—the banks of the Chickahominy—the terraces of Fredericksburgh—Antietam bridge—the grisly ravines of Manassas—the bloody promenade of the Wilderness—the varieties of the strayed dead…. the infinite dead—(the land entire saturated, perfumed with their impalpable ashes' exhalation in Nature's chemistry distill'd, and shall be so forever, in every future grain of wheat and ear of corn, and every flower that grows, and every breath we draw)—not only Northern dead leavening Southern soil—thousands, aye tens of thousands, of Southerners, crumble to-day in Northern earth.

—*from "The Million Dead"*

Malvern Hill Battlefield National Park, Virginia. 2012, 150 years after the battle

Section 1. Neither slavery nor involuntary servitude, except as a punishment for crime whereof the party shall have been duly convicted, shall exist within the United States, or any place subject to their jurisdiction.

Section 2. Congress shall have power to enforce this article by appropriate legislation.

In June 1870, all the former Confederate states had been readmitted to the Union.
During the War's four-year span, about 620,000 men and boys lost their lives to disease or in combat while serving the Union or the Confederacy. 400,000 more were wounded, many disabled for life. Sad to say, compared to later wars the toll was low. But it affected every aspect of life for every resident in the United States and its effects reached out in time and space, to other nations and even to this day.

The stone wall at Fredericksburg, 1863. From behind it, the Confederates poured devastating fire into Union troops. Before the Civil War—before photography—people outside the war zone never witnessed war with such graphic intensity. The next jolt would come to Americans with the Vietnam War, the first televised.

Walt as Nurse

"A large brick mansion...." At Chatham Manor, Falmouth, Virginia, Walt began his vocation as a nurse. Photo by Alexander Gardner, December 1862

Began my visits in the Camp Hospitals in the Army of the Potomac. Spent a good part of the day in a large brick mansion, on the banks of the Rappahannock, used as a Hospital since the battle—Seems to have receiv'd only the worst cases. Out doors, at the foot of a tree, within ten yards of the front of the house, I notice a heap of amputated feet, legs, arms, hands, &c., a full load for a one-horse cart. Several dead bodies lie near, each cover'd with its brown woolen blanket....

For nearly two years, Walt followed the War from New York. Then in December 1862, he journeyed to "a large brick mansion" near Fredericksburg, Virginia.

Walt traveled south to seek his brother George, reported as wounded at the Battle of Fredericksburg. Fortunately, the wound was minor. After spending a week with him, Walt entered "into the War," as he later said, by accompanying a group of wounded soldiers up to Washington, D.C. He would not return North, except for visits, for ten more years.

Walt became a devoted companion and nurse to soldiers wounded and ill. Although he raged against the Confederacy, his compassion transcended divisions of North and South, and he tended men and boys from both sides of the conflict.

Walt read to the soldiers, brought them necessities and treats, and most of all stayed with them through wasting and death or recovery. This physical and emotional contact with wounded men he called "perhaps the greatest interchange of magnetism human relations are capable of."

The heap of human carnage that Walt saw bore gruesome witness to rough field medicine. With no antibiotics to fight gangrene, a severely damaged limb was quickly removed. Ignorance of sanitation meant dirty instruments performed the amputations. Shortages of supplies and personnel didn't help. A surprising number of men died of drowning; many more died of disease in camp.

Technology also took a huge toll. Ease of loading and accuracy made the Minié ball (called minnie by Americans) the rifle ammunition of choice during the War. Unlike its predecessor, the solid, round musket ball, the Minié was bullet-shaped and made of relatively soft lead. Its advantages proved devastating. As one writer says, "Unlike a solid ball, which could pass through the human body nearly intact, leaving an exit wound not much larger than the entrance wound, the soft, hollow-based Minié ball flattened and deformed upon impact, while creating a shock wave that emanated outward. The Minié ball didn't just break bones, it shattered them. It didn't just pierce tissue and internal organs, it shredded them." Walt saw first hand the grief wrought by the Minié.

Minié ball exploded and intact (LEFT AND MIDDLE) and a musket ball

I devote myself much to Armory Square Hospital because it contains by far the worst cases, the most repulsive wounds, has the most suffering & most need of consolation....

Dr. Willard Bliss, chief surgeon at Armory Square, said of Walt, "From my personal knowledge of Mr. Whitman's labors in Armory Square and other hospitals, I am of [the] opinion that no one person who assisted in the hospitals during the war accomplished so much good to the soldier and for the Government as Mr. Whitman."

I go every day without fail & often at night—sometimes stay very late—no one interferes with me, guards, doctors, nurses, nor any one—I am let to take my own course.

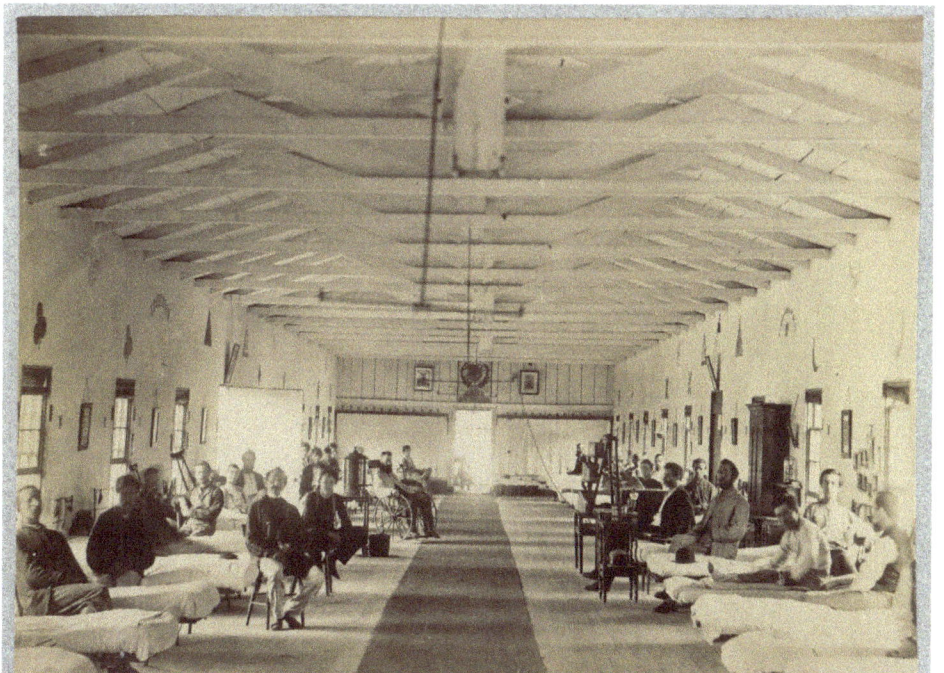

Armory Square Hospital, 1865

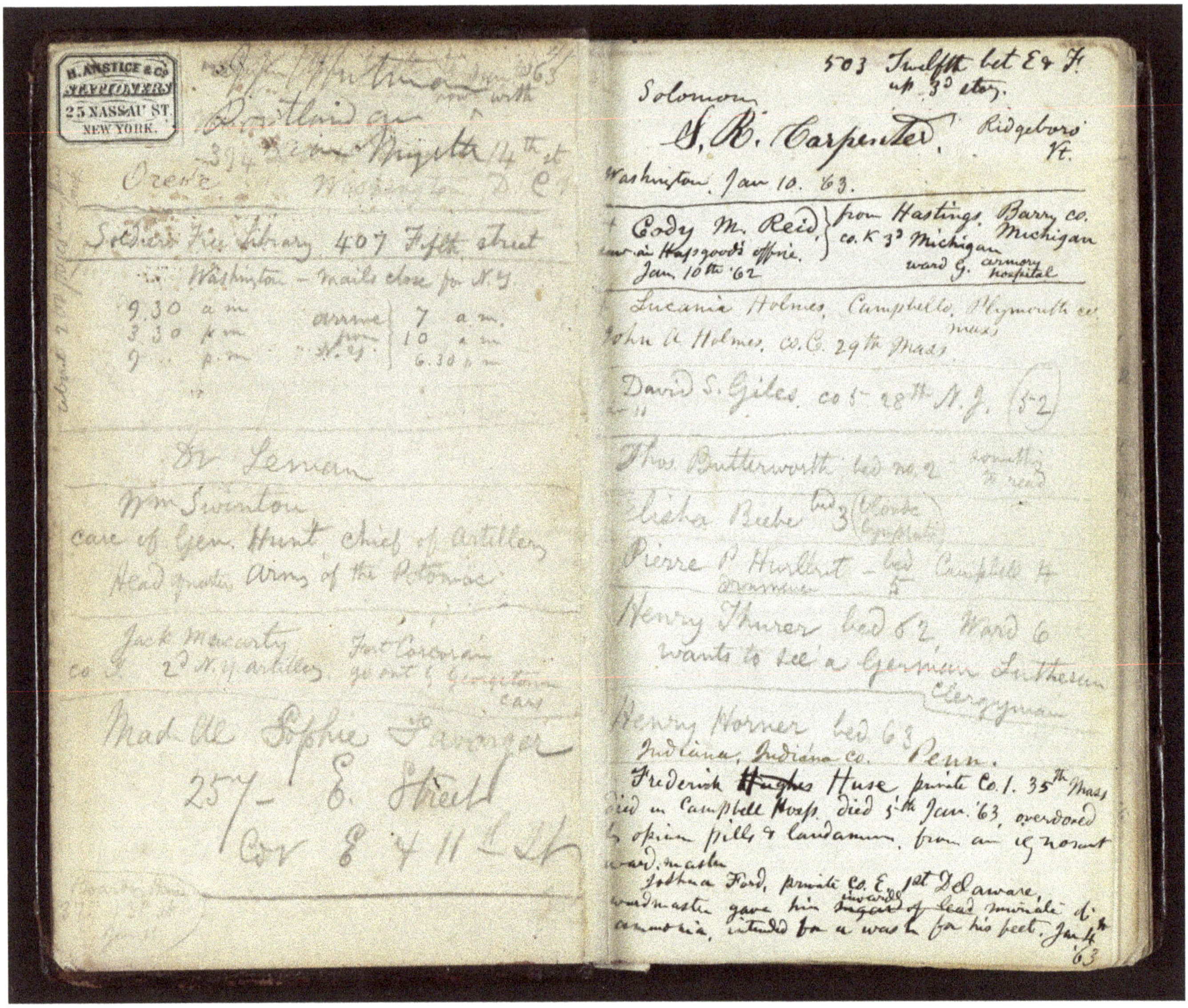

A page from Walt's notebook lists men, their location in the wards, and their requests—"something to read" and "wants to see a German Lutheran clergyman"—as well as wrongful deaths: "overdosed by opium pills and laudanum, from an ignorant ward master" and a soldier who received "inwardly" (internally) an ammonia solution "intended for a wash for his feet."

Walt's haversack, which he carried into the wards, full of treats, necessities, and comfort.

Walt wrote in letters and in memoir of kissing the soldiers, of holding their hands and embracing them. Touch and presence: "While cash is not amiss to bring up the rear," he wrote his mother, "tact and magnetic sympathy are, and ever will be, sovereign still." But Walt's vocation could be overwhelming.

Again spending a good part of the day at Harewood [hospital]. I write this about an hour before sundown. I have walk'd out for a few minutes to the edge of the woods to soothe myself with the hour and scene. It is glorious, warm, golden-sunny, still afternoon. The only noise is from a crowd of cawing crows, on some trees three hundred yards distant. Clusters of gnats swimming and dancing in the air in all directions. The oak leaves are thick under the bare trees, and give a strong and delicious perfume. Inside the wards everything is gloomy. Death is there. As I enter'd, I was confronted by it the first thing; a corpse of a poor soldier, just dead, of typhoid fever. The attendants had just straighten'd the limbs, put coppers on the eyes, and were laying it out.

Abraham Lincoln's second Inaugural Ball of 1865 took place in the Patent Building. The stunningly beautiful edifice had served as a temporary hospital.

I have this moment been up to look at the gorgeously arrayed ball and supper-rooms, for the Inauguration Dance…and I could not help thinking of the scene those rooms, where the music will sound and the dancers' feet presently tread—what a different scene they presented to my view a while since, filled with a crowded mass of the worst wounded of the war…. To-night, beautiful women, perfumes, the violins' sweetness, the polka and the waltz; but then, the amputation, the blue face, the groan, the glassy eye of the dying, the clotted rag, the odor of the old wounds and blood, and many a mother's son amid strangers, passing away untended there….

"Sleeping bunks of the First Rhode Island Regiment, at the Patent Office, Washington." Harper's Weekly, June 1, 1861

Despite the horrors witnessed, and Walt's later illnesses which were brought on, his physician believed, by the strain of his war work and exposure to pestilence:

I never once have questioned the decision that led me into the War: whatever the years have brought—whatever sickness, whatnot—I have accepted the result as inevitable and right. This is the very centre, circumference, umbillicus, of my whole career.

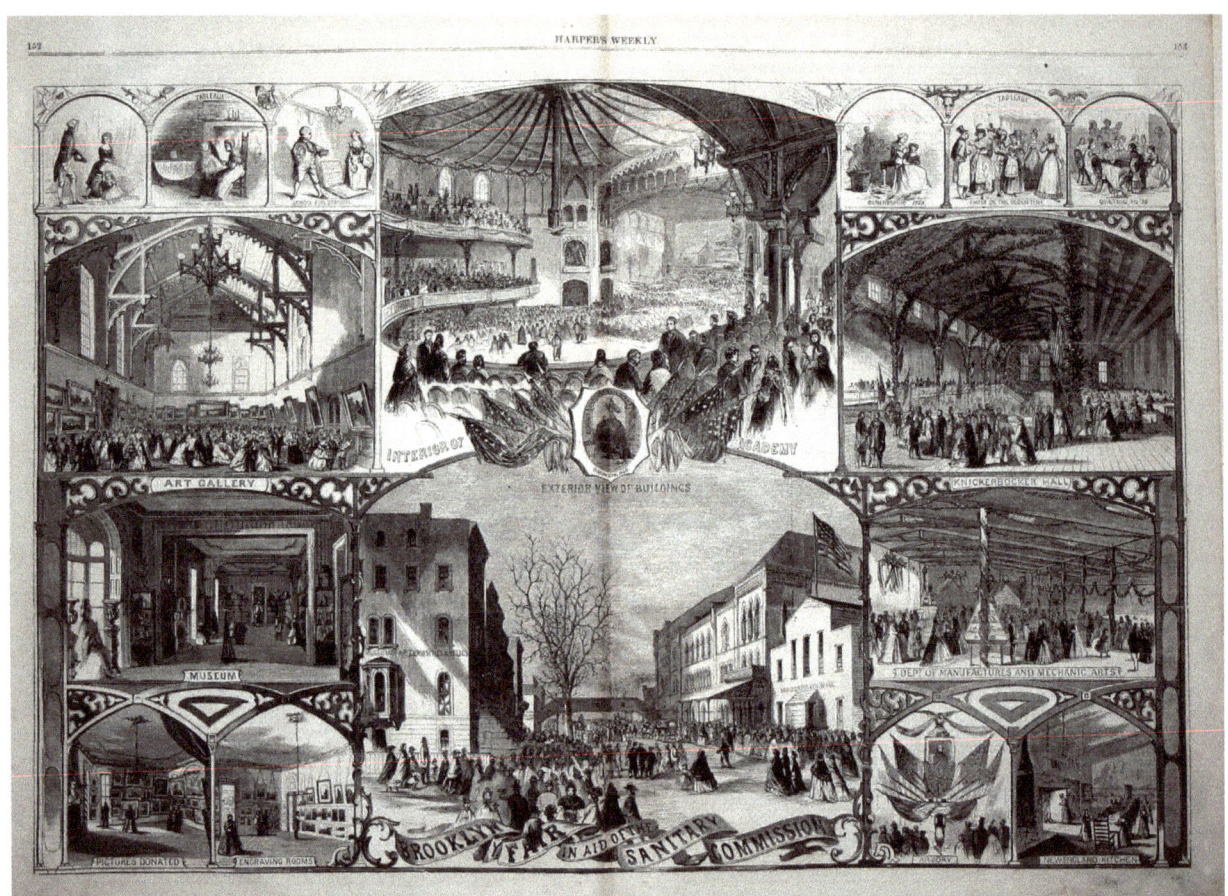

Brooklyn hosted a Fair to raise money for the U.S. Sanitary Commission, a patriotic Union charity similar to the Red Cross. Harper's Weekly. March 5, 1864

The War at Home

The Civil War, which nearly dismembered Walt's beloved America, saw the dissolution of his family. George, a Union army officer, was absent nearly throughout, on duty and as a prisoner in Georgia. His sister Hannah lived in Vermont, trapped in marriage to a man psychotically abusive. Mary lived with her family out on Long Island. Except for visits, Walt spent the War in Washington, D.C.

Jeff and his wife and daughter lived crowded with mother Louisa, oldest brother Jesse, and youngest brother Eddy. Andrew lived nearby. Jeff fumed in letters to Walt about Jesse's increasing violence, Andrew's slatternly wife, the profoundly disabled Eddy, and Louisa's excessive thriftiness. Even as Walt faced scores of men maimed and dying, he received letters from his mother with passages such as: "i have hattey [Jeff's daughter] of coarse and she is very obstropolous and her uncle Andrew says if she was his hed break her neck so you see walt what we go through every day sundays and all."

Domestic strife frays the bravest of souls; people have been known to go to war to escape it.

In 1863, Andrew died of tuberculosis. The stress pushed Jesse over the edge, and he threatened violence to little Hattie and Jeff's wife Mattie. "So help me God I would have shot him dead on the spot," Jeff declared in a letter to Walt. He begged Walt to come home and take the situation in hand. Walt came up to Brooklyn in 1864 to commit Jesse to King's County Lunatic Asylum.

George served in the Army for the duration of the War. Jeff collected and sent money for Walt to spend on the hospitalized soldiers, along with praise and encouragement for his efforts.

Writing the War

Leaves of Grass had been published in three editions—1855, 1856, and 1860—before the Civil War broke out. That would seem to give lie to Walt's claim "my book and the war are one." A friend later attributed the statement to confusion. But Walt was not at all confused about when *Leaves* was first published, nor when the War started.

Neither the War nor Walt's book are fixed dots on a line of time. The causes and conditions leading to the War, and the outcome of the War, surround *Leaves*. Its poems are "unwitting" witnesses whose accounts revolve around the War, the book's "axis," the "Old Cause," as Walt said in his poem "To Thee Old Cause."

The 'good old cause' is that which, in all its diversities, in all lands, at all times, under all circumstances, promulgates liberty, justice, the cause of the people against infidels and tyrants.

Walt's poetic purpose before, during, and after the War aligned with the "old cause," and the spirit and words of his verse entwined with his nation's very fibers.

POETRY, LETTERS & MEMORANDA

Walt's War writings include two slim poetry collections, *Drum Taps* (1865) and *Sequel to Drum Taps* (1865–66), and a collection of essays and articles, *Memoranda during the War*. His War-time letters, especially those to his mother, expose the personal doubts he reveals and conceals in *Memoranda*:

Future years will never know the seething hell and the black infernal background of countless minor scenes and interiors…and it is best they should not."

— *Memoranda during the War*

I sometimes think over the sights I have myself seen, the arrival of the wounded after a battle, & the scenes on the field too, & I can hardly believe my own recollection— what an awful thing war is—Mother, it seems not men but a lot of devils & butchers butchering each other.

— *Walt to his mother, March 1864*

The confessions Walt heard from soldiers, of "the cruelties on his surrender'd brother and mutilations of the corpse afterward," did not disillusion Walt. He was a rare one: an idealist who cherished no illusions. He tenderly nursed wounded men of both sides and extolled the common soldier's "incredible dauntlessness, habits, practices, tastes, language, his appetite, rankness, his superb strength and animality, lawless gait, and a hundred unnamed lights and shades of camp."

LEAVES OF GRASS

The 1867 edition of *Leaves of Grass* is a fascinating book. Walt's *Drum Taps* collections he bound into a revised *Leaves of Grass*. The pages of each part have their own page numbers and were evidently typeset independent of each other, *Drum Taps* in New York, *Sequel* in Washington, with another sequence, *Songs Before Parting*, added at the end.

1867 Leaves of Grass, open to Drum Taps

As scholar Luke Mancuso put it:

> The images of a coherent Union proliferate throughout all parts of the 1867 edition, but the physical "dismemberment" of the book mirrors not only the fracturing of the North from the South, but also bears the same stress marks as the contentious rhetoric across America concerned with reinstating rebel states and racial differences between whites and newly-emancipated slaves.

Sequel to Drum Taps includes elegies to Abraham Lincoln, "O Captain! my Captain!" and one of Walt's most well-known works, "When Lilacs Last in the Dooryard Bloomed."

> 1
> WHEN lilacs last in the door-yard bloom'd,
> And the great star early droop'd in the western sky in the night,
> I mourn'd…and yet shall mourn with ever-returning spring.
>
> O ever-returning spring! trinity sure to me you bring;
> Lilac blooming perennial, and drooping star in the west,
> And thought of him I love.
>
> 2
> O powerful, western, fallen star!
> O shades of night! O moody, tearful night!
> O great star disappear'd! O the blank murk that hides the star!
> O cruel hands that hold me powerless! O helpless soul of me!
> O harsh surrounding cloud that will not free my soul! …

CHAPTER 12

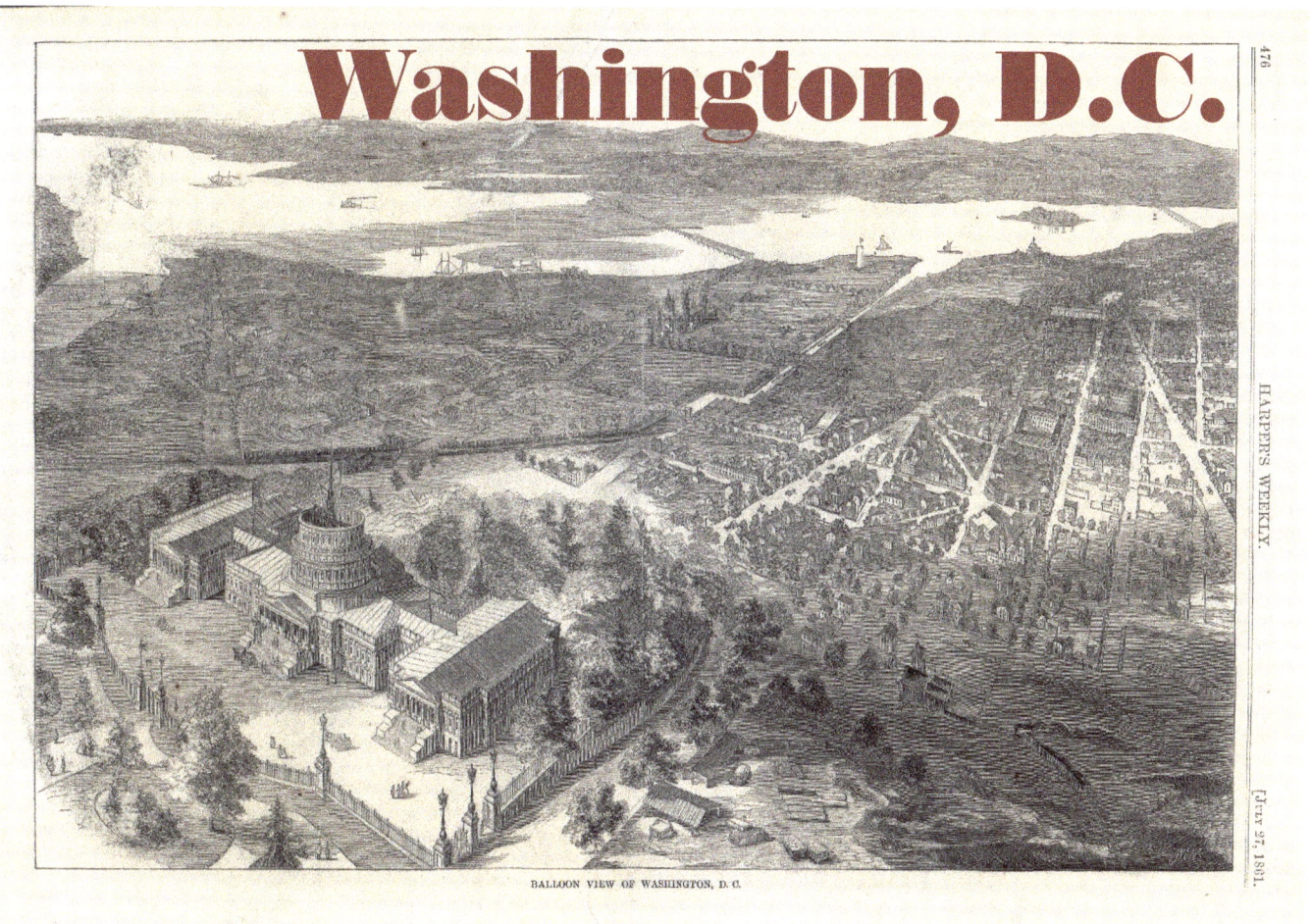

… the city of the armies of the good old cause, full of significant signs, surrounded with weapons and armaments on every hill as I look forth, and THE FLAG flying over all. The city that launches the direct laws, the imperial laws of American Union and Democracy…. The city of wounded and sick, city of hospitals, full of the sweetest, bravest children of time or lands; tens of thousands, wounded, bloody, amputated, burning with fever, blue with diarrhœa. The city of the wide Potomac, the queenly river, lined with softest, greenest hills and uplands.

Balloon View of Washington, D.C., from Harper's Weekly, July 27, 1861

A City of "Things Begun"

Washington, D.C. was more to Walt than a "city of hospitals." He loved its Southern culture and Union patriotism, its lay along the Potomac River, the neoclassical government buildings, its wide (though unpaved) streets and its open areas that mixed urban and rural toil and pleasure. For all the death he witnessed there, Walt counted Washington as a city of "romance," of "things begun."

Until the last few years of his decade in D.C., Walt felt himself to be in his prime. Helping the soldiers was deeply gratifying, and new friends rallied to champion his work. After the War, a passionate romantic friendship swept him up. A sense of physical well-being filled him to the brim.

> I often watch the city and environs from the roof of an elevated building near the Treasury. Perhaps it is sunset. Sweep the eye around now on the scene. The dazzle of red and gold from over Virginia heights there, west, is thrown across full upon us. Turning, we see the dome of the Capitol lifting itself so calmly, southeast, there, with windows yellow-red. Not far below the sombre-brown Smithsonian stands in the midst of shadows. Due east of us the severe and noble architecture of the Patent Office takes the last rich flood of the sun. The mist grows murky over in distance on the Maryland side. Northward the white barracks of the hospitals and on a hill the Soldiers' Home; southward the queenly Potomac, and the trailing smoke of a single steamer moving up this side the Long Bridge. Further down, the dim masts of Alexandria. Quite near again, the half-monument of the first President. Off far again, just visible, southeast, the low turrets of the United States Insane Asylum, on the Maryland side. But the day is fading fast.

President Lincoln did not stop construction on the Capitol's new dome during the War. In contrast to the majestic edifice, a canal polluted with everything from sewage to garbage to dead cattle ran along today's Constitution Avenue. 1860

Washington is a pleasant place in some respects—it has the finest trees, and plenty of them everywhere, in the streets and grounds. The Capitol grounds, though small, have the finest cultivated trees I ever see—there is a great variety, and not one but is in perfect condition—After I finish this letter I am going out there for an hour's recreation—The great sights of Washington are the public buildings, the wide streets, the public grounds, the trees, the Smithsonian Institute & grounds—I go to the latter occasionally—the institute is an old fogy concern, but the grounds are fine.

The Smithsonian "Castle," looking up the Mall toward the Capitol. The building was completed in 1855. Where museums stand today are houses. Photo by Mathew Brady, circa 1860

BELOW: Pennsylvania Avenue, 1860. Painting by A. Mayer

ABOVE: 15th and F Streets NW in Washington, D.C., 1865. The neoclassical building (barely visible) at the end of the street is the Treasury building, where Walt worked from January 1872 to January 1873. The block in this picture was right around the corner from where Walt lived on 15th Street, across from the Treasury. Maybe the tall building at the end of the street is where Walt climbed to view the panorama of his adopted city. All these buildings except the Treasury are gone.

Cattle on the grounds of the unfinished Washington Monument. Frank Leslie's Illustrated News, 1862

The grounds of the unfinished Washington Monument became a cattle depot. In 1862, *Frank Leslie's Illustrated News* deplored a Monument "surrounded by offal rotting two or three feet deep." But Walt had fun watching the cowboys at their work.

Among other sights are immense droves of cattle with their drivers, passing through the streets of the city. Some of the men have a way of leading the cattle by a peculiar call, a wild, pensive hoot, quite musical, prolong'd, indescribable, sounding something between the cooing of a pigeon and the hoot of an owl. I like to stand and look at the sight of one of these immense droves—a little way off—(as the dust is great.) There are always men on horseback, cracking their whips and shouting—the cattle low—some obstinate ox or steer attempts to escape—then a lively scene—the mounted men, always excellent riders and on good horses, dash after the recusant, and wheel and turn—a dozen mounted drovers, their great slouch'd, broad-brim'd hats, very picturesque—another dozen on foot—everybody cover'd with dust—long goads in their hands—an immense drove of perhaps 1000 cattle—the shouting, hooting, movement, &c.

A team of oxen hauls a cannon at Pennsylvania Avenue and 15th Street, N.W., past the tall Corcoran building, where Walt worked for the Army Paymaster. After the War, Walt lodged in the three-story brick building next to the Corcoran. Photo circa 1861–65

In the street below me a long string of army wagons defiling along Fifteenth-street, and around into Pennsylvania-avenue. White canvas coverings arch them over, and each wagon has its six-mule team. The teamsters are some of them walking along the sides of the mules, with goads in their hands. Then I notice in the half-light squads of the Provost Guard. Then a galloping cavalry company, in their yellow-braided jackets.

LODGINGS

Walt lived simply. In D.C., much of his spare money went toward his family and his soldier friends. Personal treats were fresh fruit and streetcar rides, and meals and fellowship in the homes of friends. A friend who visited Walt in his lodgings gives a picture of how he lived.

Diagonally opposite to Chase's great house, on the corner of E and 6th streets, stood one of those old wooden buildings which then and for some years afterwards lingered among the new and handsome blocks rising around them, and made the "city of magnificent distances" also a city of astonishing architectural contrasts. In the fine, large mansion, sumptuously furnished, cared for by sleek and silent colored servants, and thronged by distinguished guests, dwelt the great statesman; in the old tenement opposite, in a bare and desolate back room, up three flights of stairs, quite alone, lived the poet. Walt led the way up those dreary stairs, partly in darkness, found the keyhole of a door which he unlocked and opened, scratched a match, and welcomed us to his garret.

The Old Patent Office in the background occupies the block bounded by F, G, 7th and 9th streets. Walt's garret was a block away, at E and 6th. The buildings in the foreground are the kind that would have lodged him. The photographer who took this picture, John Plumbe, often saw Walt at his New York City gallery in the 1840s. 1846 photograph

Garret it literally was, containing hardly any more furniture than a bed, a cheap pine table, and a little sheet-iron stove in which there was no fire. A window was open, and it was a December night. But Walt, clearing a chair or two of their litter of newspapers, invited us to sit down and stop awhile, with as simple and sweet hospitality as if he had been offering us the luxuries of the great mansion across the square....

Another friend wrote:

I found him partly dressed, and preparing his own breakfast. There was a fire in the sheet-iron stove,—the open door showed a few coals,—and he was cutting slices of bread from a baker's loaf with his jackknife, getting them ready for toasting. The smallest of tin teakettles simmering on the stove, a bowl and spoon, and a covered tin cup used as a teapot comprised, with the aforesaid useful jackknife, his entire outfit of visible housekeeping utensils. His sugar bowl was a brown paper bag. His butter plate was another piece of brown paper, the same coarse wrapping in which he had brought home his modest lump from the corner grocery. His cupboard was an oblong pine box, set up a few feet from the floor, opening outward, with the bottom against the wall; the two sides one above the other, made very good shelves.

I toasted his bread for him on the end of a sharpened stick; he buttered the slices with his jackknife, and poured his tea at a corner of the table cleared for that purpose of its litter of books and newspapers; and while he breakfasted we talked.

This contemporary sheet-iron stove is very much like the kind Walt would have used in the 1860s. Cheaper, lighter, and more portable than cast iron stoves, sheet metal stoves were often used by troops in the field.

Disciples

During Walt's years in D.C., his poetic legacy began gathering pace, though an incident in his work life threatened to be a significant setback.

Shortly after the War ended, Walt worked as a clerk at the Department of the Interior. When Secretary of the Interior James Harlan found a copy of *Leaves* in Walt's desk, he deemed it obscene and sacked Walt. Through friends, Walt got another job in the Attorney General's office.

The next year, 1866, Walt and his friend William Douglas O'Connor co-wrote *The Good Gray Poet: A Vindication*, part attack on Walt's enemies, part gushing tribute, with over-the-top verbage that recalls Walt's journalism.

> When, therefore, any persons undertake to outrage and injure [Leaves'] author for having given it to the world, it is not merely as the pigmy incarnations of the depraved modesty, the surface morality, the filthy and libidinous decency of the age...

> The whole form [of Walt was] surrounded with manliness as with a nimbus, and breathing, in its perfect health and vigor, the august charm of the strong.

The title "good gray poet" stayed with Walt for the rest of his life.

1867 saw publication of *Notes on Walt Whitman as Poet and Person*, by naturalist John Burroughs. The following year English scholar and essayist William Michael Rossetti published an expurgated edition of *Leaves*, which brought Walt an English following, including Anne Gilchrist, whose important essay "A Woman's Estimate of Walt Whitman" was published anonymously in Boston in 1870.

Although Walt had a bitter falling out with O'Connor, the two eventually reconciled, and in late life Walt dubbed O'Connor his "knight errant," a pillar of the group that came to be known as Walt's "disciples."

Walt's "knight errant," William Douglas O'Connor, circa 1885

The Good Gray Poet, a copy Walt gave his friend Horace Traubel in 1888

"Washington, D.C., 1865. Walt Whitman & his rebel soldier friend Pete Doyle." Of Walt's expression, a friend said, "'Fondness, and Doyle should be a girl." Photo by M.P. Rice.

LEFT: The lock of hair is Pete Doyle's, given to Walt and kept by Walt the rest of his life.

Pete Doyle

Walt's relationship with Pete Doyle was to be the most intense and enduring romantic friendship of his life. For Pete, it was the same. Pete describes their meeting:

You ask where I first met him? It is a curious story. We felt to each other at once. I was a [streetcar] conductor. The night was very stormy.... Walt had his blanket—it was thrown round his shoulders—he seemed like an old sea-captain. He was the only passenger, it was a lonely night, so I thought I would go in and talk with him. Something in me made me do it and something in him drew me that way. He used to say there was something in me had the same effect on him. Anyway, I went into the car. We were familiar at once—I put my hand on his knee—we understood. He did not get out at the end of the trip—in fact went all the way back with me..... From that time on we were the biggest sort of friends.

    The two men could hardly have been more different. Pete was twenty-one, Walt forty-five. Pete had been a Confederate artillery man; Walt was a staunch Unionist.

Though the photo dates from circa 1880, the horse-drawn streetcar is the same kind that Pete would have worked, standing on the back platform between stops.

Pete was southern, Walt northern. Pete was a working man, a streetcar conductor, Walt a man of letters.

The difference that most bemused Walt's friends—though they all liked Pete—lay in education. A physician who occasionally rode the streetcar with Walt and Pete described the relationship as "the most taciturn mutual admiration society I ever attended; perhaps because the young Apollo was generally as uninformed as he was handsome, and Whitman's intellectual altitude was too far beyond his understanding to be reached by his apprehension or expressed by his vocabulary."

An enduring love, such as the two men had for each other, can't live on admiration alone. Yet the physician's words have a ring of truth.

Pete was Walt's type: young, handsome, masculine, and devoid of intellectual or social pretensions. Walt presented the physician's insight in another light:

A rare man, knowing nothing of books, knowing everything of life: a great big hearty full-blooded everyday divinely generous working man: a hail fellow well met…for the most part the salt of the earth. Most literary men, as you know, are the kind of men a hearty man would not go far to see: but Pete fascinates you by the very earthiness of his nobility.

Walt's love enfolded Pete into his most treasured endeavor, *Leaves of Grass:*

We would walk together for miles and miles, never sated. Oh! the long, long walks, way into the nights!—in the after hours—sometimes lasting till two or three in the

Bridge across the Eastern Branch to Anacostia, Washington, D.C., 1862. Several years later, Walt and Pete might have strolled the bridge on a moonlit night.

morning! The air, the stars, the moon, the water—what a fullness of inspiration they imparted!—what exhilaration!… It was a great, a precious, a memorable, experience. To get the ensemble of Leaves of Grass you have got to include such things as these—the walks, Pete's friendship: yes, such things: they are absolutely necessary to the completion of the story.

Pete's recollections of his times with Walt dwell on simple pleasures made golden by heart-deep camaraderie.

In the afternoon I would go up to the Treasury building [where Walt worked] and wait for him to get through if he was busy, then we'd stroll out together, often without any plan, going where we happened to get….We took great walks together—off towards or to Alexandria, often. We went plodding along the road, Walt always whistling or singing. We would talk of ordinary matters. He would recite poetry, especially Shakespeare—he would hum airs or shout in the woods. He was always active, happy, cheerful, good-natured…. We would tackle the farmers who came into town, buy a water-melon, sit down on the cellar door of Bacon's grocery, Seventh and Pennsylvania Avenue, halve it and eat it. People would go by and laugh. Walt would only smile and say, 'They can have the laugh—we have the melon.'

The tempests of love, too, joined the story. In July of 1870, a few days before leaving to visit Brooklyn, Walt vehemently wrote out his determination to break up with "164"—his code for Pete's name.

Walt must have made his intentions known, by letter to Pete. Pete must have responded with everything his friend needed. Less than a month later, Walt wrote back, "I never dreamed that you made so much of having me with you, nor that you could feel so downcast at losing me. I foolishly thought it was all on the other side."

After Walt moved to Camden, the friendship waned, then revived when Pete got a railroad job in nearby Philadelphia. After Walt's death, Walt's friends invited Pete to meetings of the Walt Whitman Fellowship, where Pete spoke on at least one occasion.

Long after Walt's death, Pete cherished their relationship and looked to Walt as a source of wisdom, as he says in this poignant account:

I have Walt's raglan here…. I now and then put it on, lay down, think I am in the old times. Then he is with me again. It's the only thing I kept amongst many old things. When I get it on and stretch out on the old sofa I am very well contented. It is like Aladdin's lamp. I do not ever for a minute lose the old man. He is always near by. When I am in trouble—in a crisis—I ask myself, "What would Walt have done under these circumstances?" and whatever I decide Walt would have done that I do.

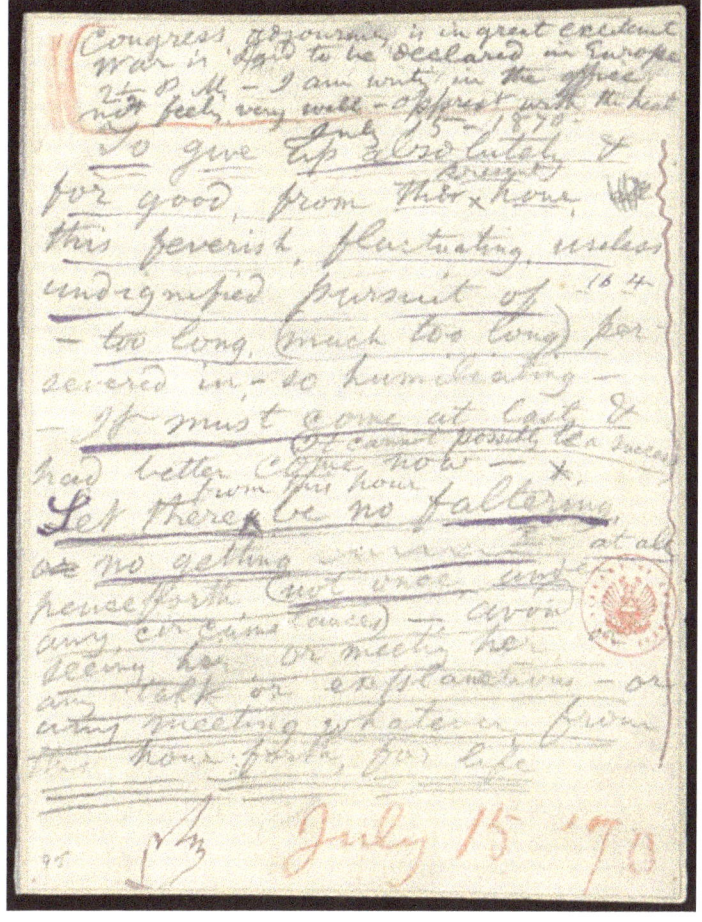

"164" was Walt's code for Pete.
"To give up absolutely & for good, from the present hour, this feverish, fluctuating, useless undignified pursuit of 164 — too long, (much too long) persevered in,—so humiliating — It must come at last & had better come now — (It cannot possibly be a success) Let there from this hour be no faltering no getting [erased] at all henceforth, (not once, under any circumstances)—avoid seeing her, or meeting her, or any talk or explanations—or any meeting whatever, from this hour forth, for life."
Walt did not keep his impetuous vow.
— Walt's notebook, July 15, 1870

After the War

This circa 1870 photograph of Walt reflects the strain inflicted by the War. Only thirteen years after writing "I, now thirty-seven years old in perfect health," Walt looks much older than his fifty-one years, as more than one person remarked on seeing him. Hands clenched, eyes hooded, the portrait conveys both tension and uncertainty.

Walt lived eight years, after the War, in D.C., with a few long sojourns in Brooklyn. He worked, he continued to visit the soldiers still hospitalized from injury or disease, he spent time with friends. He also issued two new editions of *Leaves*, the 1867 and the 1871–72. Like the 1867, the 1871–72 *Leaves* was arranged and rearranged in its several printings. The 1872 issue includes a collection, "As a Strong Bird on Pinions Free," comprised of poems and a prose preface.

In the preface dated May 31, 1872, his fifty-third birthday, Walt both acknowledged the War and put it behind, to inspire the new generation of Americans, too young to have taken part in the War:

The Four Years' War is over—and in the peaceful, strong, exciting, fresh occasions of to-day, and of the future, that strange, sad war is hurrying even now to be forgotten. The camp, the drill, the lines of sentries, the prisons, the hospitals,—(ah! the hospitals!)—all have passed away—all seem now like a dream. A new race, a young and lusty generation, already sweeps in with oceanic currents, obliterating the war, and all its scars, its mounded graves, and all its reminiscences of hatred, conflict, death. So let it be obliterated. I say the life of the present and the future makes undeniable demands upon us each and all, south, north, east, west. To help put the United States (even if only in imagination) hand in hand, in one unbroken circle in a chant—to rouse them to the unprecedented grandeur of the part they are to play, and are even now playing—to the thought of their great future, and the attitude conform'd to it—especially their great esthetic, moral, scientific future, (of which their vulgar material and political present is but as the preparatory tuning of instruments by an orchestra,) these, as hitherto, are still, for me, among my hopes, ambitions.

"Leaves of Grass," already publish'd, is, in its intentions, the song of a great composite democratic individual, male or female. And following on and amplifying the same purpose, I suppose I have in my mind to run through the chants of this volume, (if ever completed,) the thread-voice, more or less audible, of an aggregated, inseparable, unprecedented, vast, composite, electric democratic nationality.

Walt himself, though, never forgot the War or what it meant to the United States.

To thee, old Cause!
Thou peerless, passionate, good cause,
Thou stern, remorseless, sweet idea,
Deathless throughout the ages, races, lands,
After a strange sad war, great war for thee,
(I think all war through time was really fought, and ever will be
    really fought, for thee,)
These chants for thee, the eternal march of thee.

— *from "To Thee Old Cause"*

CHAPTER 13

The Verses Owning

PERHAPS the best of songs heard, or of any and all true love, or life's fairest episodes, or sailors', soldiers' trying scenes on land or sea, is the résumé of them, or any of them, long afterwards, looking at the actualities away back past, with all their practical excitations gone. How the soul loves to float amid such reminiscences!

— *from "A Backward Glance o'er Travel'd Roads"*

PREVIOUS PAGE: Whitman loved this photo and called it "the Laughing Philosopher." In it, he wears the infamous hat that his friends tried to shape and that he repeatedly knocked out of shape. He sent the photograph to fellow poet Alfred, Lord Tennyson, and was very pleased when Tennyson "liked it much—oh! so much." Photograph by George C. Cox, April 15, 1887, New York

Calamity & Recovery

The year 1873 brought disaster to Walt. Still living in D.C., at 53 years old, he suffered a debilitating stroke. Grief over the death of Jeff's wife Mattie in mid-February eroded his recovery and in May, he was forced to leave Washington. Only three days after he moved in with his brother George in Camden, New Jersey, another blow fell, the most devastating of his life: his mother died. "My physical sickness bad as it is—is nothing to it," he wrote a friend.

Slowly, though, Walt recovered a measure of health, mobility, and well being. He attended baseball games, visited friends and family, and took trips to the country and the seashore. He rode the ferry across the Delaware River to and from Philadelphia, just as in earlier days he commuted between Brooklyn and Manhattan.

What exhilaration, change, people, business, by day. What soothing, silent, wondrous hours, at night, crossing on the boat, most all to myself—pacing the deck, alone, forward or aft. What communion with the waters, the air, the exquisite chiaroscuro—the sky and stars, that speak no word, nothing to the intellect, yet so eloquent, so communicative to the soul. And the ferry men—little they know how much they have been to me, day and night—how many spells of listlessness, ennui, debility, they and their hardy ways have dispell'd.

Another stroke, in 1875, slowed but did not yet confine him. He continued to ferry to and from Philadelphia, where he browsed the bookstore of David McKay, on Ninth Street above Chestnut. McKay would publish the 1881 edition of *Leaves*.

In 1879 Walt took a trip west, all the way to Colorado. He longed to go beyond the Rockies, but illness ended his journey. On the way back to Camden, he made a long stop in St. Louis to rest and visit his brother Jeff. It would be their last reunion. Jeff died in 1890. "How we loved each other—how many jovial good times we had!" Walt wrote in the *Engineering Record* obituary.

George Whitman's house, where Walt lived when he first moved to Camden, is shown here in process of being demolished, circa 1989. George had the Italianate townhouse built around 1872; it would have been almost new when Walt moved in.

Walt befriended Henry Stafford, a tempestuous young man, in the mid-1870s. The friendship embraced the family. Henry's mother said of Walt, "I think he is the best man I ever knew." At the Stafford farm near Timber Creek, about a dozen miles from his home in Camden, Walt enjoyed health-giving sojourns. "Dear, soothing, healthy, restoration-hours—after three confining years of paralysis—after the long strain of the war, and its wounds and death." Timber Creek, near the Stafford farm, 2010

MICKLE STREET

In March 1884, Walt bought his own house on Mickle Street. William Thayer, who first visited in August 1885, described Walt's neighborhood:

It was a street of small, cheap houses, some of them serving both as little stores and dwellings, with here and there a larger building and, at a street-corner, a beer-saloon. An occasional tree, lean and starved and homesick-looking, threw a feeble shade on the sidewalk and gave the only hint of nature to that scene. Poor but respectable, with a suggestion that unrespectability was just around the corner, is the impression I recall of Mickle Street.

John Johnston, who visited Walt on Mickle Street in 1890, gave a different impression, describing it as "a quiet and retired side street, grass-grown on the roadway and side walks, and ornamented with two rows of large and graceful, leafy trees, which give it quite a pleasant, breezy, semi-rural appearance."

Increasingly immobile, Walt was attended by his live-in housekeeper Mary Oakes Davis, her adopted son Frederick Warren "Warry" Fritzinger, and devoted physicians. Friends, especially Horace Traubel, visited almost daily. Despite his declining health, Walt lived contentedly enough in the little house, the first place he could call his own.

Walt's rooms on Mickle Street were notoriously untidy; Mrs. Davis lamented her lack of access. Hamlin Garland, who visited in 1888, said, "In con-

Amidst the blight and hope that is early 21st-century Camden, Walt's house (above, left) and three neighboring houses survive. The "quiet and retired" street disappeared when Walt's section of Mickle Street widened to six lanes (renamed Dr. Martin Luther King Boulevard). Ironically, the Camden County jail (left) looms directly across from Walt's house. Mickle Street, 2014

Photo attributed to Walt's friend John Johnston shows Mickle Street in 1890. The two-story house at right was Walt's. The street is curbed, but unpaved; not surprisingly, Walt's possessions were covered with dust.

trast to his personal order and comeliness, the room was an incredible mess. Beside his chair rose a most amazing mound of manuscripts, old newspapers and clippings, with many books lying open face down at the point where he had laid them aside...."

Thankfully, Walt did not tidy up and discard his papers, and we have many of them still today.

Warren "Warry" Fritzinger, the adopted son of Walt's housekeeper on Mickle Street, attended Walt from 1889 to the very end. Walt was very fond of him and his brother Henry, who named his son after Walt. Warry wheeled Walt to the Camden Wharf for this 1890 photo.

Age and ill health increasingly confined Walt, but his friends chipped in for a horse and buggy that he kept from 1885 to 1888. Walt rides here with his driver and friend Bill Duckett. 1886

Legacy

For a dozen or so years in Camden, Walt promoted his work (and earned fees) in public appearances. In his most renowned lecture, "The Death of Abraham Lincoln," he dramatically described the assassination, then transformed it into a "ceremonial sacrifice that gives new life to the nation," as Whitman scholar Gregory Eiselein put it. (On the other hand, Walt grew heartily sick of his most popular poem, an elegy on Lincoln, "O Captain! My Captain!")

Walt wrote new essays and gathered old ones into *Specimen Days*, published in 1882. Scholars George Hutchinson and David Drews describe the collection: "The book attempts to link Whitman's life history to national and natural history while presenting itself as the casual reminiscence of a man approaching death. It therefore resembles what students of aging term 'life review.'" Although largely retrospective, many of the essays, especially those written at and about Timber Creek, his friend's rural home, have a freshness that rivals the best poems in *Leaves of Grass*.

Horace Traubel. circa 1880

What gives particular poignancy to Walt's years in Camden, especially the last decade, is the sense that his friends visited him not only to help and keep company with the living poet but, urgently, to ensure his work would live after his death. The "disciples" included readers in England, France, and other countries. The Mickle Street house became headquarters to a sort of Walt Whitman fan club. From there, Walt sent letters, photos of himself, and books to friends and strangers far and wide. Several visitors wrote adoring accounts. Walt, too, "puffed" his own work: prompting reviewers, co-authoring flattering biographical articles, exploiting reviews both good and bad, answering "fan mail" with photographs of himself, and keeping himself in print.

The Walt Whitman House as it is today contains Walt's own furniture and objects. Even his old rocker is extant. Because of the devotion Walt enjoyed in his life, his possessions were preserved rather than scattered or discarded. Their great, and for the most part only, value is that they were enjoyed by him.

From the morass of papers that surrounded Walt, Horace Traubel fished a priceless catch: letters and notes whose context, as narrated by Walt, formed the bulk of Traubel's eight-volume biography / memoir With Walt Whitman in Camden.

Among Walt's most ardent disciples was Horace Traubel. Despite the devastations Walt suffered in Camden, he told Traubel: "Camden was originally an accident—but I shall never be sorry I was left over in Camden! It has brought me blessed returns"—Traubel among them.

Traubel not only loved and cared for Walt in his old age, he preserved many of Walt's papers. On visits, he would pluck from the chaos of Walt's room a letter, a special book, a photo. Back home, he faithfully recorded his conversation with Walt on each artifact, compiled as *With Walt Whitman in Camden*, a rich record not only of Walt's life and his friends (and enemies), but also of his conversational style.

Some of the American editions of Leaves of Grass: 1855, 1856, 1860, 1867, 1876, 1871, 1892 (in a paper cover that Whitman rejected), 1882

Title page of 1891–92 Leaves of Grass, with "Come, said my Soul" as epigraph. Originally published in 1874, Walt first used the poem as an epigraph in the 1876 Leaves.

LEAVES OF GRASS

Those who dive deep into Walt Whitman's life and works find much to discuss and debate on which editions, and which poems in which editions, have more merit.

Walt spent his last strength preparing the 1891–92, "deathbed edition" of *Leaves of Grass*, an amended reprint of the 1881–82 edition annexed with collections "Sands at Seventy" and "Goodbye My Fancy," and the final essay "A Backward Glance O'er Travel'd Roads."

Walt said, of the 1891–92 publication of *Leaves of Grass*:

As there are now several editions of L. of G., different texts and dates, I wish to say that I prefer and recommend this present one, complete, for future printings, if there should be any; a copy and fac-simile, indeed, of the text of these 438 pages. The subsequent adjusting interval which is so important to form'd and launch'd work, books especially, has pass'd; and waiting till fully after that, I have given my concluding words.

Come, said my Soul

On March 26, 1892, with Warry and Horace attending, Walt died.

The cane Walt holds in this late-life portrait poignantly echoes the cane he so jauntily sported as a young man looking into a life unfolding. Here, an old man faces eternity: marked deeply with joy and sorrow, stoic, perhaps resigned, eclipsed in shadow, looking into the light.

Walt in his room, sitting in his rocking chair with the wolf-fur comforter.

Photo by Dr. William Reeder. 1891

the strongest & SWEETEST SONGS YET REMAIN to be SUNG

ending words of Walt Whitman's LEAVES OF GRASS, 1892

Sources

Many sources were used for this book, but the grandest of them all is The Walt Whitman Archive, directors Ed Folsom and Kenneth M. Price, an online and searchable record of just about everything ever said, done, and written by and about Walt Whitman.

The source entries are ordered by artwork, quotes (alphabetized), and general reference sources.

PRINCIPLE SOURCES

The first group of sources are those used frequently enough that abbreviations (given first) are justified.

CW. Whitman, Walt. *The Complete Writings of Walt Whitman*. Richard Maurice Bucke, Thomas Biggs Harned, Horace Traubel, and Oscar Lovell Triggs, eds. New York: G.P. Putnam's Sons, circa 1902. Collection of University of California Libraries. via archive.org

LOC. Library of Congress. Prints and Photographs Division. via loc.gov/pictures

CPW. Whitman, Walt. *Complete Prose Writings of Walt Whitman*. New York & London, G.P. Putnam's Sons, 1902. via gutenberg.org

WE. J.R. LeMaster and Donald D. Kummings, eds.. *Walt Whitman: An Encyclopedia*. New York: Garland Publishing, 1998.

WWA. The Walt Whitman Archive. Folsom, Ed, and Kenneth M. Price, eds. via WWA

WWWC. Traubel, Horace. *With Walt Whitman in Camden*. 9 vols. Vols. 1-3. 1906-1914. New York: Rowman and Littlefield, 1961; Vol. 4. Ed. Sculley Bradley. Philadelphia: U of Pennsylvania P, 1953; Vol. 5. Ed. Gertrude Traubel. Carbondale: U of Southern Illinois P, 1964; Vol. 6. Ed. Gertrude Traubel and William White. Carbondale: U of Southern Illinois P, 1982; Vol. 7. Ed. Jeanne Chapman and Robert Maclsaac. Carbondale: U of Southern Illinois P, 1992; Vols. 8-9. Ed. Jeanne Chapman and Robert Maclsaac. Oregon House, CA: W.L. Bentley, 1996. via WWA

Folsom, Ed, and Kenneth Price. "Walt Whitman." WWA.

Folsom, Ed. "Whitman Making Books / Books Making Whitman." Iowa City, IO: Obermann Center for Advanced Studies, University of Iowa, 2005. WWA

Kaplan, Justin. *Walt Whitman: A Life*. New York: Simon and Schuster, 1980.

Loving, Jerome. *Walt Whitman: The Song of Himself*. Berkeley, CA: University of California Press, 1999.

Miller, Edwin Haviland, ed. *Selected Letters of Walt Whitman*. Iowa City: University of Iowa Press, 1990. via WWA

Reynolds, David S. *Walt Whitman's America*. New York: Alfred A. Knopf, 1995.

Traubel, Horace. *Intimate with Walt*. Gary Smidgall, ed. Iowa City: Iowa University Press, 2001. via WWA

Whitman, Walt. *Leaves of Grass*. Brooklyn: 1855. Collection of University of Iowa Libraries, Special Collections & University Archives. via WWA

Whitman, Walt. *Leaves of Grass*. Boston: Thayer and Eldridge, 1860. Collection of Kenneth M. Price. via WWA

Whitman, Walt. *Leaves of Grass*. New York: 1867. Private collection.

Whitman, Walt. *Leaves of Grass*. Philadelphia: David McKay, 1891–2. Albert and Shirley Small Special Collections Library, University of Virginia. via WWA

Whitman, Walt. *Memoranda during the War*. 1876. Reprint. Mineola, NY: Dover Publications, 2011.

Whitman, Walt. *Specimen Days*. In *Complete Prose Writings of Walt Whitman*. New York & London, G.P. Putnam's Sons, 1902. via gutenberg.org

Whitman, Walt. *The Uncollected Poetry and Prose of Walt Whitman.* Emory Holloway, ed. Garden City, NY: Doubleday, Page & Company, 1921. via archive.org

Zweig, Paul. Walt Whitman: The Making of the Poet. New York: Basic Books, Inc., 1984.

PRELIMINARIES

Walt Whitman. Photo by Thomas Eakins. 1891. Hirshhorn Museum and Sculpture Garden, Smithsonian Institution. via WWA

CHAPTER 1 | WALT WHITMAN: HIMSELF

Walt Whitman. Engraving by William J. Linton. Circa 1871. Collection of Gay Wilson Allen Papers, Duke University Library. via WWA

Walt Whitman. 1854. Etching by Samuel Hollyer, based on a daguerreotype by Gabriel Harrison (original lost). LOC.

Edward J. Roye. Daguerrotype. Circa 1870. American Colonization Society Records, 1792-1964. LOC.

MAKING A CHART, MAKING THE MAN

Photograph of Samuel Robert Wells, Charlotte Fowler Wells, and Lorenzo N. Fowler standing in the doorway of S.R. Wells & Co., ca. 1880. Division of Rare and Manuscript Collections, Cornell University Library. via digital.library.cornell.edu

"The Symbolical head, illustrating all the phrenological developements of the human head." Circa 1842. Fowler and Strachan. LOC.

"This man…" Fowler, L.N. "Phrenological Notes on W. Whitman." July 1849. Quoted in Stern, Madeleine B., Heads & Headlines: The Phrenological Fowlers. Norman, OK: U. of Oklahoma Press, 1971.

"I am not yet past the phrenology phase…" WWWC. I: 386.

"The laziest fellow…" "Editor's Table." Aurora, April 1, 1876.

"He would lie abed …" Traubel, Horace, Richard Maurice Bucke, and Thomas B. Harned, eds. In Re Walt Whitman. Philadelphia: David McKay, 1893.

"You eat too hearty…" Barrus, Clara. Whitman and Burroughs: Comrades. via archive.org

Fowler, Orson Squire. Fowler's Practical Phrenology. New York: O.S. Fowler, 1840. via archive.org

Fowler, Orson Squire. Self-Culture. New York: Fowler & Wells, 1856.

SEEING WALT WHITMAN

Walt Whitman. 1854. Attributed to Gabriel Harrison. LOC.

Louis Jacques Mandé Daguerre. 1844. LOC.

Mathew Brady. Circa 1875 LOC.

Walt Whitman. 1889. Frederick Gutekunst. LOC.

"He is too brawny…" Alcott quoted in Myerson, Joel, ed. *Walt Whitman in His Own Time.* Iowa City: University of Iowa Press, 1991.

"A very grand one…" Gilchrist quoted in Myerson, Joel, ed. *Walt Whitman in His Own Time.* Iowa City: University of Iowa Press, 1991.

Appleton's Journal quotes from "Pictures and Sound: Gallery of Images." WWA.

"No man has…" WWWC. Vol. 3, p. 378.

Quotations on photography in Folsom, Ed, "This Heart's Geography's Map: The Photographs of Walt Whitman." WWA.

HEARING WALT WHITMAN

Thomas Edison. Circa 1878. LOC.

"America" recording attributed to Walt Whitman. LOC.

Folsom, Ed. "The Whitman Recording." Walt Whitman Quarterly Review, vol. 9, no. 4 (Spring 1992) pp. 214–216.

Israel, Paul, ed. "Edison and Poetry: Did Edison Record Walt Whitman?" The Edisonian. Volume 10 (February 2013). via edison.rutgers.edu

CHAPTER 2 | THE CRADLE

Long Island Homestead. Painting by Andrew W. Warren. 1859. Oil on canvas. American Art Museum, Smithsonian Institution. via commons.wikimedia.org

Walt Whitman Birthplace. Circa 1933. LOC.

ORIGINS

Louisa Whitman. Daguerrotype in case. Circa 1851–1860. LOC.

Walter Whitman. Circa 1850. LOC.

Schooner "John R. Beigen." Jackson & Shark Co., builder, Wilmington. Circa 1890. LOC.

Mount Mansfield. Painting by Charles Louis Heyde. Circa 1857. Oil on canvas. Robert Hull Fleming Museum, University of Vermont. via uvm.edu

Brooklyn Navy Yard. Harper's Weekly. 1861 Aug. 24, p. 534. LOC.

George Whitman. Circa 1880. LOC.

Thomas Jefferson Whitman. Circa 1863. LOC.

Levins, Sandy. "Camden County's First Lunatic Asylum." Camden County Historical Society. via historiccamdencounty.com

"Leaves of Grass is the flower…" WWWC. Vol. 2, p. 113.

"Daily and daring rider…" SD.

Ceniza, Sherry. "Whitman, Louisa Van Velsor [1795-1873]." WE.

"So your writing again leaves of grass…" Quoted in Cineza, Sherry. Walt Whitman and Nineteenth-Century Woman Reformers. Tuscaloosa, AL: University of Alabama Press, 1998. p. 22.

"A large, slow, good natured man…" Quoted in Miller, p. 81. via WWA

"Keep good heart…" Quoted in Kaplan, p. 58.

Roper, Robert. "Jesse Whitman, Seafarer." Walt Whitman Quarterly Review. 26:1, 35–41.

Re Jesse's employment. Walt Whitman to Samuel Livingston Breese, November 1861. LOC. via WWA

"Your Book came last night…" Hannah Whitman Heyde to Walt Whitman, November 1881 LOC. via WWA

"Walt we have a splendid…" George Whitman to Walt. 25 February 1863. Trent Collection of Whitmaniana, Duke University Rare Book, Manuscript, and Special Collections Library. via WWA

Murray, Martin G. "George Washington Whitman." WE.

Dennis Berthold and Kenneth M. Price, eds. *Dear Brother Walt: The Letters of Thomas Jefferson Whitman.* Kent, Ohio: Kent State University Press, 1984.

"Eddy is helpless…" WWWC. Vol. 2, p. 56.

CHAPTER 3 | BROOKLYN TO MONTAUK POINT

On Long Island near Shelter Island. Painting by John Carleton Wiggins. Circa 1860. Oil on canvas. Private collection. via the-athenaeum.org

RURAL LONG ISLAND

A Sunny Afternoon, Shinnecock Hills. Painting by William Merritt Chase. 1898. Oil on canvas. Private collection. via wikipaintings.org

Long Island, detail of Map of Southern part of the State of New York. P. Maverick, engraver. New York: W. Damerum, 1815. David Rumsey Map Collection. davidrumsey.com

Long Island Sound at Dawn. Painting by John Frederick Kensett. Circa 1865. Oil on canvas. Private collection. via the-athenaeum.org

Montauk Lighthouse. Painting by Sanford Robinson Gifford. 1877. Oil on canvas. Private collection. via hamiltonauctiongalleries.com

Fire Island Beach. Painting by Sanford Robinson Gifford. 1878. Oil on canvas. Private collection. via the-athenaeum.org

Pool in the Forest. Painting by Thomas Moran. 1883. Oil on canvas. Private collection. via the-athenaeum.org

Brinton, Daniel B. "A Visit to West Hills." Conserving Walt Whitman's Fame: Selections from Horace Traubel's Conservator, 1890–1919. Ed Folsom, ed. Iowa City: University of Iowa Press, 2006. p. 41. via WWA

BROOKLYN

View of New York from Brooklyn Heights. John William Hill. Circa 1837. The Miriam and Ira D. Wallach Division of Art, Prints and Photographs: Print Collection, The New York Public Library. The New York Public Library Digital Collections. NYPL.org

Winter Scene in Brooklyn. Painting by Guy Francis. Circa 1820. Painting. Private collection. via americangallery.wordpress.com.

Dr. James Tillary House, 15 Tillary Street, Brooklyn. Erected circa 1813–1820, demolished circa 1935. Photograph by E.P. MacFarland, Historic American Buildings Survey. LOC.

Brooklyn map (detail). New York: G.W. & C.B. Colton, 1866. David Rumsey Map Collection. davidrumsey.com

Wallabout and Brooklyn Navy Yard. Engraving, 1847. Unattributed. via whitmans-brooklyn.org

Baseball. Circa 1887. Aquarelle print by L. Prang & Co. LOC.

"Its situation for grandeur…" Whitman, Walt. "Brooklyniana; A Series of Local Articles, on Past and Present." Daily Standard, 1861. via WWA.

"Its streets were poorly paved…" Stiles, Henry R. A History of the City of Brooklyn. Brooklyn, NY: 1869.

"The style exhibits…" The Historical American Buildings Survey. December 1935. LOC.

"We occupied them…" SD.

"Without concurrence…" Quoted in Kaplan.

"I believe in all that …" WWWC. Vol. 1, p. 267.

"It's our game…" WWWC. Vol. 4, p. 508.

Lawrence, Deidre. "Whitman and the Arts in Brooklyn." Brooklyn Museum. brooklynmuseum.org

Ostrander, Stephen. A History of the City of Brooklyn and Kings County. 1894. via archive.org

CHAPTER 4 | SHAPING FORCES

Young America. Painting by Thomas Le Clear, circa 1860. Private collection. via writersgang.com

AMERICAN REVOLUTION

Washington & Lafayette. Reproduction of 1907 John Ward Dunsmore painting, by Brown & Bigelow, St. Paul and Toronto. LOC.

FREE THOUGHT

Thomas Paine. Circa 1792. Painting by Laurent Dubos. National Portrait Gallery, Smithsonian Institution, Washington, D.C.

Frances Wright. From Stanton, Elizabeth Cady, Susan B. Anthony and Matilda Joslyn Gage. History of Woman Suffrage. 1887. via wikipedia.org

"It was on that occasion that the corner-stone …" SD.

"I swore when I was a young man…" WWWC. Vol. 2, p. 206.

Paine, Thomas. The Age of Reason. 1796. via us.archive.org

Wright, Francis. Course of Popular Lectures. 1829. via digitalhistory.uh.edu

QUAKER CURRENTS

Elias Hicks. Drawn by H. Inman; engraved by Peter Maverick. New York : Edward Hopper, c1830. LOC.

"Did you know…" WWWC. Vol. 2, p. 19.

"Some may query…" Quoted by Walt in Walt Whitman, "Endnotes (such as they are) founded on Elias Hicks." CPW.

SCHOOL

Rhode Island schoolhouse room. Woody Hill School. Exeter Memory Project (website). Exeter, RI, Public Library. exetermemoryproject.org

Goodrich, Charles A. A history of the United States of America…. Bellows Falls, VT: James I. Cutler & Co, 1825. via archive.org

Kimber, Thomas. The American Class Book. Philadelphia: Kimber & Richardson, 1812. University of Pittsburgh, Digital Research Library. via digital.library.pitt.edu

Todd, Rev. John. The Student's Manual. Northampton, Mass, 1835. via archive.org

Taylor, Rev. Isaac. Scenes in America for the Amusement and Instruction of Little Tarry-at-Home Travellers. 1848. via archive.org

READING

Apprentice library. Brooklyn Museum Archives. Photograph Collection [S06]. Museum building: former sites. Apprentices' Library Association, Corner of Henry and Cranberry Streets, 1825. via whatwasthere.com

Humboldt in his library. Chromolithograph copy of watercolor drawing by Eduard Hildebrant, 1856. Berlin: Storch & Kramer. Graphic Arts Collection, Princeton University.

The Arabian Nights. Chiswick, U.K.: C. Whittingham, College House: 1828. Private collection. via antiqbook.com

Stereoscope of wilderness. William England. LOC.

Scene from "The Last of the Mohicans," Cora Kneeling at the Feet of Tamenund. Painting by Thomas Cole. 1827. Oil on canvas, 25-3/8 x 35-1/16 in. Bequest of Alfred Smith, 1868.3. Wadsworth Atheneum Museum of Art, Hartford, Connecticut. Photo: Allen Phillips/Wadsworth Atheneum.

Homer. The Odyssey of Homer. Translated by Alexander Pope. London: 1853. via archive.org

Sand, George. Consuelo. London: 1847. via archive.org

"Astor Place Opera-House Riots." Art and Picture Collection, The New York Public Library. New York Public Library Digital Collections. via digitalcollections.nypl.org

Humboldt, Alexander von. Kosmos. Translated by E.C. Otte. NY: Harper & Bros., 1858.

"I have a crazy…" Humboldt letter. Quoted in Reynolds, p. 244.

Arabian Nights. Edward Forster, transl. 1815. via archive.org

Cooper, James Fenimore. The Last of the Mohicans. New York : Stringer and Townsend, 1856. via archive.org

Scott, Sir Walter. The Ministrelsy of the Scottish Border. 1806.

"How much I am indebted…" WWWC. Vol. 1, p. 96.

"I regard her as the brightest woman…" WWWC.

"I have already spoken of Shakspere.…" CPW. p. 324.

PRINTING

Great Fire of NY. Lithograph by Hoffy, printed by H.H. Robinson, New York. LOC.

Composing room. Photo by Mangoman88. Private collection. via commons.wikimedia.org

Compositor's stick. Photo by Wilhei. Private collection. via wikipedia.org

Composing room. Encyclopédie; ou, Dictionnaire raisonné des sciences, des arts et des métiers.… Paris, 1751-72. LOC.

"The printers and foremen…" Walt Whitman to Thomas Jefferson Whitman, 10 May 1860. Walt Whitman House, Camden, NJ. via WWA

"If I had been a little more vigilant…" WWWC. Vol. 1, p. 357.

"I like to supervise…" WWWC.

"I am almost in a hurry…" WWWC.

CHAPTER 5 | THE PARTI-COLORED WORLD

Broadway from Barnum's Museum Looking North. 1860. Edward Anthony and Henry T. Anthony. From Anthony's Instantaneous Views No. 321. Hand-colored albumen silver prints from glass negatives (stereoscopic views). Published by E. & H. T. Anthony & Company. Robert N. Dennis Collection of Stereoscopic Views, Miriam and Ira D. Wallach Division of Art, Prints and Photographs, The New York Public Library, Astor, Lenox and Tilden Foundations.

Fulton Street from the Ferry. Ballou's Pictorial. 1857. Unattributed. via whitmans-brooklyn.org

South Street Seaport, Piers 17 & 18, South Street into East River at Fulton Street, New York, New York County, NY. Circa 1870. LOC.

THE STREETS OF NEW YORK

Haughwout building. Photo by Elisa Rolle. Private collection. via commons.wikimedia.org

Macy's. Circa 1860. Unattributed. via forgottendelights.com

Life of a Fireman. Hand-colored lithograph. New York: Published by Currier & Ives, circa 1861. LOC.

Dead Rabbit. Painting by George Henry Hall. 1858. Oil on canvas. National Academy Museum, New York. via cuny.edu

F.S. Chanfrau in the Character of Mose. 1848. Theatre poster. Harvard Theatre Collection, Houghton Library, Harvard University. via wikipedia.org

Broadway Hospital. Circa 1869. Unattributed. via weill.cornell.edu/archives

Prostitutes. Circa 1830. Lithograph, Serrell & Perkins. Museum of the City of New York

Cholera brandy. New York: Robertson, Seibert & Shearman, 93 Fulton St., circa 1860. LOC.

SOUNDS OF THE CITY

Radish vendor. From The Cries of New York, by Francis Osgood. New York: John Doggett, Jr., 1846. Yale University Library.

Bucket boy. Circa 1890. via growlergaragevt.com

ENTERTAINMENT

"Amusements this evening." New York Times. Sept. 1, 1860, p. 5.

Castle Garden. [New York]: N. Currier, 1848. LOC.

Crystal Palace. Nagel & Weingärtner, printmaker. New York : Goupil & Co., c1853. LOC.

Winter Scene in front of Barnum Museum. 1855. By Thomas Benecke. Printed by Nagel & Lewis. LOC.

Barnum lecture room. Chapin, artist, and Avery, engraver. Unattributed. via commons.wikimedia.org

Barnum: Ticket to Barnum's American Museum, 1867. Museum of the City of New York. via mcnyblog.org

Barnum: Chang & Eng. Currier & Ives lithograph. 1860. National Library of Medicine. via commons.wikimedia.org

Barnum: Quaker giants. LOC.

Barnum: Wonderful Albino Family. New York: Lithogd. by Currier & Ives, [circa 1860]. LOC.

Barnum: Tom Thumb. Currier & Ives print. Cira 1849. LOC.

Barnum: Feejee mermaid. Unattributed. via mermaidmania.de

THE ARTS

Brooklyn Institute. Photo by Wallace Goold Levison. June 10, 1891. LOC.

Mathew Brady gallery. A. Berghaus, artist. 1861. Wood engraving. LOC.

Poster, Egyptian Museum. Brooklyn Museum Libraries. Wilbour Library of Egyptology. Special Collections. brooklynmuseum.org

Picture Gallery, Smithsonian Institute. 1858. Made by American Stereoscopic Co., Langenheim, Lloyd & Co. Albumen print on paper. LOC.

Autumn along the Hudson. Painting by Jesse Talbot. Circa 1845. Private collection. via mutualart.com

Bowery Theatre. 1867. Unknown photographer. From a stereoscopic print. Miriam and Ira D. Wallach Division of Art, Prints and Photographs, New York Public Library.

Park Row & Park Theatre. Drawn & Engraved by H. Fossette. 1831. via commons.wikimedia.org

Marietta Alboni. Photograph by Jeremiah Gurney, circa 1862. via wikipedia.org

Chadwick, Henry. "Oh! Susanna." Sheet music. New York: C. Holt, Jr., 1850. LOC.

Morris, George P. (lyrics) and Russell, Henry (music). "My Mother's Bible." In Cottage Melodies: a hymn and tune book, for prayer and social meetings and the home circle. 1859 Unattributed. via hymnary.org

Howe, Julia Ward. "Battle Hymn of the Republic." Philadelphia: Supervisory Committee for Recruiting Colored Regiments, [1863?]. LOC.

Langenschwartz, Max. "The Soldier's Farewell to His Bride." Baltimore: Charles Magnus, 1864. The Lester S. Levy Sheet Music Collection, Johns Hopkins University. levysheetmusic.mse.jhu.edu

New York with the city of Brooklyn in the distance. From the steeple of St. Paul's Church looking east, south, and west. Circa 1855. Drawing by J.W. Hill; engd. by Henry Papprill. LOC.

"The entire length…"Gleason's Pictorial. III: 371. Quoted in No. 361 Broadway Building. Landmarks Preservation Commission. July 27, 1982. via neighborhoodpreservationcenter.org

"Twenty years ago…" Harper's Weekly. 1862. Quoted in No. 361

Broadway Building. Landmarks Preservation Commission. July 27, 1982. via neighborhoodpreservationcenter.org

"Belongs yet to the fire clubs…" WWWC. Vol. 1, p. 102.

"We 'go' heartily…" Quoted in Reynolds.

WW on theaters. SD.

Anon. "History of Engine 6 Tigers." fdnyengine6.org

Cutler, Edward. "Passage to Modernity: Leaves of Grass and the 1853 Crystal Palace Exhibition in New York." Walt Whitman Quarterly Review. Vol 16, no. 2. Fall 1998. pp 65-89 via WWA

Kray, Elizabeth. "Walking Tour: Walt Whitman's Printing House Square in New York City." poets.org.

Krieg, Joann P. Walt Whitman and the Irish. University of Iowa Press, 2000. via WWA

CHAPTER 6 | LETTERS

Walt Whitman. Notebook. 1847. LOC

PROSE

Walt Whitman. Circa 1850. Gay Wilson Allen Papers, Duke University Library. via WWA

Brooklyn Daily Eagle office. Brooklyn Museum Archives. Lantern Slide Collection [S10]. Views: U.S., Brooklyn Daily Eagle. Old Eagle Building (front view), Lower Fulton Street, Brooklyn, n.d. via brooklynmuseum.org

Brooklyn Eagle. April 1, 1846. via newspapers.com

Whitman, Walt. "Franklin Evans." The New World. New York: November 1842. Part of "Walt Whitman at the Lilly," designed and written by Christoph Irmscher, Indiana University Bloomington. Collection of Lilly Library, Indiana University, Bloomington. via indiana.edu

"We took our cane…" & "tall and graceful in appearance." Aurora, 1842. Quoted in "Pictures and Sound: Gallery of Images." via WWA

The Aurora and Walt's tenure there. In Conserving Walt Whitman's Fame. via WWA

"The great Ann Street Bamboozle…" "There is in this city…" Quoted in Kray, Elizabeth. "Walking Tour: Walt Whitman's Printing House Square in NYC." 2009. via poets.org.

LITERARY SCENE

Sketch of Walt Whitman. From Notebook 91. Circa 1860. LOC.

Henry Clapp. Photo from Winter, William. Old Friends: Being Literary Recollections of Other Days. New York: Moffat, Yard and Company, 1909. "The Vault at Pfaff's," pfaffs.web.lehigh.edu

Adah Isaacs Menken photo. Napoleon Sarony, photographer. Circa 1866. LOC

Anne Charlotte Lynch Botta. Carte de visite. Unattributed.

"The vault at Pfaff's…" Whitman, Notebooks. Quoted at pfaffs.web via pfaffs.web.lehigh.edu

"They were gifted men…" Hemstreet, Charles. Literary New York. New York: G.P. Putnam's Sons, 1903. via gutenberg.org

Stansell, Christine. "Whitman at Pfaff's." Walt Whitman Quarterly Review. 10: 3 (Winter 1993), pp 107-126. via WWA

"In person she is…" Poe, Edgar Allen. "The Literati of New York City. No. V." Godey's Lady's Book. Vol. 33, 1846, p. 133. via librarycompany.org

"Walt Whitman (b. 1819) writes with great force…" Botta, Anne C. Lynch. Handbook of universal literature. Boston: Houghton, Mifflin and Compay, 1889. p. 535 via archive.org

WRITERS OF WALT'S TIME

Kindred Spirits. Painting by Asher Brown Durand. 1849. Oil on canvas. Crystal Bridges Museum of American Art, Bentonville, Arkansas. via commons.wikimedia.org

Emily Dickinson. Daguerrotype. Todd-Bingham picture collection, 1837-1966 (inclusive). Manuscripts & Archives, Yale University Library. via yale.edu

Carriage. Unattributed. via readmycanvas.wordpress.com

Bryant, William Cullen. Poems. New York: Harper & Brothers, 1842. via archive.org

William Cullen Bryant portrait. From Graham's Illustrated Magazine of Literature, Romance, Art, and Fashion. 1843 via commons.wikimedia.org

Nathaniel Hawthorne. Painting by Charles Osgood. 1840. Peabody Essex Museum.

Hawthorne, Nathaniel. The Scarlet Letter. Boston: Ticknor, Reed, and Fields, 1850. via archive.org

Longfellow, Henry Wadsworth. The Song of Hiawatha. London: G. Routledge & Co., 1856. via archive.org

Henry Wadsworth Longfellow. Print of daguerrotype by Southworth and Hawes. Circa 1850. Unattributed. via commons.wikimedia.org

Whittier, John Greenleaf. Songs of Labor and Other Poems. Boston: Ticknor, Reed, and Fields, 1850. via archive.org

John Greenleaf Whittier. Circa 1840–60. Ambrotype. Boston Public Library. via wikipedia.org

Edgar Allan Poe portrait. 1848. Copy of daguerreotype by W.S. Hartshorn. LOC.

Poe, Edgar Allan. The Poetical Works of Edgar Allan Poe. James Hannay, ed. London: Charles Griffin and Company, 1852. via archive.org

Tennyson, Alfred. In Memoriam. London: Edward Moxon & Co., 1863. Collection of University of Michigan. via openlibrary.org

Alfred, Lord Tennyson. Circa 1870. Attributed to Juliet Margaret Cameron. Private collection. via wikimedia.org

Herman Melville. Reproduction of photograph, frontispiece to Journal Up the Straits. Ca. 1860. LOC.

Melville, Herman. Moby Dick. New York: Harper & Brothers, 1851. via archive.org

Louisa May Alcott. 1870. Photo by George Kendall Warren. LOC.

Alcott, Louisa May. Little Women. Boston: Roberts Brothers, 1868. University of California Libraries. via archive.org

Folsom, Ed, and Jerome Loving. "The Walt Whitman Controversy: A Lost Document." Virginia Quarterly Review. Spring, 2007. On Mark Twain and Walt Whitman.

Ludlow, Fitz Hugh. The Hasheesh Eater. London: 1857. via archive.org

Kirkland, Caroline. A New Home—Who'll Follow? or, Glimpses of Western Life. New York: 1855. LOC.

Neal, John. Randolph. 1823. via archive.org

Morris, George Pope. "Woodman! Spare that Tree!" Sheet music cover. New York: Firth and Hall, circa 1837.

Fern, Fanny. Fern Leaves (cover). 1853. From Folsom, Ed. "Whitman Making Books/Books Making Whitman: A Catalog and Commentary." Iowa City: Obermann Center for Advanced Studies, University of Iowa, 2005. via WWA

Fern, Fanny. Fern Leaves. Auburn, NY: Derby and Miller, 1853. New

York Public Library. via archive.org

Taylor, Bayard. "Our Own Dear America." New York: circa 1850. LOC.

"A feature in Bryant…" WWWC. Vol 2, p 553

"The dirtiest book…" WWWC. Vol. 1, p. 124.

"He has all that in him…" WWWC. Vol. 2, p. 196.

"Toward the last…" Whitman, Walt. "A Backward Glance o'er Travel'd Roads." CPW.

THE TRANSCENDENTALISTS

The Catskills. Painting by Asher Brown Durand. 1858. Oil on canvas. The Walters Art Museum, Baltimore.

Ralph Waldo Emerson. Print of circa 1850–60 photo. LOC.

The Potato Harvest. Painting by Jean-François Millet. 1855. Oil on Canvas. The Walters Art Museum, Baltimore.

Emerson's house, Concord, Mass. Postcard circa 1900. Detroit Publishing Co. LOC.

Henry David Thoreau. 1856. Daguerreotype by Benjamin D. Maxham. National Portrait Gallery, Smithsonian Institution, Washington, D.C.

Thoreau, Henry David. Walden Pond. Boston: Ticknor and Fields, 1854. Boston Public Library. via archive.org

Anon. "Transcendentalism." Aurora. March 8, 1842, p 1. (Article is tentatively attributed to WW.) Paterson Free Public Library, Paterson, NJ. via WWA

"I have always been best pleased…." WWWC. Vol. 6, p. 386

"Millet has the right idea…" WWWC. Vol. 9, p. 120.

"So subordinate that…" WWWC. Vol. 6, p. 386.

Emerson. "The Poet." Essays: Second Series. 1844. via poetryfoundation.org

"I find it…" "Leaves of Grass." The Saturday Review. 1 (15 March 1856). via WWA

"He was a far-fetching force…" (on Emerson) WWWC. Vol 3, p. 185. via WWA

"He is a great fellow…" Henry David Thoreau. "Leaves of Grass." The Boston Globe. 13 November 1881: 8. via WWA

CHAPTER 7 | COMRADES, FRIENDS, SPOUSE

COMRADES

"To a new personal admirer." Walt Whitman, notebook. 1857–59. Albert and Shirley Small Special Collections Library, University of Virginia. via WWA

Calamus. Photo by Christian Fischer. Private collection. via commons.wikimedia.org

NYC stagecoach. Circa 1900–06. Detroit Publishing Co. LOC.

Fred Gray. Photo by Brassart, Johnson, and Williams, Photographers. 1862. Bryn Mawr College Library Special Collections.

"Why be there men I meet…" Walt Whitman: Daybooks and Notebooks. William White, ed. New York: New York U Press, 1977. Vol. III, p. 764.

"He is always…" WWWC. Vol. 1, p. 74.

"Many will say…" "Democratic Vistas." CPW.

"Ever since…" Doris Kearns Goodwin quote of Stanton letter to Chase, in Fudge, Tom, "Our Gay President?" KPBS.org

"'Calamus' is a common word…" Walt Whitman to Moncure D. Conway. Nov. 1, 1867. Manuscripts Division, Department of Rare Books and Special Collections, Princeton University Library. via WWA

"I heard [Emerson] lecture…" Fred Vaughan to Walt Whitman, 27 March 1860. LOC. via WWA

"I am fain to hope…" Quoted in Schmidgall, Gary, ed., Intimate with Walt. Iowa City: U of Iowa Press, 2001. p. xiii. via WWA

Blalock, Stephanie M. "'My Dear Comrade Frederickus.'" Walt Whitman Quarterly Review. 27:1 (Summer 2009), pp 49-65. via WWA

Higgins, Andrew C. "Symonds, John Addington [1840-1893]." WE.

Miller, James E., Jr. "Sex and Sexuality." WE. via WWA

Murray, Martin G. "Pete the Great: A Biography of Peter Doyle." Walt Whitman Quarterly Review 12 (Summer 1994), 1-51. via WWA

Olsen-Smith, Steven. "The Inscription of Walt Whitman's 'Live Oak, with Moss' Sequence: A Restorative Edition." Scholarly Editing. 33 (2012). scholarlyediting.org

FRIENDS

Abby Hills Price. Circa 1875. Unattributed. via adinballou.org

Gilchrist, Anne. Circa 1870. Photo by Misses Davison Royal Polytechnic Studio, 309 Regent Street, W. LOC.

Hubble Explores the Mysteries of UGC 8201. NASA.

"LofG is essentially a woman's book…" WWWC. 1888.

"Democracy, in silence,…" CPW. p. 225.

"[Woman] needs to have her whole nature…" Cerniza, Sherry. "Walt Whitman and Abby Price." Walt Whitman Quarterly Review. Vol. 7, no. 2, pp 49–67. via WWA

"You can imagine…" WWWC. Vol. 1, p. 218.

"I have that sort of feeling…" WWWC. Vol. 1, p. 218.

Gilchrist, Anne. "A Woman's Estimate of Walt Whitman." in Thomas B. Harned, ed., The Letters of Anne Gilchrist and Walt Whitman. New York: Doubleday, Page & Co., 1918.

SPOUSE

Old Man. Photo by George Hodan. Old man. Private collection. via publicdomainpictures.net

"I suppose the chief reason why I never married…" In Bucke, p. 36.

"I was aware of a certain radiant power in him…" In Carpenter, Edward, Days with Walt Whitman. New York: Macmillan, circa 1906. p. 6. via archive.org

CHAPTER 8 | VOYAGER

Map of USA with Walt's annotations. LOC.

"If I rested 'Leaves of Grass' on the usual claims…" WWWC, v 2, p 108

TRANSPORTS

Pullman sleeper car, circa 1870. Unattributed. via smithosonianmag.com

Horsecar. "Manhattan: 4th Avenue - 12th Street (East)." 1838. Irma and Paul Milstein Division of United States History, Local History and Genealogy, The New York Public Library; NYPL Digital Collections.

Brooklyn, L.I., as seen from Trinity Church, New York. 1853. Artist, John William Hill. New York : Smith Brothers & Co., 225 Fulton St., 1853. LOC.

Fulton Ferry photo, with inscription. 1890. LOC.

NEW ORLEANS

New Orleans flower girl. Harper's Weekly. Feb. 16, 1861. via sonofthesouth.net

New Orleans French Market. Picture by Alfred R. Waud. Harper's Weekly. August 18, 1866. Mariner's Museum. via amhistory.si.edu

New Orleans French Market. Photo by William Henry Jackson. 1880—97. Detroit Publishing Co. LOC.

Lithograph "New-Orleans (Louisiana)". Late 1840s, by Henry Lewis. Published in Das illustrirte Mississippithal, 1854–1857. via commons.wikimedia.org

New Orleans artillery officer. Photograph by Samuel Anderson. Notations on back: Jackson [Banades?], New Orleans, La., April 26, 1859. LOC.

Auction area, St. Louis Hotel, New Orleans. Detroit Publishing Co., circa 1906. LOC.

New Orleans wharf. Photo 1875. Unattributed. via americanhistory.si.edu

Steamboat race. Circa 1859. Attributed to Weingärtner. LOC.

Steamboat pilot room. Harley, John. From Twain, Mark, Life On The Mississippi. Boston: James R. Osgood & Company, 1883.

"Miss Dusky Grisette." Daily Crescent. March 16, 1848.

"Often, of a Sunday morning…" Daily Crescent. April 4, 1848.

"Following a brilliant campaign…" SD.

"I used to wander…" "November Boughs." CW.

"I used to wander…" CW.

"One of my choice amusements…" "November Boughs." CW.

"Passed down Conti Street…" Daily Crescent.

"Live Oak with Moss" draft manuscript. Valentine-Barrett Collection, University of Virginia. via WWA

Walt in New Orleans. 1848. Daguerrotype. Walt Whitman House, Camden, New Jersey. via WWA

Parker, Herschel. "The Real 'Live Oak, with Moss': Straight Talk about Whitman's 'Gay Manifesto.'" Nineteenth-Century Literature. 51 (September 1996), pp. 145-60. via WWA

VOYAGES

The Sidewheeler "The City of St. Paul" on the Mississippi River, Dubuque, Iowa. Painting by Alfred Thompson Bricher. 1872. Oil on canvas mounted on board, Image: 20 1/8 x 38 1/8 in. (51.1 x 96.8 cm) Frame: 35 x 52 3/4 in. (88.9 x 134.0 cm), Terra Foundation for American Art, Daniel J. Terra Collection, 1992.18

View on the Hudson at West Point. New York: Published by John Walsh & Co., 37 Spring St., [circa 1870] N.Y. : Printed by J.F. Smart & Kahlmann, 14 Cortland St. LOC.

Wisconsin Road. Photo by the author.

Lake Michigan. Photo by the author.

City of Cleveland, Ohio.1872. Steel engraving from a study by A. C. Warren, engraved by R. Hinshelwood. In Picturesque America. New York: D. Appleton & Company, 1872. 1:529. via media.ctsfw.edu

Chicago as It Was. New York: Currier & Ives, circa 1856–1907. LOC.

View of Front Street. Lithograph by John Caspar Wild. 1840. Missouri History Museum. via stl250.org

Spanish Peaks, Colorado. Painting by Samuel Colman. Circa 1870. Oil on canvas. Private collection. via christies.com

Denver. Circa 1898. Hand-tinted photograph by William Henry Jackson. Detroit Publishing Co. LOC.

Coreopsis verticillata. Photograph by chrumps. Private collection. via commons.wikimedia.org

Atlantic Ocean off Ocracoke Island, North Carolina. 2010. Photo by author.

"Pete this is a wonderful country…" Walt Whitman to Pete Doyle. November 5, 1879. LOC.

"The attractions…" SD

CHAPTER 9 | AMERICA

Flag – 34 stars. 1861. Curator Branch, Naval History and Heritage Command. via commons.wikimedia.org

ONE NATION

1835 U.S. Map. From Bradford, T.G., A Comprehensive Atlas, Geographical, Historical & Commercial. Boston: American Stationers' Company, 1835. David Rumsey Map Collection. via davidrumsey.com

1847 U.S. Map. Published by Phelps, Ensigns & Thayer, New York. David Rumsey Map Collection. via davidrumsey.com

1860 U.S. Map. By Samuel Augustus Mitchell, Jr., Philadelphia. David Rumsey Map Collection. via davidrumsey.com

Portrait of Andrew Jackson. Painting by Thomas Sully. 1824. U.S. Senate. via senate.gov

Boss Tweed on tobacco label. Circa 1869. LOC.

Jackson, Andrew. "Farewell Address," March 4, 1837. Online by Gerhard Peters and John T. Woolley. The American Presidency Project. via presidency.ucsb.edu

McCormick reaper, in Iles, George. Leading American Inventions. 1912. via commons.wikimedia.org

The Times. Lithograph by Edward Clay. New York, 1837. Political Cartoon Collection at the American Antiquarian Society, Worcester, Massachusetts. via common-place.org

"My father was always a Democrat…" WWWC. Vol. 3, p. 109.

A CHANGING "US"

Henry Ward Beecher. Circa 1855–60. LOC.

Plymouth Church. Photo by E.P. MacFarland. April 26, 1934. LOC.

American Patriot. Boston. 1854. via historicipswitch.org

In the Land of Promise, Castle Garden. Painting by Charles Friedric Ulrich. 1884. Oil on canvas. Corcoran Gallery of Art. via wikimedia.org

WOMEN'S RIGHTS

Elizabeth Cady Stanton, seated, and Susan B. Anthony, standing. Circa 1880–1902. LOC.

Lucretia Mott. Circa 1860. LOC

Price, Kenneth M. "To Walt Whitman, America." WWA

SLAVERY

Stowe, Harriet Beecher. Uncle Tom's Cabin. Cleveland: John P. Jewett & Company, 1852.

Auction & Negro Sales, Whitehall Street, Atlanta, Georgia. Photograph by George Bernard. September – November 1864. LOC.

Slave cells, Alexandria, Virginia. Photo by Mathew Brady. Circa 1861–65. New York : E. & H. T. Anthony & Co., American and Foreign Stereoscopic Emporium, 501 Broadway. LOC.

Frederick Douglass. Circa 1856. Ambrotype. National Portrait Gallery, Smithsonian Institution. via commons.wikimedia.org

John Brown. Daguerreotype attributed to Martin M. Lawrence. 1859. LOC.

Harriet Tubman. 1911. LOC.

"The Americans of all nations…" Preface. Leaves of Grass. 1855.

"The young men…" Quoted in Klammer, Martin, "Slavery and Abolitionism." WE.

WESTWARD

American Progress. Painting by John Gast, print by George Cruffit. 1873. LOC.

1823 U.S. Map. Cartographer John Melish. David Rumsey Map Collection. davidrumsey.com

Robert E. Lee. New York : E. Anthony, 501 Broadway, circa 1846. LOC.

War News from Mexico. Painting by Richard Caton Woodville. 1848. Oil on canvas. Crystal Bridges Museum of American Art, Bentonville, Arkansas.

Osceola. Lithograph from painting by George Catlin. 1838. LOC.

Generals Wesley Merritt, Philip Sheridan, George Crook, James William Forsyth, and George Armstrong Custer. 1865. Photo by Alexander Gardner; print by Moses P. Rice. LOC.

"There is certainly not one government in Europe …" Memoranda During the War. p. 63.

Folsom, Ed. "Native Americans (Indians)." WE

Whitman, Walt. "Mexican War." The Brooklyn Daily Eagle. May 11 and June 6, 1846. via nationalhumanitiescenter.org

CHAPTER 10 | POETRY

COMING TO POETRY

Walt Whitman. "Each Has His Grief." The New World. 3 (20 November 1841): 1. via WWA

Walt Whitman. Notebook. 1847. LOC.

"Different objects…" Whitman, Walt. Notebook LC #80. 1847. p. 26. LOC.

LEAVES OF GRASS

Ralph Waldo Emerson, to Walt Whitman. 1855. LOC.

CHAPTER 11 | THE CIVIL WAR

Catalpa tree at Chatham house, Virginia. 2012. Photo by author.

THE CIVIL WAR

Walt Whitman. Photo attributed to Mathew Brady or William Kurtz. 1863. LOC.

Malvern Hill Battlefield National Park, Virginia. 2012. Photo by author.

WALT AS NURSE

Fredericksburg wall. Photo by Andrew J. Russell. 1863. LOC.

Chatham Manor / Lacy House. Circa 1861–65. National Archives. via research.archives.gov

Minie ball and musket ball. Ralphe Poore. via poorboysingray.wordpress.com

Armory Square Hospital. 1865. LOC.

Walt's notebook #94. LOC.

Walt's haversack. (Photo contrast altered to enhance details.) LOC.

Sleeping bunks of 1st RI. Harper's Weekly. June 1, 1861. via sonofthesouth.net

"A poet's bag of compassion." Ruane, Michael E. "A poet's bag of compassion in the Civil War." The Washington Post. Reprinted in The Richmond Times-Dispatch. May 19, 2013, p. A15.

"The picture is by some…" Walt Whitman to William M. Rossetti, 9 December 1869. Walt Whitman Collection, 1842–1957, Rare Book & Manuscript Library, University of Pennsylvania. via WWA

"I devote myself much…" Walt Whitman to Louisa Whitman. June 1863.

"Unlike a solid ball…" Leonard, Pat. "The Bullet that Changed History." Disunion, New York Times. Aug 31, 2012.

"From my personal knowledge…" Dr. Willard Bliss. Quoted in Murray, Martin G. "Traveling with the Wounded: Walt Whitman and Washington's Civil War Hospitals." Washington History: Magazine of the Historical Society of Washington, D.C. 8 (Fall/Winter 1996–1997), 58-73, 92-93. via WWA

"Again spending a good part of the day at Harewood…" CPW. p. 77.

"I have this moment…" New-York Times. 12 March 1865: 3. via WWA

"I have never once questioned…" WWWC. Vol. 3, p. 95.

THE WAR AT HOME

Brooklyn Sanitary Fair. Harper's Weekly. March 5, 1864. via sonofthesouth.net

"I have hattey…" Louisa Whitman to Walt Whitman. October 30 (?), 1863. Quoted in Dennis Berthold and Kenneth M. Price, ed. Dear Brother Walt: The Letters of Thomas Jefferson Whitman. Kent, Ohio: Kent State University Press, 1984. via WWA

"So help me…" Jeff Whitman to Walt Whitman. 15 December, 1863. LOC. via WWA

WRITING THE WAR

"Future years will never know…. the cruelties…. Incredible dauntlessness…" Whitman, Walt. Memoranda during the War. pp. 3–4.

"I sometimes think…" Walt Whitman to Louisa Van Velsor Whitman, 22 March 1864. LOC. via WWA

"The images of…" Mancuso, Luke. WE.

CHAPTER 12 | WASHINGTON, D.C.

Balloon view of D.C. Harper's Weekly. 1861 July 27. Wood engraving. Private collection. via philaprintshop.com

"The city of the armies…" New-York Times. 4 October 1863: 2 via WWA

CITY OF "THINGS BEGUN"

The U.S. Capitol under construction. 1860. National Archives.

Smithsonian "Castle." Photo by Mathew Brady. Circa 1860–65. National Archives. via commons.wikimedia.org

Pennsylvania Avenue. Painting by A. Mayer. 1860. LOC. via ghostsofdc.org

15th and F streets NW. LOC.

Cattle on the grounds of the Washington Monument. Frank Leslie's Illustrated Newspaper. 1862. via civilwarwashingtondc1861-1865.blogspot.com

Ox team with cannon. Circa 1861–65. LOC.

"I often watch…" "Letter from Washington." New-York Times. 4 October 1863: 2.

"Washington is a pleasant place…" Walt Whitman to Louisa Whitman. 7 July 1863. LOC. via WWA

"Among other sights…" SD.

"In the street below me…" New-York Times. 4 October 1863: 2. via WWA

The Old Patent Office building. Photo by John Plumbe. 1846. LOC.

Tea kettle. via liveauctioneers.com

Sheet iron stove. via greatwestmetal.ca

"Diagonally opposite to Chase's great house…" Trowbridge, John Townsend, Walt Whitman in His Time. p 115

"I found him partly dressed…" Trowbridge, John Townsend, Walt Whitman in His Time. p. 228

DISCIPLES

O'Connor, William Douglas. The Good Gray Poet: A Vindication. New York: Bunce & Huntington, 1866. LOC.

William Douglas O'Connor. Circa 1880–89. Gelatin silver print. LOC.

Lott, Deshae E. "O'Connor, William Douglas [1832-1889]." WE.

PETE DOYLE

Pete Doyle's hair. LOC.

Walt Whitman and Pete Doyle. Photo by M.P. Rice. 1865. LOC.

Horse-drawn trolley streetcar. Historical Society of Washington, D.C. via nlm.nih.gov

Bridge over Potomac. 1865. LOC.

Walt Whitman, notebook. 1870. LOC

"You ask where I met him…" CW. p. 23.

"The most taciturn mutual admiration society…" Quoted in Murray, Martin G. "Pete the Great." Walt Whitman Quarterly Review. 12 (Summer 1994), 1-51. via WWA

"A rare man…." WWWC. Vol. 3, p. 543.

"We would walk together…" WWWC. Vol. 2, p. 511.

"To give up absolutely…" Walt Whitman's notebook. 1870. LOC.

"In the afternoon I would go up…" Pete Doyle quoted in CW.

"I have Walt's raglan here…." Pete Doyle quoted in CW, p. 11.

Murray, Martin G. "Pete the Great." Walt Whitman Quarterly Review. 12 (Summer 1994), 1-51. via WWA

AFTER THE WAR

Walt Whitman. Circa 1870. Photograph by G. Frank Pearsall. Ohio Wesleyan University, Bayley Collection.

CHAPTER 13 | THE VERSES OWNING

Walt Whitman. Photo by George C. Cox. 1887. LOC

CALAMITY AND RECOVERY

George Whitman's house. Unattributed. via curatorofshit.com

Timber Creek, North Branch. Photo by milkbreath. via wikimedia.org

Walt Whitman's house. Photo by author. 2012.

Camden County jail. Photo by author. 2012.

Mickle Street. Attributed to John Johnston. 1890. LOC.

Warren Fritzinger and Walt Whitman. 1890. LOC.

Walt Whitman with Bill Duckett in buggy. Tintype photo attributed to Lorenzo F. Fisler of Fisler & Gaubert. 1886. Ohio Wesleyan University, Bayley Collection.

"A quiet and retired…" Johnston, John. Diary Notes of a Visit to Walt Whitman and Some of His Friends. London: The "Clarion" Office, 1898.

"Camden was originally…" WWWC. Vol. 2, p. 29.

"In contrast to…" Quoted in Myerson, Joel, ed. *Walt Whitman in His Own Time*. Iowa City: University of Iowa Press, 1991. p. 319.

LEGACY

Horace Traubel. Circa 1885. Unattributed. via greatthoughtstreasury.com

Walt in his room. Photo by Dr. William Reeder. 1891. LOC

Leaves of Grass editions, from "Revising Himself: Walt Whitman and Leaves of Grass." Online exhibition "American Treasures," at Library of Congress. LOC.

COME, SAID MY SOUL

Walt Whitman. Photograph by Thomas Eakins. 1891. LOC.

"The Strongest and Sweetest Songs Yet Remain to be Sung." Wooden type handset and printed by Jean Huets, at Richmond Visual Arts Center, Richmond, Virginia. 2014.

ACKNOWLEDGMENTS

Antietam. Photo by author. 2011.

Always, to my husband, Bruce Frostick: Your love and support keep me going.

Thank you for your insights and enthusiasm: Ron Andrea, Marta Bliese, Ben Cleary, Dan Cox, Helen Montague Foster, Lenore Gay, and Laura Jones.

To Ed Folsom and Kenneth M. Price, directors of The Walt Whitman Archive, and to the many other men and women who have contributed to the Archive: I could not even have begun this work without the work you have done. The searchable contents of Horace Traubel's With Walt Whitman in Camden, as well as images of the original editions of Leaves of Grass are only a few of the invaluable sources you make available to anyone in the world with access to the internet. I extend additional thanks to Ed Folsom for his friendly interest in *With Walt Whitman, Himself*.

The Library of Congress furnished many of the images used in this book. Other public institutions, including the Smithsonian, also contributed. My deepest gratitude to the staff members, and to the American people, whose taxes support the work to conserve, study, and exhibit our priceless heritage, and to share much of it all over the world with anyone who has access to the internet. I appreciate the generosity of the museums that acquire, conserve, and exhibit works that would otherwise be closeted in private collections.

Finally, my dear love to Walt's disciples. From his lifetime to this day, you hold Walt close with memoirs, photos, and conservation of his works and belongings, as well as countless websites, blogs, books, readings, and other activities.

www.ingramcontent.com/pod-product-compliance
Lightning Source LLC
Chambersburg PA
CBHW051333110526
44591CB00026B/2988